CAMBRIDGE PRIMARY
Mathematics

Teacher's Resource

Cherri Moseley and Janet Rees

CAMBRIDGE
UNIVERSITY PRESS

University Printing House, Cambridge CB2 8BS, United Kingdom

One Liberty Plaza, 20th Floor, New York, NY 10006, USA

477 Williamstown Road, Port Melbourne, VIC 3207, Australia

4843/24, 2nd Floor, Ansari Road, Daryaganj, Delhi – 110002, India

79 Anson Road, #06–04/06, Singapore 079906

Cambridge University Press is part of the University of Cambridge.

It furthers the University's mission by disseminating knowledge in the pursuit of education, learning and research at the highest international levels of excellence.

Information on this title: education.cambridge.org

First published 2014
20 19 18 17 16 15 14 13 12 11 10 9 8

Printed in Great Britain by CPI Group (UK) Ltd, Croydon CR0 4YY

A catalogue record for this publication is available from the British Library

ISBN 978-1-107-66889-8 Paperback

Cover artwork: Bill Bolton

Contents

Term 3

The Ethos of the *Cambridge Primary Maths* project

Cambridge Primary Maths is an innovative combination of curriculum and resources designed to support teachers and learners to succeed in primary mathematics through best-practice international maths teaching and a problem-solving approach.

Cambridge Primary Maths brings together the world-class Cambridge Primary mathematics curriculum from **Cambridge International Examinations**, high-quality publishing from **Cambridge University Press** and expertise in engaging online eFment materials for the mathematics curriculum from **NRICH**.

Cambridge Primary Maths offers teachers an online tool that maps resources and links to materials offered through the primary mathematics curriculum, NRICH and Cambridge Primary Mathematics textbooks and e-books. These resources include engaging online activities, best-practice guidance and examples of *Cambridge Primary Maths* in action.

The Cambridge curriculum is dedicated to helping schools develop learners who are confident, responsible, reflective, innovative and engaged. It is designed to give learners the skills to problem solve effectively, apply mathematical knowledge and develop a holistic understanding of the subject.

The Cambridge University Press series of *Teacher's resources* printed books and CD-ROMs provide best-in-class support for this problem-solving approach, based on pedagogical practice found in successful schools across the world. The engaging NRICH online resources help develop mathematical thinking and problem-solving skills.

The benefits of being part of *Cambridge Primary Maths* are:
- the opportunity to explore a maths curriculum founded on the values of the University of Cambridge and best practice in schools
- access to an innovative package of online and print resources that can help bring the Cambridge Primary mathematics curriculum to life in the classroom.

To get involved visit www.cie.org.uk/cambridgeprimarymaths

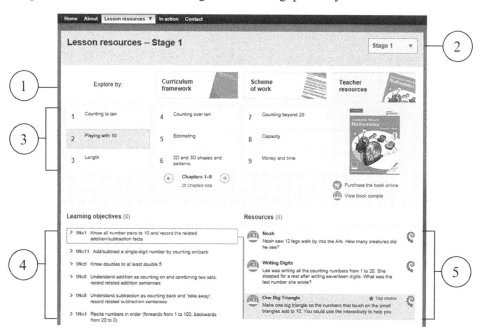

1 You can explore the available resources on the *Cambridge Primary Maths* website by curriculum framework, scheme of work, or teacher resources. In this example, the 'Teacher resources' tab has been selected.
2 The drop-down menu allows selection of resources by Stage.
3 Following selection of the 'Teacher resource' and 'Stage 1', the chapters in the Cambridge University Press textbook *'Teacher's resource 1'* are listed.
4 Clicking on a chapter ('2 Playing with 10' in this example) reveals the list of curriculum framework objectives covered in that chapter. Clicking on a given objective (1Nc1 in this example) highlights the most relevant NRICH activity for that objective.
5 A list of relevant NRICH activities for the selected chapter are revealed. Clicking on a given NRICH activity will highlight the objectives that it covers. You can launch the NRICH activity from here.

The *Cambridge Primary Maths* project provides a complete support package for teachers. The *Teacher's Resource* is a standalone teaching textbook that can be used independently or together with *Cambridge Primary Maths* website. The free to access website maps the activities and games in the *Teacher's Resource* to the Cambridge Primary curriculum. It also highlights relevant online activities designed by the NRICH project team based at the University of Cambridge.

The additional material that the *Cambridge Primary Maths* project provides can be accessed in the following ways:

As a Cambridge Centre:
If you are a registered Cambridge Centre, you get free access to all the available material by logging in using your existing Cambridge International Examinations log in details.

Register as a visitor:
If you are not a registered Cambridge Centre you can register to the site as a visitor, where you will be free to download a limited set of resources and online activities that can be searched by topic and learning objective.

As an unregistered visitor:
You are given free access an introductory video and some sample resources, and are able to read all about the scheme.

Introduction

The *Cambridge Primary Maths* series of resources covers the entire content of the Cambridge Primary Mathematics curriculum framework from Cambridge International Examinations. The resources have been written based on a suggested teaching year of three, ten week terms. This can be amended to suit the number of weeks available in your school year.

The Cambridge Primary Mathematics framework provides a comprehensive set of learning objectives for mathematics. These objectives deal with what learners should know and be able to do. The framework is presented in five strands: the four content strands of Number (including mental strategies), Geometry, Measures and Handling Data are all underpinned by the fifth strand, Problem Solving. Problem solving is integrated throughout the four content strands. Whilst it is important to be able to identify the progression of objectives through the curriculum, it is also essential to bring together the different strands into a logical whole.

This series of printed books and CD-ROMs published by Cambridge University Press is arranged to ensure that the curriculum is covered whilst allowing teachers flexibility in approach. The Scheme of Work for Stage 3 has been fully covered and follows in the same 'Unit' order as presented by Cambridge International Examinations (1A–C, 2A–C and then 3A–C) but the order of objective coverage may vary depending on a logical pedagogy and teaching approach.

The components of the printed series are as follows:
- *Teacher's Resource* (printed book and CD-ROM)
  This resource covers all the objectives of the Cambridge framework through lessons referred to as '*Core activities*'. As a 'lesson' is a subjective term (taking more or less time depending on the school and the learners) we prefer to use the terms '*Core activity*' and 'session' to reinforce that there is some flexibility. Each *Core activity* contains the instructions for you to lead the activity and cover the objectives, as well as providing expected outcomes, suggested dialogue for discussion, and likely areas of misconception. A section called '*More activities*' provides you with suggestions for supplementary or extension activities.

The *Teacher's Resource* can be used on its own to **completely cover** the course. (The *Learner's Book* and *Games Book* should **not** be used without the associated teacher resource, as they are not sufficient on their own to cover all the objectives.)

The accompanying CD-ROM contains:
- a Word version of the entire printed book. This has been supplied so that you can copy and paste relevant chunks of the text into your own lesson plans if you do not want to use our book directly. You will be able to edit and print the Word files as required but different versions of Word used on different PCs and MACs will render the content slightly differently so you might have some formatting issues.
- *Questioning* – This document outlines some of the different types of question techniques for mathematics and how best to use them, providing support for teachers.
- *Letters for parents* – a template letter is supplied along with a mapping grid to help you to write a letter per Unit of material in order to inform parents what work their child is doing, and what they can do to support their child at home.
- *Photocopy masters* – resources are supplied as PDFs, and as Word files so that you can edit them as required.

- *Learner's Book* (printed book)
  This resource is **supplementary** to the course. As the ethos of the *Cambridge Maths Project* is to avoid rote learning and drill practice, there are no accompanying workbooks. The *Learner's Book* instead combines consolidation and support for the learner with investigations that allow freedom of thought, and questions that encourage the learner to apply their knowledge rather than just remembering a technique. The investigations and questions are written to assess the

learner's understanding of the learning outcomes of the *Core activity*. Learners can write down their answers to investigations and questions in an exercise book in order to inform assessment. The overall approach of the *Teacher's Resource* accompanied by the *Learner's Book* allows a simple way for you to assess how well a learner understands a topic, whilst also encouraging discussion, problem-solving and investigation skills.

At Stage 3, each *Learner's Book* page is designed to help learners to consolidate and apply knowledge. All pages of the *Learner's Book* are associated with a *Core activity from Teacher's Resource 3*. Some of the *Learner's Book* pages start with an introductory investigation called *"Let's investigate"*, which is an open-ended question to get the learners thinking and investigating. These are often 'low threshold, high ceiling' so that learners can approach the question at many levels. All pages contain a series of questions and/or activities to develop problemsolving skills and support learning through discovery and discussion. New vocabulary is explained, and where possible this is done using illustrations as well as text in order to help visual learners and those with lower literacy levels. Hints and tips provide direct support throughout. Ideally, the session should be taught using the appropriate *Core activity* in the *Teacher's Resource* with the *Learner's Book* being used at the end of the session, or set as homework, to consolidate learning; but, how the *Learner's Book* page is used (independently, in groups or as a class) will depend on the confidence of your learners.

There is generally a single page in the *Learner's Book* for each associated *Core activity* in the *Teacher's Resource* for Stage 3. The *Teacher's Resource* will refer to the *Learner's Book* page by title and page number, and the title of the *Core activity* will be at the bottom of the *Learner's Book* page. **Please note** that the *Learner's Book* does not cover all of the Cambridge objectives on its own; it is for supplementary use only.

• *Games Book* (printed book and CD-ROM)
This resource is complete in its own right as a source of engaging, informative maths games. It is also a **supplementary** resource to the series. It can be used alongside the *Teacher's Resource* as a source of additional activities to support learners that need extra reinforcement, or to give to advanced learners as extension. Each game comes with a '*Maths* focus' to highlight the intended learning/reinforcement outcome of the game, so that the book can be used independently of any other resource. For those who are using it as part of this series, relevant games are referred to by title and page number in the '*More activities*' section of the *Teacher's Resource*. The accompanying CD-ROM contains nets to make required resources; it also contains a mapping document that maps the games to the other resources in the series for those who require it. **Please note** that the *Games Book* does not cover all of the Cambridge objectives on its own; it is for supplementary use only.

Each chapter in the Teacher's Resource includes

• A *Quick reference* section to list the title of each of the *Core activities* contained within the chapter. It provides an outline of the learning outcome(s) of each *Core activity*. (See page vii and later in this list, for a reminder of what is meant by a *Core activity*.)
• A list of the *Objectives* from the Cambridge Primary Mathematics curriculum framework that are covered across the chapter as a whole. **Please note** that this means that not all of the listed objectives will be covered in each of the chapter's *Core activities*; they are covered when the chapter is taken as a whole. The objectives are referenced using subheadings from the framework, for example '**1A: Calculation** (*Mental strategies*)' and the code from the Scheme of Work, for example, '2Nc3'.

Please be aware that the content of an objective is often split across different *Core activities* and/or different chapters for a logical progression of learning and development. Please be assured that provided you eventually cover all of the *Core activities* across the whole

Teacher's Resource, you will have covered all of the objectives in full. It should be clear from the nature of a *Core activity* when parts of an objective have not been fully covered. For example, a chapter on length will list 'Measure' objectives that also include weight, such as '1MI1' (Compare lengths and weights by direct comparison…) but the weight aspect of the objective will not be covered in a chapter on length(!); that part of the objective will be covered in a chapter on weight. Or a chapter focusing on understanding teen numbers as 'ten and some more' might cover the action 'recite numbers in order' but only up to 20 and therefore only partially cover objective '1Nn1' (Recite numbers in order … from 1 to 100…). But please be reassured that, by the end of the *Teacher's Resource*, all of objectives 1MI1 and 1Nn1 will have been covered in full; as will all objectives. The *Summary* bulleted list at the end of each *Core activity* lists the learning outcome of the activity and can add some clarity of coverage, if required.

- A list of key *Prior learning* topics is provided to ensure learners are ready to move on to the chapter, and to remind teachers of the need to build on previous learning.
- Important and/or new *Vocabulary* for the chapter as a whole is listed. Within the *Core activity* itself, relevant vocabulary will be repeated along with a helpful description to support teaching of new words.

The *Core activities* (within each chapter) collectively provide a comprehensive teaching programme for the whole stage. Each *Core activity* includes:

- A list of required *Resources* to carry out the activity. This list includes resources provided as photocopy masters within the *Teacher's Resource* printed book (indicated by '(pxx)'), and photocopy masters provided on the CD-ROM (indicated by '(CD-ROM)'), as well as resources found in the classroom or at home. '(Optional)' resources are those that are required for the activities listed in the '*More activities*' section and thus are optional.
- A main narrative that is split into two columns. The left-hand (wider) column provides instructions for how to deliver the activity, suggestions for dialogue to instigate discussions, possible responses and outcomes,

as well as general support for teaching the objective. Differences in formatting in this section identify different types of interactivity:

- ○ Teacher-led whole class activity
  The main narrative represents work to be done as a whole class.
- ○ Teacher-Learner discussion
  "Text that is set in italics within double-quotation marks represents suggested teacher dialogue to instigate Teacher-Learner disccusion."
- ○ Learner-Learner interaction

  Group and pair work between learners is encouraged throughout and is indicated using a grey panel behind the text and a change in font.

The right-hand (narrow) column provides,
- ○ the vocabulary panel
- ○ side-notes and examples
- ○ a *Look out for!* panel that offers practical suggestions for identifying and addressing common difficulties and misconceptions, as well as how to spot advanced learners and ideas for extension tasks to give them
- ○ an *Opportunity for display* panel to provide ideas for displays.
- A *Summary* at the end of each *Core activity* to list the learning outcomes/expectations following the activity. This is accompanied by a *Check up!* section that provides quick-fire probing questions useful for formative assessment; and a *Notes on the Learner's Book* section that references the title and page number of the associated *Learner's Book* page, as well as a brief summary of what the page involves.
- A *More activities* section that provides suggestions for further activities; these are not required to cover the objectives and therefore are optional activities that can be used for reinforcement and differentiation. The additional activities might include a reference to a game in the *Games Book*. You are encouraged to also look on the *Cambridge Maths Project* website to find NRICH activities linked to the Cambridge objectives. Together, these activities provide a wealth of material from which teachers can select those most appropriate to their circumstances both in class and for use of homework if this is set.

We would recommend that you work through the chapters in the order they appear in this book as you might find that later chapters build on knowledge from earlier in the book. If possible, work with colleagues and share ideas and over time you will feel confident in modifying and adapting your plans.

Teaching approaches

Learners have different learning styles and teachers need to appeal to all these styles. You will find references to group work, working in pairs and working individually within these materials.

The grouping depends on the activity and the point reached within a series of sessions. It may be appropriate to teach the whole class, for example, at the beginning of a series of sessions when explaining, demonstrating or asking questions. After this initial stage, learners often benefit from opportunities to discuss and explain their thoughts to a partner or in a group. Such activities where learners are working collaboratively are highlighted in the main narrative as detailed in the previous section. High quality teaching is oral, interactive and lively and is a two-way process between teacher and learners. Learners play an active part by asking and answering questions, contributing to discussions and explaining and demonstrating their methods to the rest of the class or group. Teachers need to listen and use learner ideas to show that these are valued. Learners will make errors if they take risks but these are an important part of the learning process.

Talking mathematics

We need to encourage learners to speak during a maths session in order to:
- communicate
- explain and try out ideas
- develop correct use of mathematical vocabulary
- develop mathematical thinking.

It is important that learners develop mathematical language and communication in order to (using Bloom's taxonomy):

Explain mathematical thinking (I think that … because …)
Develop understanding (I understand that …)
Solve problems (I know that … so …)
Explain solutions (This is how I found out that …)
Ask and answer questions (What, why, how, when, if …)
Justify answers (I think this because …)

There is advice on the CD-ROM about the types of questioning you can use to get your students talking maths (*Questioning*).

Resources, including games

Resources can support, assist and extend learning. The use of resources such as *Ten frames, 100 squares*, *number lines*, *digit cards* and *arrow cards* is promoted in the *Teacher's Resource*. Games provide a useful way of reinforcing skills and practising and consolidating ideas. Learners gain confidence and are able to explore and discuss mathematical ideas whilst developing their mathematical language.

Calculators should be used to help learners understand numbers and the number system including place value and properties of numbers. However, the calculator is not promoted as a calculation tool before Stage 5.

NRICH have created an abundance of engaging and well-thought-out mathematical resources, which have been mapped to the Cambridge Primary scheme of work, and are available from the *Cambridge Primary Maths* website. Their interactive and downloadable activities can provide an alternative learning style or enrichment for some of the core concepts.

1A   1 Place value (1)

Quick reference

Core activity 1.1: Hundreds, tens and ones (Learner's Book p4)
Learners explore three-digit numbers using place value cards.

Core activity 1.2: To 1000 (Learner's Book p6)
Learners make three-digit numbers and mark them on a 0 to 1000 number line marked in multiples of ten.

Core activity 1.3: Place value (Learner's Book p8)
Learners take note of all three digits when placing a number on a number line. They develop their understanding of the value of each digit through a range of activities.

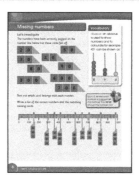

Prior learning	Objectives* – please note that listed objectives might only be partially covered within any given chapter but are covered fully across the book when taken as a whole
• Experience of using place value cards to at least 100. • Counting on and back in tens and ones from any single digit number. • Finding one and 10 less or more than any two-digit number.	**1A: Numbers and the number system** 3Nn1 – Recite numbers 100 to 200 and beyond. 3Nn3 – Count on and back in ones, tens and hundreds from two- and three-digit numbers. 3Nn2 – Read and write numbers to at least 1000. 3Nn5 – Understand what each digit represents in three-digit numbers and partition into hundreds, tens and units. 3Nn6 – Find 1, 10, 100 more/less than two- and three-digit numbers. 3Nn9 – Place a three-digit number on a number line marked off in multiples of 100. 3Nn10 – Place a three-digit number on a number line marked off in multiples of 10. **1A: Using understanding and strategies in solving problems** 3Ps3 – Explore and solve number problems and puzzles. 3Ps6 – Identify simple relationships between numbers.

*for NRICH activities mapped to the Cambridge Primary objectives, please visit www.cie.org.uk/cambridgeprimarymaths

Vocabulary

abacus • hundreds • ones • place value • tens • units

Resources: Large *100 square* (p12). Sets of *Place value cards* photocopy master (CD-ROM), prepare a set of cards up to the value of 900 per pair. *Hundreds, tens and ones* photocopy master (CD-ROM). *0 to 9 digit cards* photocopy master (CD-ROM). Base ten equipment (if available). (Optional: *Hundreds, tens and ones* photocopy master (CD-ROM), one copy per pair; *0 to 9 digit cards* photocopy master (CD-ROM) one copy per pair and a pot of mixed counters per pair; *Less and more* photocopy master (CD-ROM) and *Place value cards* photocopy master (CD-ROM); *Stamp, clap, click* photocopy master (CD-ROM).)

Display a large 100 square and begin by checking that the learners remember what they are counting in when they count along a row or column of the 100 square. Ask the learners to imagine there is another 100 square below the current one. This 100 square starts at 101 and finishes at 200. It is exactly the same as the one they can see, but every number (except 200!) begins with one hundred and '...'. Point to a few random numbers, asking the learners to tell you what this number would be on the 101–200 number square. Challenge the learners to count on from any single digit in tens to about 200. Repeat starting from a different number. Finish by counting in ones from 101 to around 130.

Give each pair of learners a set of *Place value cards* and ask them to arrange them into three columns, with hundreds on the left, tens in the middle and ones on the right. Explain that some people call the ones 'units' and talk about hundreds, tens and units. So, if they hear the word 'units' elsewhere, it simply means ones. Call out a range of two- and three-digit numbers for the learners to make with the cards. After several numbers, check that the learners have replaced their place value cards in order. Ask one learner to hold the 300 card while the second learner matches ten with it to make 310. Count on together in tens, with the second learner changing the ten card to match. The first learner must change the hundreds card when the next hundred is reached. Occasionally pause and ask the learners to show you the number they have just said. Count forward and back in ones, tens or hundreds from any two- or three-digit number in this way. Occasionally pause to ask questions such as, "*What are we counting in now? Which number is ten (or hundred) less (or more) than this number.*" Collect in the place value cards.

Either enlarge a copy of the *Hundreds, tens and ones* sheet or draw a large copy of it where everyone can see. Shuffle the digit cards and explain that you are Player 1 and the class is

Look out for!

- Learners who find it difficult to recognise how many hundreds, tens or ones in each number. *Ask them to make a two-digit number with place value cards and then match it with ten sticks and ones. Take the 100 card and match it with a 100 plate (or ten tens if you do not have any). Put the numbers together, then increase the number in steps of 100, matching the apparatus to the number. Do the same changing the tens. Encourage learners to continue using base ten apparatus for support until they feel confident to work without it.*
- Learners who can visualise the changing hundreds, tens or ones. *Encourage them to work without using the place value cards for support.*

Player 2. Explain that the aim of the game is to make the highest number you can, but once a digit is placed in a space, it cannot be moved until the game is complete. Turn over the top digit card and model making the decision of where to the place the digit by talking out loud. So if the digit is a 7, you could say, *"This is quite a high digit. I could put it in the tens or the hundreds. If I put it in the hundreds, there are only two higher digits, 8 and 9. If you pick up 8 or 9 you will win. But there are more lower digits, 0, 1, 2, 3, 4, 5 and 6, so I think it is more likely that I will make the highest number if I put it in the hundreds."*

Ask a learner to turn over the next digit and then ask the learners to talk to their partner about where to place it. Invite the learners to share their opinions until agreement is reached. If necessary, ask questions such as, *"Is that the best place to put it? Is it likely you will get a higher (or lower) digit than that? Which digits must be left?"*

After the first round of the game, ask, *"Were the numbers we made the highest possible numbers with those digits? What other numbers could we have made?"* Play another round, this time aiming to make the lowest number possible. Ask the learners how the two games were the same and how they were different. If there is time, play a third round, asking the learners whether they would like to play for the highest or lowest number. Remind learners that some people call ones units so they would call this game the HTU game.

Summary

Learners recognise the value of each digit in a three-digit number and are beginning to count on and back in hundreds, tens and ones from any two- or three-digit number.

Notes on the Learner's Book
Hundreds, tens and ones (p4): learners identify which place value cards have not been used and which three-digit numbers could be made with the missing cards. Some learners could go on to predict and then investigate how three-digit numbers they could make with any two hundreds, two tens and two ones place value cards.

Check up!
- Show pairs of learners a three-digit number and ask them questions such as, *"How many hundreds (or tens or ones)? How do you know?"*
- Challenge them to count on or back in ones, tens or hundreds from that number.

More activities

<u>HTO</u> (in small groups as teams or pairs)

> You will need the *Hundreds, tens and ones* photocopy master (CD-ROM), one copy per pair, *0 to 9 digit cards* photocopy master (CD-ROM) one copy per pair and a pot of mixed counters per pair.

The aim is to make the highest/lowest number (as above), or the number nearest to 500 or any agreed number. Players take it in turns to turn over the top *digit card* and decide where to place it; remind them that, once placed, the *digit card* cannot be moved. The winner of each round is awarded a counter. The first player to collect ten counters is the winner. Playing as a team gives learners the opportunity to discuss where to place a particular digit and why, so it may be better to play in this way, at least initially.

Less and More (in pairs)

> You will need the *Less and more* photocopy master (CD-ROM) and *Place value cards* photocopy master (CD-ROM) one copy per pair.

Learners write a three-digit number in the middle of the *Less and more* grid, then write the numbers which are one, 10 or 100 less or more in the labelled boxes. A learner makes the three-digit number for their partner using *Place value cards*. Differentiate numbers appropriately.

Stamp, clap, click (small groups or whole class)

> You will need the *Stamp, clap, click* photocopy master (CD-ROM).

Stamp your feet for 100, clap for 10 and click your fingers for one. So stamp, stamp, stamp, clap, clap, clap, clap, click is 341. Stamp, clap and click in that order at first, but then move on to doing the actions in a different order. Learners can take it in turns to make a number. Display the *Stamp, clap, click* sheet for support. Ask learners to suggest an action or sound for 1000. Stick to just one thousand until learners are more familiar with higher numbers.

Games Book (ISBN 9781107694019)

Place value games (p1) are a set of four games for pairs, groups, or the whole class. They develop understanding of place value.

Resources: *Place value cards* photocopy master (CD-ROM). *Number line 0 to 1000 (marked in 10s)* photocopy master (p13) large version for class displays, and one regular copy per pair. Scissors. Glue. *Abacus sheet* photocopy master (CD-ROM). (Optional: *0 to 9 digit cards* photocopy master (CD-ROM); stop watch and counters for each small group; *Hundreds, tens and ones* photocopy master (CD-ROM); pot of mixed counters, for each pair or group.)

Give each pair of learners a set of *Place value cards* and ask them to arrange them into three columns, with hundreds on the left, tens in the middle and ones on the right. Ask one learner to hold the 500 card while the second learner matches ten with it to make 510. Count on in tens together, with the second learner changing the tens cards to match what is said. The first learner must change the hundreds card when the next hundred is reached. Count forward and back in ones, tens or hundreds from any two- or three-digit number in this way. Occasionally pause to ask questions such as, *"What are we counting in now? Which number is ten (or hundred) less (or more) than this number? How many tens (or hundreds or ones) in this number?"* Collect in the *Place value cards*. An explanation of this concept should be given or modelled before learners attempt this activity.

Show the learners an enlarged copy of the *Number line 0 to 1000 (marked in 10s)*. Give each pair of learners a copy of the *Number line* and show them how to cut along the dotted line and glue the two pieces together to make a *0 to 1000 Number line*.

Ask the learners to talk with their partner about what they notice about this number line. Check that they have noticed that the line begins at 0, ends at 1000 and is marked in tens.

Talk through where you would find numbers between 200 and 300 and so on. Describe a mark on the number line, for example as, *"The second mark after 200"* or *"The mark three marks before 300,"* and ask the learners use their number line to help them find out which number the mark represents.

Make nine three-digit numbers using a set of hundreds and tens *Place value cards* and ask the learners where you should mark each number on the line. All the numbers will have zero ones to make it easier to find their position on the number line. Talk through looking at the hundreds to know which section of the line to go to. Then talk through looking at the

Vocabulary

abacus: an abacus is used to show numbers and to calculate for example 421 can be shown as:

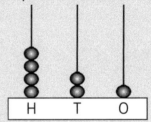

Look out for!

- Learners who find it hard to identify the value of each digit. *Encourage them to make the number with place value cards, then separate the cards to see the value of each digit. Making the number using base 10 apparatus will also help to develop understanding.*
- Learners who are able to identify the value of each digit. *Give them the ones place value cards too. Ask them to place the three-digit number on the number line as accurately as they can, taking note of the ones digit as well.*

tens to know where in that section to mark the number. Repeat with several other numbers until there is a number in every hundred section of the number line, except 0 to 100. Ask the learners to explain why there is no number to mark in that section. Occasionally ask one of the learners to come and mark the number on the number line, explaining why they are positioning it where they are.

Give each pair of learners a set of hundreds and tens *Place value cards*. Explain that they need to create nine three-digit numbers and mark them on their number line, using the marks on the line to help them.

Finish the session by asking each pair of learners to come and mark one of their numbers on the enlarged number line, explaining why they are positioning where they are.

Summary

Learners can mark a three-digit number on a 0 to 1000 number line marked in tens.

Notes on the Learner's Book
Missing numbers (p6): nine numbers were made with place value cards and pegged in the correct place on a number line. Some of the place value cards fell off the line. Learners identify the missing card for each number. They then read numbers on an abacus and draw an abacus to show a number using the *Abacus* photocopy master.

Check up!
- Say a three-digit number and ask learners to quickly draw the matching abacus.
- Say a three-digit number and ask pairs of learners to count on or back in tens from that number. Use numbers with and without ones.

More activities

<u>3 by 3</u> (small group)

You will need the *0 to 9 digit cards* photocopy master (CD-ROM), a stop watch and counters for each small group.

Shuffle a set of *digit cards* (excluding 0) and place them face down on the table. Turn over the cards one at a time, arranging them in a 3 by 3 grid. The three-digit numbers can be read across from left to right or right to left, up, down or diagonally. Either use a stop watch to time 10 seconds or count to 10, then cover the grid. Challenge everyone in the group to write down the largest number and smallest number they noticed and the number closest to 500. Compare numbers and check the grid, awarding a counter to the player (or players) who correctly identified the numbers. After each group member has had a turn at laying out the cards, who has the most counters?

HTO (pairs or groups)

> You will need the *Hundreds, tens and ones* photocopy master (CD-ROM), *0 to 9 digit cards* photocopy master (CD-ROM), and a pot of mixed counters for each pair or group.

Learners aim to make the highest/lowest number, or the number nearest to 500 or any agreed number. Players take it in turns to turn over the top *digit card* and decide where to place it on the *Hundreds, tens and ones* sheet; remind them that, once placed, the digit card cannot be moved. The winner of each round is awarded a counter. The first player to collect 10 counters is the winner.

Guess my number (small groups or whole class)

Choose a number on the number line and invite learners to ask questions to identify the number. You can only answer 'yes' or 'no'. Questions might include, "*Is it more than 200? Is it less than 500?*" Learners could cross out the parts of the number line where they know the number is not located to help them. Allow 20 questions at first, then challenge learners to find the number after 10 questions.

Resources: One copy of *Number line 0 to 1000 (marked in 10s)* photocopy master (p13). Scissors. Glue. One copy of *Number line 0 to 1000 (marked in 100s)* photocopy master (p14) per learner. *Hundreds, tens and ones* photocopy master (CD-ROM). *0 to 9 digit cards* photocopy master (CD-ROM). (Optional: *Place value cards* photocopy master (CD-ROM) and *Abacus sheet* photocopy master (CD-ROM) one copy per learner; *What's my value?* photocopy master (CD-ROM) one copy per learner.)

Give each learner a copy of the *0 to 1000 Number line (marked in 10s)* and ask them to quickly make up the number line. Explain that they are going to use the number line to help them count in tens, forwards and back. Ask everyone to put a finger on 300 and, keeping track of where they are on the number line, count forwards in tens to 500. Choose a different starting point and repeat, counting both forwards and back in tens. Initially, start on a hundreds number, changing to other numbers which are multiples of ten, as the learners become more confident. Collect in the number line to reuse on another day.

Give each learner a copy of the *0 to 1000 Number line (marked in 100s)* and ask them to quickly make up the number line. Ask the learners what is the same and what is different about this number line compared to the one they were using earlier. Explain that to mark a three-digit number on the line now, they need to estimate roughly where that number would be within each hundred. Talk through what sort of numbers would go in the middle of each section, towards the beginning and towards the end.

Show the learners an enlarged copy of the number line with three additional marks on it. Ask the learners to mark the same positions on their own lines, then talk to their partner to decide which number each mark represents. Ask the learners to share their ideas. Draw up a list of the suggested numbers for each mark.

Ask questions such as, "*What makes you think that? Would it be so close to (or far away from) X00?*" Agree a possible range of numbers for each mark.

> Ask each learner to mark a number on their number line without labelling it, but also writing the number on the back of their number line. Each learner can then challenge their partner to identify the marked number. Once both partners have had a go at identifying each other's numbers, they can swap partners with another pair and have a go at identifying each other's numbers.

Finish the session by playing three rounds of the HTO game against the class. Aim for the highest, then lowest number, then the number closest to 500.

Look out for!

- Learners who find it hard to read along a number line which is not marked. *Give them time to mark the numbers on the line before expecting them to join in with the counting. Alternatively, they may find it useful to continue to use place value cards for support.*
- Learners who find reading along a number line straightforward. *Challenge them by expecting them to be more accurate in placing numbers on the number line. They should take notice of the hundreds, tens and ones digits.*

Summary

Learners can estimate the position of a three-digit number on a number line marked in hundreds. They can identify the value of each digit in a three-digit number.

Notes on the Learner's Book

Learners need to play the HTO game before attempting *Which game is which?* (p8): three unfinished games of HTO are pictured. One game was trying to make the highest number, another game was trying to make the lowest number and another game was trying to make numbers closest to 500. The learners use their understanding of place value to identify which game is which and explain how they know.

Check up!

- Show pairs of learners a number marked on a number line, either one marked in tens or hundreds.
- Ask the learners to decide what the number is.
- Listen carefully to their conversation and give support if necessary.

More activities

Abacus numbers (individual)

> You will need the *Place value cards* photocopy master (CD-ROM) and *Abacus sheet* photocopy master (CD-ROM), one copy per learner.

Learners use a set of *Place value cards* to make nine three-digit numbers, then draw the matching abacus for each number using the *Abacus sheet*.

What's my value? (individual)

> You will need the *What's my value?* photocopy master (CD-ROM), one copy per learner.

Learners identify the value of the digit circled or shown on the abacus on the *What's my value?* sheet. They then draw abacus figures for the three-digit numbers shown made from place value cards.

Games Book (ISBN 9781107694019)

On the line (p2) is a game for two players. Players generate and place a three-digit number on a number line marked off in multiples of 10. The winner is the first person to mark three numbers in a row without the other player marking a number between.

100 square

1	2	3	4	5	6	7	8	9	10
11	12	13	14	15	16	17	18	19	20
21	22	23	24	25	26	27	28	29	30
31	32	33	34	35	36	37	38	39	40
41	42	43	44	45	46	47	48	49	50
51	52	53	54	55	56	57	58	59	60
61	62	63	64	65	66	67	68	69	70
71	72	73	74	75	76	77	78	79	80
81	82	83	84	85	86	87	88	89	90
91	92	93	94	95	96	97	98	99	100

Number line 0 to 1000 (marked in 10s)

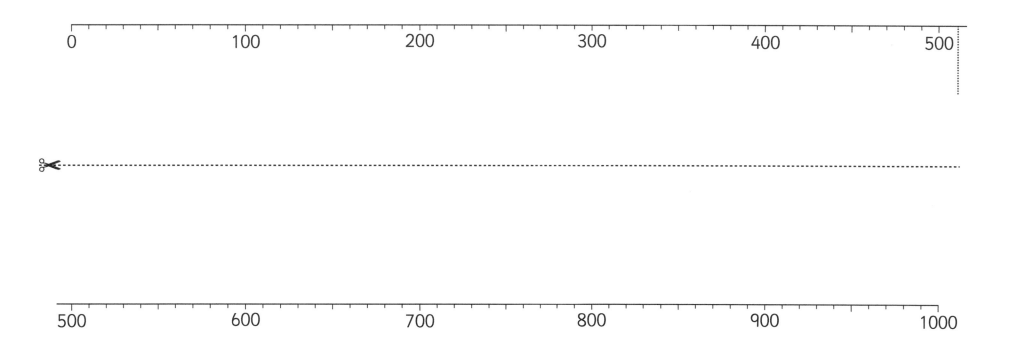

Number line 0 to 1000 (marked in 100s)

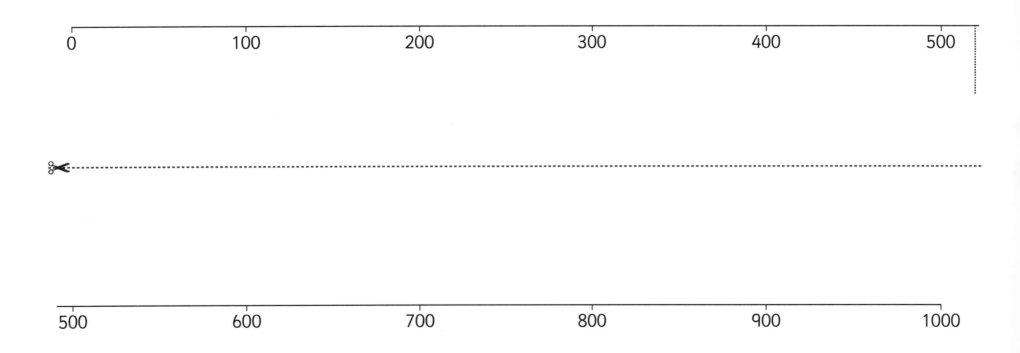

Quick reference

Core activity 2.1: 10 less and 10 more (Learner's Book p10)

Learners use their understanding of place value to add and subtract 10 and multiples of 10 to two- and three-digit numbers. They also explore adding 100 and multiples of 100.

Prior learning	Objectives* – please note that listed objectives might only be partially covered within any given chapter but are covered fully across the book when taken as a whole
• Counting on and back in tens from any two-digit number. • Exploring three-digit numbers.	**1A: Numbers and the number system** 3Nn3 – Count on and back in ones, tens and hundreds from two- and three-digit numbers. 3Nn2 – Read and write numbers to at least 1000. 3Nn5 – Understand what each digit represents in three-digit numbers and partition into hundreds, tens and units. **1A: Calculation** (*Addition and subtraction*) 3Nc9 – Add and subtract 10 and multiples of 10 to and from two- and three-digit numbers. 3Nc10 – Add 100 and multiples of 100 to three-digit numbers. **1A: Problem solving** (*Using techniques and skills in solving mathematical problems*) 3Pt1 – Choose appropriate mental strategies to carry out calculations. 3Pt3 – Make sense of and solve word problems and begin to represent them. **1A: Using understanding and strategies in solving problems** 3Ps1 – Make up a number story to go with a calculation. 3Ps2 – Explain a choice of calculation strategy and show how the answer was worked out. 3Ps3 – Explore and solve number problems and puzzles. 3Ps6 – Identify simple relationships between numbers.

*for NRICH activities mapped to the Cambridge Primary objectives, please visit www.cie.org.uk/cambridgeprimarymaths

Vocabulary

hundreds • multiple • solve • tens

Resources: Copies of *Number lines 0 to 1000 (marked in 10s)* assembled in *Core activity 1.3*. A large *100 square* (chapter 1, p12). *Star numbers* photocopy master (p18) and a 1–6 dice or spinner (CD-ROM), per pair. *All stars* photocopy master (CD-ROM) one copy per learner. 1–9 spinner. (Optional: *Snakes* photocopy master (CD-ROM) one copy per learner, pencil or pen; *Place value cards* photocopy master (CD-ROM); *Number cards* photocopy master (CD-ROM) and *Tens and hundreds cards* photocopy master (CD-ROM), one copy per learner, scissors.)

Using the *0 to 1000 Number lines* for support, count forward and back in tens from any two- or three-digit number with zero ones. Count from 200 to 400 in tens. Ask the learners how the count would change if they started at 207. If necessary, remind the learners how they counted on from 7, using the large 100 square for support. Count on and back in tens from any two- or three-digit numbers. Remind the learners that each number they said was ten more than the one before when they were counting forward in tens. Ask the learners what they could say about the numbers when they were counting back. Check that they understand that each number is 10 less than the one before when they are counting back.

Write a three-digit number where everyone can see it. Ask the learners what 10 more would be. Write the matching number sentence, for example 323 + 10 = 333. Ask the learners what 323 – 10 would be. Invite one of the learners to come and write the matching number sentence. Check that the learners have noticed that the tens digit changes, but the ones digit stays the same. Repeat for 393. This time adding 10 changes the hundreds digit too, to 403. Discuss adding and subtracting other multiples of ten, working through a few examples together. Include crossing the hundreds barrier when subtracting as well as adding.

Give each pair of learners a copy of the *Star numbers* sheet and a dice or spinner. Each learner will also need a copy of the *All Stars* sheet. Learners choose a star on the *Star numbers* sheet, they then roll the dice or spin a spinner to tell them how many tens to add or subtract to/from the numbers in their chosen star. They record their answers in one of the stars on the *All Stars* sheet. Two stars must be used for addition and two for subtraction. Once a star has been completed, learners record one of the calculations they carried out in a number sentence next to the star.

Finish the session by looking at the second star on the *Star numbers* sheet. Pick one of the numbers and ask the learners how the number would change if 100 or 1000 was added to it. Choose another number to add 200 and 2000 to, and another to add 300 and 3000 to and so on. Ask the learners which digit is changing each time. Make sure they have realised that only the hundreds digit changes, the tens and ones digits stay the same.

Vocabulary

solve: find the answer.

multiple: when we start counting at 0 and count in steps of equal size, we say the number are multiples of the step size. For example, 2, 4, 6, 8 ... are all multiples of 2.

Look out for!

- Learners who find it hard to add or subtract 10 and multiples of 10. *Encourage them to make the number using place value cards to help them. This will also help when adding 100 or multiples of 100 to three-digit numbers. Some learners may find the patterns in the 100 square more helpful, so give them the opportunity to use one if they prefer.*

- Learners who are confident in adding and subtracting 10 and multiples of 10. *Give them a 1 to 9 spinner to use with the star numbers. This will make it likely that some of their numbers will be greater than 1000, extending their number range. You could also adapt the activity, asking some learners to add hundreds rather than tens.*

Summary

Learners can add 10, multiples of 10, 100 or multiples of 100 to a two- or three-digit number, recognising which digits change. They can subtract 10 or a multiple of 10 from a two- or three-digit number, recognising which digits change. They can write the matching number sentence for their calculations.

Notes on the Learner's Book

At the store (p10): learners solve problems involving changing quantities, choosing which operation is needed to find the answer. Challenge some learners by telling them that there are 10 or 12 sweets in each pack in Question 1 and asking how many sweets did the shop have before and after the delivery.

Check up!

Ask the learners to tell you a story for a number sentence such as:

$42 + 10 = 52$, or $327 - 200 = 127$.

More activities

Snakes (individual)

> You will need the *Snakes* photocopy master (CD-ROM), one copy per learner, and a pencil or pen, and might need copies of *Place value cards* photocopy master (CD-ROM).

Learners complete the *Snakes* by counting on or back in 10, multiples of 10 or counting on in hundreds or multiples of hundreds. Some learners may find *Place value cards* useful for this activity.

Number stories (individual)

> You will need the *Number cards* photocopy master (CD-ROM) and *Tens and hundreds cards* photocopy master (CD-ROM), one copy per learner, and pairs of scissors.

Cut out the *Number cards* and mix them up in pile face down. Do the same with the *Tens and hundreds cards*. Learners take a card from each pile and add them, writing the number sentence. If the second number can be subtracted from the first, they carry out that calculation too, again writing the matching number sentence. After writing six number sentences, learners choose a number sentence to tell a story to a friend about. For example: the shop had 39 books left when a box of 200 arrived. The book shop now has 239 books.

Star numbers

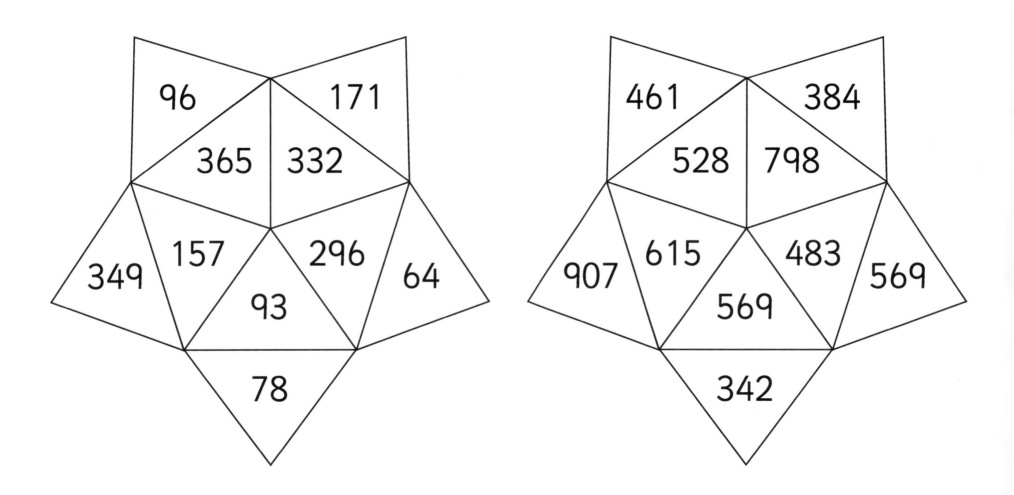

Quick reference

Core activity 3.1: Adding several small numbers (Learner's Book p12)

Learners explore a range of strategies for adding several small numbers, including finding unknown numbers.

Prior learning	Objectives* – please note that listed objectives might only be partially covered within any given chapter but are covered fully across the book when taken as a whole
• Number pairs for 10. • Doubles and near doubles. • Place value. • Addition to at least 20.	**1A: Numbers and the number system** 3Nn3 – Count on and back in ones, tens and hundreds from two- and three-digit numbers. **1A: Calculation** (*Addition and subtraction*) 3Nc12 – Add several small numbers. 3Nc16 – Re-order an addition to help with the calculation. **1A: Problem solving** (*Using techniques and skills in solving mathematical problems*) 3Pt1 – Choose appropriate mental strategies to carry out calculations. 3Pt3 – Make sense of and solve word problems and begin to represent them. 3Pt4 – Check the results of adding two numbers using subtraction, and several numbers by adding in a different order. **1A: Using understanding and strategies in solving problems** 3Ps2 – Explain a choice of calculation strategy and show how the answer was worked out. 3Ps3 – Explore and solve number problems and puzzles.

*for NRICH activities mapped to the Cambridge Primary objectives, please visit www.cie.org.uk/cambridgeprimarymaths

Vocabulary

addition • total

Resources: The *Number line 0 to 1000 (marked in 10s)* assembled in *Core activity 1.3*. A large *100 square* (chapter 1, p12). *0 to 9 digit cards* photocopy master (CD-ROM). (Optional: *Puzzles* photocopy master (CD-ROM) one copy per learner; *Addition grids 9* photocopy master (CD-ROM); *0 to 9 digit cards* photocopy master (CD-ROM); calculators, pens or pencils; *Addition grids 16* photocopy master (CD-ROM); *1–9 spinner* (CD-ROM).)

Begin by counting on and back in ones, tens and hundreds from any two- or three-digit number. Some learners may need the *Number line 0 to 1000 (marked in 10s)* from *Core activity 1.3* for support. Revisit counting in twos on the large 100 square, identifying odd and even numbers, then count on in twos from an even three-digit number initially, then from an odd three-digit number.

Display five single digit numbers 7, 2, 9, 8 and 4. Ask the learners to talk to their partner about how they could find the total. After giving the learners a few moments, confirm that they know the total is 30. Invite various learners to describe how they found the total and, as they do so, draw up a list of strategies, including using:

- number pairs for 10, • doubles, • near doubles, • place value, •...

Ask if any of the learners added the numbers in the order in which they were written. Someone may well have done so, adding 7 and 2 to make 9, then doubling 9 to make 18, then adding 2 of the 8 to make 20 and another 6 to make 26, then 26 + 4 = 30. Alternatively, they could have added 7 and 2 to make 9, then doubled 9 to make 18. Double 8 is 16 add 10 is 26, add 4 is 30. Explain that it is often easier to notice relationships between the numbers first, then add. Here, it could be 8 + 2 = 10, 7 + 4 = 1 more than 10, add that extra 1 to 9 to make another 10, 30 altogether.

Shuffle a set of *0 to 9 digit cards* and display five of them for the learners to add in pairs again. Agree the total and add any further strategies used to the list, for example, near number pairs for 10.

Vocabulary

total: how many altogether; i.e. how much of something there is.

addition: putting more than one amount together; the symbol is +.

Look out for!

- Learners who cannot recall the number pairs for 10. *Suggest that they draw up a list first. They could also list doubles to double 10. They can then use their lists for support. When adding totals in Addition grids 9 and 16, some learners may need to use a calculator.*

- Confident learners who are completing their tasks easily. *Challenge them to find the grand total in Addition Grids 9 and 16 by applying the same strategies as they did when adding several small numbers.*

Opportunities for display!

Display the learners' own puzzles, with the solutions in an envelope next to each puzzle. Challenge the learners and visitors to the classroom to work out the value of each picture or shape in a puzzle before checking the solution.

Draw the following puzzle where everyone can see it:

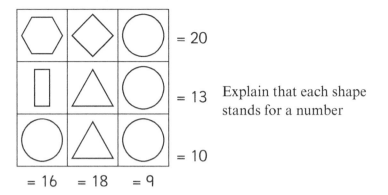

= 20

= 13   Explain that each shape
        stands for a number

= 10

= 16   = 18   = 9

Ask the learners to talk to their partner for a few moments about how they could find the value of each shape. Talk through, beginning with the circle. Since there are three of them in the column, we know the three lots of a circle makes 9, so a circle must be worth 3. The bottom row shows us that two circles (6) and a triangle makes 10. Using our number pairs for 10, the triangle must be 4 because 6 + 4 = 10.

Continue until the learners know what each shape in the puzzle is worth. Make sure they check across and down to be sure they are right.

Summary

Learners use their understanding of numbers to add several small numbers and to identify missing numbers.

Notes on the Learner's Book
Wildlife puzzle (p12): learners add small numbers and reason about numbers to find the value of each animal. They then use the animals as shorthand for numbers in a range of addition and subtraction calculations.

Check up!
- Use a set of digit cards to challenge learners whenever appropriate.
- Show pairs of learners four or five cards and ask them to rearrange them to show how they would add them.

More activities

Puzzles (individual)

> You will need the *Puzzles* photocopy master (CD-ROM), one copy per learner.

Learners work out the value of each picture in the *Puzzles* grid. They could go on to make their own puzzles.

Addition grids 9 (individual)

> You will need one copy of *Addition grid 9* (CD-ROM) per learner, *0 to 9 digit cards* photocopy master (CD-ROM), one copy per learner (without the 0), calculators, pens or pencils.

Learners shuffle a set of *digit cards* (without 0) and write the numbers in the 3 by 3 grid: *Addition grid 9* as they turn over each card. They then add the numbers in each row and column, then finally add these totals to reach a grand total. They may need to reorder these numbers to find the total. Ask the learners what they notice about the totals they find. Can they work out why?

Addition grids 16 (individual)

> You will need one copy of *Addition grid 16* per learner, 1–9 spinner, calculators, pens or pencils.

There are now 16 spaces in the grid, so learners will need to generate the numbers by rolling a dice or spinning a spinner. After completing the grid, they add the numbers in each row and column, then finally add these totals to reach a grand total. They may need to reorder these numbers to find the total. The numbers in the grid can now vary so different totals can be made. Ask the learners what helps them to make the largest total. What is the largest total that could be made? What is the smallest total that could be made?

Games Book (ISBN 9781107694019)

Addition game (p4) is a game for two players. Players add together several small numbers and then find the totals of a series of two-digit numbers, reordering as they choose to help with the calculation.

4 Doubling and halving

Quick reference

Core activity 4.1: Doubling and halving (Learner's Book p14)

Learners explore what happens when they halve a doubled number and double a halved number.

Prior learning	Objectives* – please note that listed objectives might only be partially covered within any given chapter but are covered fully across the book when taken as a whole
• Doubled numbers to at least 10. • Halved even numbers to at least 10.	**1A: Numbers and the number system** 3Nn3 – Count on and back in ones, tens and hundreds from two- and three-digit numbers. 3Nn4 – Count on and back in steps of 2, 3, 4 and 5 to at least 50. **1A: Calculation** (*Multiplication and division*) 3Nc19 – Understand the relationship between doubling and halving. **1A: Problem solving** (*Using techniques and skills in solving mathematical problems*) 3Pt1 – Choose appropriate mental strategies to carry out calculations. 3Pt3 – Make sense of and solve word problems and begin to represent them. **1A: Using understanding and strategies in solving problems** 3Ps1 – Make up a number story to go with a calculation. 3Ps3 – Explore and solve number problems and puzzles. 3Ps6 – Identify simple relationships between numbers.

*for NRICH activities mapped to the Cambridge Primary objectives, please visit www.cie.org.uk/cambridgeprimarymaths

Vocabulary

double • half • inverse

Resources: The *Number line 0 to 1000 (marked in 10s)* assembled in *Core activity 1.3*. *Doubling and halving* photocopy master (p26), one copy per learner. (Optional: *Doubling towers* photocopy master (CD-ROM), one copy per learner, pencil or pen.)

Count on and back in ones, two, tens and hundreds from any two- and three-digit number. Some learners may need the *Number line 0 to 1000 (marked in 10s)* from *Core activity 1.3* for support. Ask the learners to tell you what they know about even numbers. They should be able to tell you that an even number of objects can be arranged in pairs (twos) with none left over and that even numbers have 0, 2, 4, 6 or 8 ones.

Give each learner a copy of the *Doubling and halving* sheet and ask them to look at the first set of columns. The middle column is the even numbers. Each number can then be doubled and written in the right hand column, then halved and written in the left hand column. Ask the learners to complete all three columns. They can work down each column or across the three columns.

Once the learners have completed the three columns, ask them to look at the numbers in each column and tell you what they notice. They should notice that the first column increases in ones, the second in twos and the third in fours. Remind the learners that they started with the middle column and halved each number to get the column labelled 'half'. Ask them to look at the half column and mentally double the first few numbers. Ask what they notice. They should notice that when they double the numbers in the column labelled half, they get the numbers they started with. So halving is 'undone' by doubling. We could say that doubling and halving are opposites.

Ask the learners to look at the column labelled 'double' and mentally halve the first few numbers. They should notice that when they halve the numbers in the column labelled 'double', they get the numbers they started with. So doubling is 'undone' by halving – again, they are opposites. Explain that the mathematical word for this is **inverse**.

Ask the learners to complete the second set of columns. You may need to work through the first few with learners to make sure they get the idea. You could continue to support some groups while others continue on their own. Once completed, they should check if the doubling is undone or reversed by halving, and if halving is undone or reversed by doubling. Talk the learners through the checking if necessary.

End the session by asking the learners to describe how doubling and halving are related to each other.

Vocabulary

double: twice as much; multiply to 2.

half: one part of something that has been split into two equal pieces; divided by 2.

inverse: the opposite to or reversing of something. So doubling reverses (undoes) halving, and halving reverses (undoes) doubling.

Look out for!

- Learners who find doubling and halving difficult. *Give them cubes or counters to work with. For two-digit numbers, give them place value cards and counters or cubes to work with so that they can halve (or double) the tens and ones practically before adding the two parts together.*
- Learners who find these tasks straightforward. *Challenge them to extend the repeated doubling on the doubling towers even further. In addition, they could start with an even three-digit number and try repeatedly halving.*

Opportunities for display!

There are many possibilities for display here. Paired towers showing a number and its double; paired circles showing a number and its double; twins labelled with the same number and each pointing at the double, and so on.

Summary

Learners begin to understand that doubling and halving are inverse operations, they each reverse or undo the other.

Notes on the Learner's Book

Double and half (p14): learners answer doubling and halving questions and match up the inverse calculations. Challenge some learners to make up a grid of doubles and halves for a friend to indentify inverses.

Check up!
- Give learners a number to double and then ask them to undo (or reverse) the doubling, saying what they did.
- If you gave learners four, they could say, "*Double 4 is 8 and half of 8 is 4.*"

More activities

Doubling towers (individual)

> You will need the *Doubling towers* photocopy master (CD-ROM), one copy per learner, and a pencil or pen.

Double the number on each floor to climb to the next floor. Tell the learners that splitting the number into hundreds, tens and ones will make it easier to double two- and three-digit numbers.

Doubling and halving stories (individual)

Give the learners a doubling or halving fact such as, "*Double 2 is 4,*" and ask them to make up a story about that calculation. For example, "*Bananas were 2 for the price of 1, so I paid for 2 but got 4.*" Or, "*Half of 10 is 5 – I had 10 marbles but lost half of them, so I only have 5 left.*"

Games Book (ISBN 9781107694019)

Double and half pelmanism (p4) is a game for two players. Learners recognise the relationship between doubling and halving by finding pairs of numbers which are the double and half of each other.

Doubling and halving

Odd numbers

half	number	double
	1	
	3	
	5	
	7	
	9	

Even numbers

half	number	double
1	2	4
2	4	8
	6	
	8	
	10	

5 Number pairs

Quick reference

Core activity 5.1: Fact families (Learner's Book p15)
Learners revise addition and subtraction facts to 20 and explore other addition and subtraction fact families. They also explore equivalence.

Core activity 5.2: Calculation strips (Learner's Book p16)
Learners explore the relationship between addition and subtraction and equivalence. They begin to develop a sense of number.

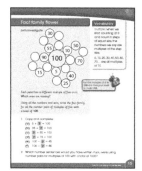

Prior learning	Objectives* – please note that listed objectives might only be partially covered within any given chapter but are covered fully across the book when taken as a whole

• Explored addition and subtraction facts for numbers to 20.
• Explored multiples of 10.
	1A: Calculation (*Mental strategies*)
	3Nc1 – Know addition and subtraction facts for all numbers to 20.
	3Nc2 – Know the following addition and subtraction facts:
	    Multiples of 100 with a total of 1000
	    Multiples of 5 with a total of 100.
	1A: Calculation (*Addition and subtraction*)
	3Nc11 – Use the = sign to represent equality.
	1A: Problem solving (*Using techniques and skills in solving mathematical problems*)
	3Pt1 – Choose appropriate mental strategies to carry out calculations.
	3Pt3 – Make sense of and solve word problems and begin to represent them.
	3Pt4 – Check the results of adding two numbers using subtraction, and several numbers by adding in a different order.
	3Pt5 – Check subtraction by adding the answer to the smaller number in the original calculation.
	3Pt12 – Consider whether an answer is reasonable.
	1A: Using understanding and strategies in solving problems
	3Ps2 – Explain a choice of calculation strategy and show how the answer was worked out.
	3Ps3 – Explore and solve number problems and puzzles.
	3Ps6 – Identify simple relationships between numbers.

*for NRICH activities mapped to the Cambridge Primary objectives, please visit www.cie.org.uk/cambridgeprimarymaths

Vocabulary
calculation • multiple

Resources: (Optional: *Fun fact families* photocopy master (CD-ROM), one copy per learner, a pen; *Multiple target board* photocopy master (CD-ROM), one copy per learner, a pen.)

Begin the session counting forward and back in tens from any two- or three-digit number. Choose a two-digit number and count on and back in hundreds, ending with counting from 0 to 1000 and back again in hundreds.

Draw the fact family triangle for 3, 16 and 19, and ask the learners to quickly write the four number sentences for the triangle. After a few moments, ask four different learners to tell you one of the number sentences. Record them next to the triangle so that everyone can check that they are correct.

$3 + 16 = 19$
$16 + 3 = 19$
$19 - 3 = 16$
$19 - 16 = 3$

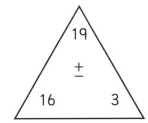

Write up the number sentence □ + ◇ = ⌂. Explain that we do not know what any of the numbers are, but we can still write the other three number sentences in the family. Give learners a few minutes to work with their partner to write the sentences.

□ + ◇ = ⌂

◇ + □ = ⌂

⌂ − □ = ◇

⌂ − ◇ = □

Ask some learners to explain what they did to find the other sentences. Tell the learners that ⌂ stands for 500 and □ and ◇ are multiples of 100. Challenge the learners to write all the possible addition and subtraction number sentences using 500 and multiples of 100 to 500.

Vocabulary

multiple: when we start counting at 0 and count in steps of equal size, we say the numbers are multiples of the step size. For example, 0, 10, 20, 30, 40, 50, 60, 70…are all multiples of 10. Multiples of 10 are the numbers in the ten times table. This is true for all multiples, so multiples of two are the numbers in the two times table, multiples of three are the numbers in the three times table and so on.

calculation: another word for a number sentence.

Look out for!

- Learners who find it hard to see how the facts relate to each other. *Explore fun fact families with them to help them to recognise the relationship between the numbers.*
- Learners who can see how the facts relate to each other. *Challenge them by giving them a single number, such as 97, and asking them to find three different fact families using the given number in any way they wish.*

Check that the learners have correctly identified the multiples of 100 and written the fact families for each set of calculations. Remind them that the equals sign means the same total is on both sides. Ask the learners to pair their number sentences using the equals sign, for example:
100 + 400 = 400 + 100. Alternatively, they could write,
100 + 400 = 300 + 200.

Draw up a list of paired sentences, asking the rest of the class to check they are correct. There are many possibilities, so do not try to collect them all. End with some missing number problems, for example 30 + □ = □ + 50. Ask the learners which numbers could be in the boxes and how these numbers are related to each other. In this example, the difference between 30 and 50 is 20, so there must be a difference of 20 between the two missing numbers and the higher number must be paired with 30 or both sides of the equals sign will not have the same total.

Summary

Learners can write the fact family for an addition or subtraction number sentence. They can use the equals sign to show equivalence.

Notes on the Learner's Book
Fact family flower (p15): learners complete the multiples of 5 to 100 then write the fact families for pairs of multiples of 5 to 100.

Check up!
Give the learners a number sentence and ask them to tell you one or more of the other facts in the fact family.

More activities

Fun fact families (individual)

> You will need the *Fun fact families* photocopy master (CD-ROM), one copy per learner, and a pen.

Learners write the fact families for objects that go together to make a third article.

Multiple target boards (individual)

> You will need the *Multiple target board* photocopy master (CD-ROM), one copy per learner, and a pen.

These target boards help the learners to practise the addition and subtraction facts specified in objective 3Nc2. The target boards focus on the multiples of 100 with a total of 1000 and the multiples of five with a total of 100. Learners find the calculations which total 100 or 1000, identify which multiples have been used and write the fact family for each calculation.

> **Resources:** Strips of paper approximately 15 cm wide and as long as you can make them, one per learner, pens. (Optional: cards showing 20 random numbers between 20 and 100; *Equivalence* photocopy master (CD-ROM); strips of paper as above, one per learner, pens; *Blank target board* photocopy master (CD-ROM), one copy per learner.

Begin the session counting forward and back in ones, twos, fives or tens from any two- or three-digit number.

Write three additions where everyone can see them:

$15 + 4$
$12 + 5$
$11 + 8$

Confirm the totals of 19, 17 and 19 with the learners and write them in. Ask the learners to talk to their partner about how they could check they were correct, then share ideas. If necessary, remind the learners that they can change the order of the numbers when they add. They could also subtract one of the numbers from the total to check. Ask the learners to look at the additions again. Explain that they could also compare calculations. If $15 + 4$ = 19, then swap $12 + 5$ around to make $15 + 2$. The previous calculation was $15 + 4$ so $15 + 2$ must be 2 less, 17. Also talk about having an idea what the total must be. Looking at the ones digits, none of the additions have enough ones to make another 10, so the totals must be under 20. Any total over 20 cannot be right.

Write up three subtractions where everyone can see them.

$15 - 4$
$12 - 5$
$11 - 8$

Confirm the totals of 11, 7 and 3. Ask the learners how they could check they were correct. If necessary, remind them that they cannot subtract in any order but they could add the answer to the smaller number. Explain that they can also compare the calculations. The last two must be less than 10 because they are taking away more ones than the two-digit number has in the ones space.

Look out for!

- Learners who use just one strategy for addition (or subtraction). *Ask them to complete a calculation, then talk through different ways of tackling it and the occasions when a different method would be useful.*
- Learners who are using the techniques confidently. *Encourage them to contribute calculations involving both addition and subtraction or to use more than two numbers on the calculation strips.*

Opportunities for display!

Display the strips of equivalent calculations with the heading 'Equivalence' and label with questions such as, 'Can you think of another calculation for each strip?' You could also display some incomplete strips for people to continue.

Tell the learners that it is useful to have all these things in mind when they are adding or subtracting.

Give each pair of learners a strip of paper and ask them to write any addition or subtraction and the equals sign on the left of the strip.

37 – 19 =

Learners pass the strips around the room, writing a new calculation with the same totals on the strips, until all pairs of learners have contributed to every strip. Each pair then check that all the calculations on the strip they end up with have the same total, correcting any mistakes.

Summary

Learners have developed a range of strategies to support addition and subtraction. They use the equals sign to show equivalence.

Notes on the Learner's Book
Target 11 (p16): you will need the *Blank target board* photocopy master (CD-ROM) one copy per learner. Alternatively, learners could draw their own 8 by 8 grid on squared paper. Learners find the addition number sentences which total 11, then link them with the equals sign. They also find other totals to link and explore subtraction of 11. Some learners could go on to colour all the same totals in one colour, another total in a different colour and so on.

Check up!
Give learners a number sentence without a total and ask them to tell you an equivalent calculation.

More activities

Equivalence (individual)

You will need cards showing 20 random numbers between 20 and 100 and the *Equivalence* photocopy master (CD-ROM) one copy per learner.

Give learners a random selection of 20 numbers between 20 and 100. Learners shuffle the cards and turn over the top two cards, writing the numbers in any of the boxes either side of the equals sign on their *Equivalence* sheet. They then work out which numbers could go in the other two boxes to make both sides equal. Challenge some learners to use numbers up to 1000.

Calculation strips (small group, as for core activity)

> You will need strips of paper approximately 15 cm wide and as long as you can make them, one per learner, pens.

Each learner starts a calculation strip. The strips can be passed around the group until they return to the starter, who then checks it and corrects any errors. This allows the numbers and calculations to be tailored to the group. For example, you could say that the calculation must include three numbers and two subtraction signs or three numbers and both addition and subtraction.

Games Book (ISBN 9781107694019)

Target dice (p9) is a game for two players. Players add and subtract three or more small numbers to reach a target number.

Quick reference

Core activity 6.1: Sorting multiples (Learner's Book p17)
Learners explore two- and three-digit multiples of 2, 5 and 10.

Core activity 6.2: Multiple fact families (Learner's Book p18)
Learners explore the fact family triangles for multiplication and division.

Core activity 6.3: Multiple patterns (Learner's Book p20)
Learners explore patterns in multiplication and pair facts.

Prior learning	Objectives* – please note that listed objectives might only be partially covered within any given chapter but are covered fully across the book when taken as a whole
• Counting on and back in steps of 2, 5 or 10 from any two- or three-digit number. • Explored counting in multiples of 3 from zero. • Multiplication as an array and grouping.	**1A: Numbers and the number system** 3Nn4 – Count on and back in steps of 2, 3, 4 and 5 to at least 50. **1A: Calculation** (*Mental strategies*) 3Nc3 – Know multiplication/division facts for 2×, 3×, 5×, and 10× tables. 3Nc4 – Begin to know 4× table. 3Nc5 – Recognise two- and three-digit multiples of 2, 5 and 10. **1A: Calculation** (*Addition and subtraction*) 3Nc11 – Use the = sign to represent equality. **1A: Calculation** (*Multiplication and division*) 3Nc20 – Understand the effect of multiplying two-digit numbers by 10. 3Nc25 – Understand and apply the idea that multiplication is commutative. **1A: Problem solving** (*Using techniques and skills in solving mathematical problems*) 3Pt1 – Choose appropriate mental strategies to carry out calculations. 3Pt3 – Make sense of and solve word problems and begin to represent them. **1A: Using understanding and strategies in solving problems** 3Ps1 – Make up a number story to go with a calculation. 3Ps2 – Explain a choice of calculation strategy and show how the answer was worked out. 3Ps3 – Explore and solve number problems and puzzles. 3Ps5 – Describe and continue patterns which count on or back in steps of 2, 3, 4, 5, 10 or 100. 3Ps6 – Identify simple relationships between numbers.

Vocabulary
commutative • divisible by • multiple • Venn diagram

*for NRICH activities mapped to the Cambridge Primary objectives, please visit www.cie.org.uk/cambridgeprimarymaths

Resources: *Blank Venn diagram* photocopy master (p42), one copy per pair, pens and large sheets of paper. (Optional: *100 cent square* photocopy master (CD-ROM), one copy per learner.)

Begin by counting forward and back in twos, tens and hundreds from any two- or three-digit number. Tell the learners that they can count in twos, tens and hundreds because they understand the patterns the numbers make. Ask the learners to explain how they can tell whether a number is a multiple of 2, 5 or 10. Draw a simple Venn diagram labelled 'Multiples of 2 and Multiples of 5' and discuss with the learners where a few single digit numbers belong. Then add a third oval labelled 'Multiples of 10'. Ask the learners to talk with a partner about what kind of numbers should be placed in each section.

After a few moments, share the learner's ideas. Enclose the Venn diagram in a box and tell the learners that you want to focus on the numbers 75 to 125, deciding where to write each number. Delete any previous numbers and invite various learners to write 75, 76, 77, 78 and 79 on the diagram. Check each number with the rest of the class.

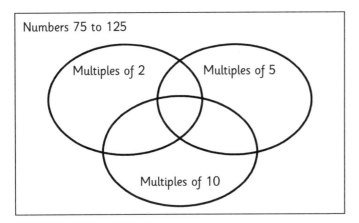

Give each pair of learners a copy of the *Blank Venn diagram*. They should copy the diagram and work through the numbers between 75 and 125, writing each number in the relevant sections. As the learners work, circulate around the room asking pairs of learners questions such as, *"How did you decide where to put that number? Why is it in this space rather than that one? Which number has been multiplied by 2 (or 5 or 10) to make that number? How many twos (or fives or tens) in that number?"*

Look out for!

- Learners who find it difficult to move from a Venn diagram with two overlapping circles to one with three. *They may need to look at the three pairs of overlapping circles separately to get the idea. Encourage them to write which type of numbers can be written in each of the overlaps for support.*
- Learners who quickly recognise the patterns in the numbers for each section of the Venn diagram. *Challenge them to create their own three oval Venn diagram, deciding how to label each oval and the range of numbers to work with.*

Opportunities for display!

Display different Venn diagrams on the wall with an explanation of what a Venn diagram is. Label with questions such as, 'Can you put another number on this Venn diagram?' and, 'Where would 250 be?' Venn diagrams created in science sessions or other areas could also be displayed.

Once the learners have worked through the majority of the numbers, bring them back together to talk about what they notice. In the multiples of 2 oval but not in any overlap will be the multiples of 2 with 2, 4, 6 and 8 ones. In the multiples of 5 oval, but not in any overlap will be the multiples of 5 with 5 ones. In the multiples of 10 oval, all the multiples of 10 should be placed in the overlap of all three ovals. Talk through the overlaps, asking questions such as "*Are there any numbers that are multiples of 2 and 5? Are there any numbers that are multiples of 2 and 10? Are there any numbers that are multiples of 5 and 10?*" The answer to all three questions is the tens numbers, so they must go in the overlap of all three ovals, leaving the overlaps of the tens oval with the other two ovals and the rest of the tens oval empty.

Summary

Learners recognise two and three-digit multiples of 2, 5 and 10, including those which are multiples of more than one of them.

Notes on the Learner's Book
Will you won't you? (p17): learners explore counting on and back in twos, fives and tens, checking whether or not they will say a particular number.

Check up!
- Give learners a number and ask them if it is a multiple of 2, 5 or 10, or more than one of those.
- Alternatively, ask learners to tell you a multiple of 2 (or 5 or 10), and another, and another.

More activities

Numa Island (individual)

> You will need the *100 cent square* photocopy master (CD-ROM), one copy per learner.

On Numa Island, you can buy three different postage stamps – 2 cents, 5 cents and 10 cents. Ask questions such as "*If a letter costs 47c to post, how many different ways can you put the correct stamps on the letter? If a parcel costs 91 cents to post, how many different ways can you put the correct stamps on the parcel? 2 cent stamps are in short supply. Customers can only buy two each, though they can buy as many 5c and 10c stamps as they like.*" Which amounts can you make? Which amounts are you unable to make?" Give learners a copy of the *100 cent square* to help them keep a record of which amounts they can and cannot make.

Paired Facts (individual)

Ask learners to quickly write the 2, 5 and 10 times table. They then look for facts with the same total and pair them, using the equals sign to show equality, for example $2 \times 5 = 1 \times 10$. Challenge some learners to use the division facts as well.

Resources: Paper, pens, counters, cubes or squared paper. *Multiplying by 10* photocopy master (CD-ROM), one copy per learner. (Optional: learners will need pens, paper and counters, cubes or other objects for counting; *Multiplication grids* photocopy master (CD-ROM), one copy per learner; *Times ten aliens* photocopy master (CD-ROM) one copy per learner.)

Begin the session by asking learners to quickly write the 10 times table. Draw a large triangle and label it as shown.

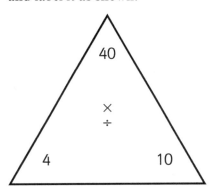

Ask the learners to talk to their partner about the triangle and what it shows. After a few moments, share ideas. If necessary, remind the learners that they have seen triangles like this before. They used them to summarise all the addition and subtraction facts in the fact family for those particular numbers. Explain that this triangle is the same, but the fact family is for multiplication and division.

Ask the learners to work with their partner to write the four facts shown in the triangle, if they have not done so. After a few moments, invite four different learners to tell you one of the facts and list them where everyone can see.
Draw a matching array and show all four facts.

$4 \times 10 = 40$

$10 \times 4 = 40$

$40 \div 4 = 10$

$40 \div 10 = 4$

| × × × × × × × × × × |
| × × × × × × × × × × |
| × × × × × × × × × × |
| × × × × × × × × × × |

Vocabulary

commutative: we can add or multiply two or more numbers in any order and the total will be the same. Multiplication and addition are commutative.

Look out for!

- Learners who cannot see the link between multiplication and division. *Ask them to tell you a multiplication calculation and solve it together by modelling it with an array. Then show how the same array is a model of the matching division calculations, so the numbers are in the same family. Alternatively, model the four calculations from one fact family triangle with an array to show that the four arrays are identical.*

- Learners with older siblings who may have told them that when you multiply by 10, you just add a zero. *Explain that they will find out as they move through school that this does not always work, so it is not a good shortcut to learn.*

- Learners who immediately see the link between multiplication and division and do not need to make arrays. *Challenge them to find different fact families for the same total.*

Write the ten times table where everyone can see it. Ask the learners to write the matching division facts for at least three of the facts in the ten times table. They may find it useful to use counters, cubes or squared paper to make the matching array to help them at first.

Ask the learners to look carefully at each number before and after it is multiplied by 10. Ask them to describe how the number changes. Although learners may say a zero has been added to the end of the number, make sure they realise that every 1 has become a 10 because we have multiplied by 10. If necessary, explain that is what multiplying is – when we multiply by 5, each 1 becomes a 5; when we multiply by 2, each 1 becomes a 2. When we multiply by 10, this has the effect of moving all the digits one place to the left. We then need a zero in the ones place to stop them from slipping back. Write a '3' where everyone can see it and pretend to push it to the left and write a zero in after the three to stop it moving back. Talk through what happens with two more single digit numbers. Give each learner a copy of the *Multiplying by 10* sheet and talk through completing the first three multiplications, reminding the learners that each 1 becomes a 10 because we have multiplied by 10, the number is 10 times bigger. Skip forward to the second column and talk through 10 tens. As before, pretend to push the 10 to the left and write a zero in after the 10 to stop it moving back.

Repeat with 20, then ask the learners to complete all the multiplications.

Finish the session by checking that the learners have recognised that the multiplication and division facts can be grouped into families just like addition and subtraction facts. Ask the learners what this tells them about the facts. If necessary, explain that multiplication can be done in any order, just like addition. So $4 \times 10 = 10 \times 4$. Explain that mathematicians have a special word for this. They say that that multiplication is **commutative**, which simply means that it can be done in any order, just like addition. Explain that division is like subtraction, it undoes multiplication. But multiplication also undoes division, they are each the **inverse** of the other.

Opportunities for display!

Take photographs of the learners' arrays and display them next to times tables and fact family triangles.

Summary

Learners recognise the link between multiplication and division using arrays and fact families. They understand what commutative means.

Notes on the Learner's Book

Assorted multiples (p18): learners work through various questions and problems about multiples.

Check up!

- Give the learners half of a paired number sentence, for example 2×5, and ask them to tell you the rest of the sentence, for example 5×2 or 1×10.
- You could also ask them to explain what commutative means.

More activities

<u>Times tables fact families</u> (individual)

> Learners will need pens, paper and counters, cubes or other objects for counting.

Focus on the 5 (or 2 or 10) times table. Ask learners to write out the 5 (or 2 or 10) times table, then draw the fact family triangle for each fact. They should choose three triangles to write out the fact family for and make the matching array using counters, cubes or something else.

<u>Multiplication Grids</u> (individual)

> You will need the *Multiplication grids* photocopy master (CD-ROM), one copy per learner, pens.

Learners complete the *Multiplication grids*. They then write the fact families for the indicated facts.

<u>Times ten aliens</u> (individual)

> You will need the *Times ten aliens* photocopy master (CD-ROM), one copy per learner, pens.

Learners complete the calculations to find out which alien got the most correct.

Resources: Large *100 square* (chapter 1, p12). *Multiples of 3 and 4* photocopy master (CD-ROM), one copy per learner. Colouring pencils. (Optional: 1–6 dice (CD-ROM); sticky labels; *Multiples of 2, 3, 4 and 5* photocopy master (CD-ROM), one copy per learner; colouring pencils.

Begin the session by counting forward and back in twos, tens and hundreds from any two- or three-digit number. Tell the learners that you know they can count in fives from 0, but what if they started at three, could they count in fives then? Look at the pattern together on the large 100 square, making sure the learners realise that the numbers alternate between three and eight ones. Count from three to 98 in fives. Then challenge the learners to count on from 103. Ask them what the pattern would be if they started at four. Count on from 104 in fives.

Give each learner a copy of the *Multiples of 3 and 4* sheet. Ask them to choose two different colouring pencils. They need to count along the 100 square in threes first of all to find the multiples of 3, and then in fours to find the multiples of 4. They should colour the top half of the square using one colour if a number is a multiple of 3 and the bottom half of the square using the other colour if the number is a multiple of 4. After the learners have coloured the multiples to at least 50, ask them to write out the 3 and 4 times tables.

Finish the session by talking to the learners about what they have noticed. Ask them to describe the patterns they can see for threes and fours. Check that they have noticed that they have coloured every other number from the 2 times table, or in other words, every other even number. Ask which squares have been coloured in using both colours. Check that the learners have identified 12, 24, 36, 48, 60, 72, 84 and 96. Ask the learners to tell you as much as they can about these numbers – for example, they are multiples of 4, multiples of 3, divisible by 3 and divisible by 4. Ask them to write some paired facts about those numbers, for example $9 \times 4 = 12 \times 3$ or $36 \div 4 = 3 \times 3$

Vocabulary

divisible by: a number is divisible by another number if there is no remainder after dividing.

Look out for!

- Learners who find it very difficult to recognise the pattern of counting in fives from three and four. *Give them a copy of a 100 square to colour in the numbers, counting on five each time. The colouring can be done quite quickly with a thick marker pen so that the pattern is quickly revealed.*
- Learners who find it straightforward to describe the pattern created by the multiples of three. *Encourage them to recognise that the pattern repeats itself in chunks of 30. Ask them to predict whether numbers such as 123, 139 or 156 are multiples of three.*

Opportunities for display!

Display the coloured multiple sheets with the other work on multiples from this unit.

Summary

Learners recognise the patterns produced when multiplying by 2, 3, 4 and 5. They can use the equals sign to show equivalence in multiplication and division.

Notes on the Learner's Book

Multiple multiples (p20): you will need the *Multiples of 2, 3, 4 and 5* photocopy master (CD-ROM) one copy per learner and colouring pencils. Learners explore the patterns when counting in multiples of 2, 3, 4 and 5 from 0, including multiples which occur in more than one count.

Check up!

- Say the first part of a ×3 number sentence and ask the learners to complete it.
- Challenge some learners by asking them a ×4 question.
- You could also ask, "*How many threes in 12? How many fours in 8?*" and so on.

More activities

Target 100 (pairs)

> You will need a 1–6 dice and a sticky label for each pair.

Place a sticker over each 6 on the dice and write 0 or miss a turn on it. Give each pair of learners two dice. They take it in turns to roll the dice and multiply the two numbers together. They keep a running total of their scores. Set a target of 100 or 200 and challenge the learners to get as close to the target as they can.

Games Book (ISBN 9781107694019)

The multiples game (p9) is a game for two or three players. Players recognise multiples of 2, 3, 4 and 5 to 50.
Domino multiplication (p11) is a game for two or three players. Players multiply by 0, 1, 2, 3, 4 and 5 and add the totals.

Blank Venn diagram

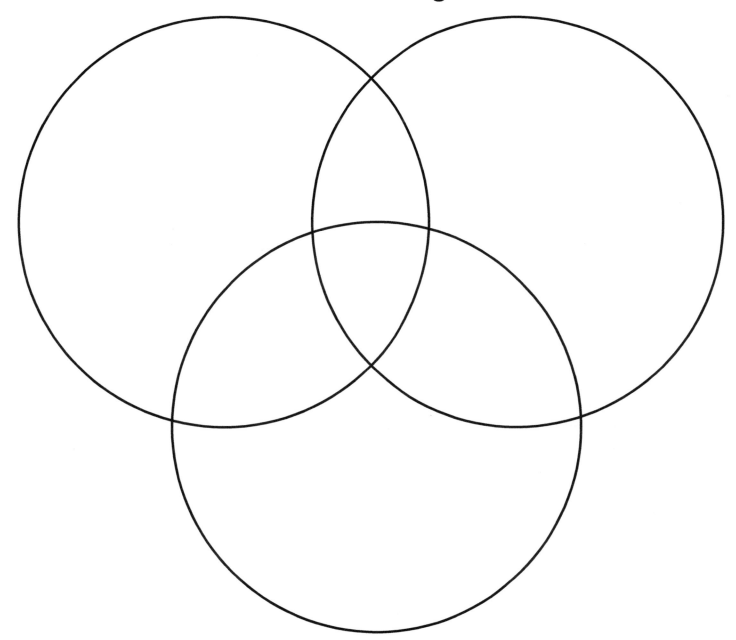

7 Shapes, shapes and more shapes

Quick reference

Core activity 7.1: 2D shapes (Learner's Book p24)

Learners revise 2D shape which leads on to recognising and drawing regular and irregular 2D shapes.

Core activity 7.2: 3D shapes (Learner's Book p26)

Learners revise knowledge and understanding of 3D solids and build on this when constructing, comparing and discussing shapes.

Core activity 7.3: Nets of 3D shapes (Learner's Book p28)

Learners apply knowledge and understanding of 3D shape by identifying, making and describing prisms and pyramids. This activity also includes using correct mathematical vocabulary and language in order to describe what the learners did and what they found out.

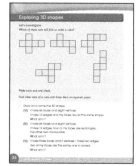
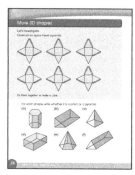

Prior learning	Objectives* – please note that listed objectives might only be partially covered within any given chapter but are covered fully across the book when taken as a whole
• Names and properties of 2D shapes. • Knowledge and understanding of right angles. • Some knowledge of classifying shapes. • Understanding how the net of the shape builds into the shape itself.	**1B: Geometry** 3Gs8 – Identify right angles in 2D shapes. 3Gs1 – Identify, describe and draw regular and irregular 2D shapes including pentagons, hexagons, octagons, semi-circles. 3Gs2 – Classify 2D shapes according to the number of sides, vertices and right angles. 3Gs3 – Identify, describe and make 3D shapes including pyramids and prisms, investigate which nets will make a cube. 3Gs4 – Classify 3D shapes according to the number and shape of faces, number of vertices and edges. 3Gs6 – Relate 2D shapes and 3D solids to drawings of them. **1B: Problem solving** 3Pt8 – Recognise the relationships between different 2D shapes. 3Pt9 – Identify the differences and similarities between different 3D shapes.

*for NRICH activities mapped to the Cambridge Primary objectives, please visit www.cie.org.uk/cambridgeprimarymaths

Vocabulary

circular • cone • cube • cuboid • cylinder • edges/sides • hexagon • hexagonal • irregular • octagon • pentagon • pentagonal • prism • pyramid • quadrilateral • rectangular • regular • semi-circle • right angle • sphere • symmetric • triangular • vertices

Resources: *Shape cards* photocopy master (p53), one copy. A6 paper ($\frac{1}{4}$ of A4) or post-it stickers. Pencils. A large Venn diagram for display and *Labels for Venn diagram* photocopy master (CD-ROM), one copy. (Optional: *Shape cards* photocopy master (p53), one set per pair; scissors; 5×5 pin boards, elastic bands (or spotty paper and a ruler); paper, pens/pencils.)

Begin the session with a quiz in order to find out what learners already know and understand about 2D shape. This can be done as a team game or by individuals. Begin with:

"I have one side, I have no corners, I have one curved edge. What am I?" When learners have decided upon the answer (**circle**) ask, *"How do you know that? Could it have been anything different? What if I had one straight edge and one curved edge? Would that still be a circle? Why not? What is it called?"* (**semi-circle**) *"Who can tell me what 'semi' means?"* (**half**)

Continue with, *"I have four straight sides. I have four corners. What could I be?"* Allow learners to talk together to discuss the options, then say, *"I could be a square; I could be a rectangle. I could be any shape with four sides. If a shape has four sides, we call it a quadrilateral (quad means four) Let me give you the next clue. All my sides are the same length."* Give time for the class to answer. Confirm that, *"I am a square. Could I have been anything else? Why not?"*

Finally, say, *"I have three straight sides, I have three corners, and sometimes two of my sides meet at a right angle."* When learners have decided upon the answer (**triangle**) ask, *"Could it have been anything else? Why not? Who can tell me what a right angle is?"* Give time for discussion between pairs or groups and ask for responses.

Using the *Shape cards* sheet, read the first description and ask the class to draw what they think it is on A6 paper or a post-it sticker. This can be done individually, in pairs or as small groups. When all of the description cards have been read, each learner/pair/group will have drawn a set of 2D shapes.

Display the large Venn diagram and say, *"We are going to sort these shapes using a Venn diagram."* Choose two of the *Labels for Venn diagram* and read them to the class. Put the labels on to the Venn diagram. Read the left-hand one. Ask, *"Who has a shape that can go here? Any more?"*

Vocabulary

right angle: is a quarter trun; it has a size of 90 degrees (90°).

regular: a shape that has all sides the same length and all angles the same size.

irregular: a shape that is not regular; lengths of all sides are not the same.

polygon: a shape with three or more straight sides.

pentagon: a five-sided polygon.

hexagon: a six-sided polygon.

octogan: an eight-sided polygon.

quadrilateral: 2D shape with four sides.

semi-circle: 2D shape of a half circle, formed by cutting a whole circle along a diameter line.

Look out for!

- Learners experiencing difficulties sorting the shapes into the Venn diagram. *Allow them to use a Venn diagram with no intersection so that they have only two attributes. Give them a set of shapes so that they have a visual reference on the table.*

Ask two or three other learners to bring their shapes for that left-hand circle. Some shapes may need to be in the centre of the Venn diagram, but place them where the learners say, as they can be moved later.

Ask, "*How do you know this one fits here? Show me where your shape has this property.*" Repeat for the right-hand side. Then say, "*We need to put some shapes into this middle part. Which shapes can go here? What does it mean when we have the circles overlapping? Do we need to move any of the shapes into this part of the Venn diagram? Why?*"

Encourage discussion between the learners so that they can give you reasons for moving any shapes. Display the completed Venn diagram to use as reference for later sessions.

Revise the meaning of quadrilateral. Ask, "*What do we call a four-sided shape?*" (**quadrilateral**) "*Tell me the name of a quadrilateral*" (**square, rectangle**). "*What about this shape?*" Draw an irregular quadrilateral on the board. "*How many sides does it have?*" (**4**) "*What is a four-sided shape called?*" (**quadrilateral**) "*Any shape that has four sides is a quadrilateral.*" Choose some learners to draw an example of a four-sided shape that is not regular. Count the sides. Ask "*Are all of these quadrilaterals? How do you know?*" Repeat with regular and irregular pentagons, hexagons and octagons, ensuring that learners recognise that any five-sided shape is a pentagon, and so on.

- Learners who are confident using a Venn diagram. *Encourage them to use one with three overlapping circles for sorting and classifying shapes. Learners can choose the criteria for sorting. Alternatively, use a Carroll diagram.*

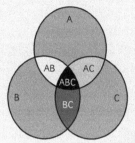

	Straight edge	Not straight edge
Quadrilateral		
Not quadrilateral		

Opportunities for display!

Completed Venn diagram.

Any photos of work done using the pin boards.

Summary

By the end of this activity learners will have revised and learnt new 2D shapes and will be able to name them, talk about their properties and use that knowledge to solve a problem of classification using a Venn diagram.

Notes on the Learner's Book

2D shapes (p24): learners will need pin boards and elastic bands. This exercise begins by taking the core activity into a more practical context, allowing learners to explore different quadrilaterals using a geoboard and elastic bands; it then moves on to more formal activities which allow learners to show what they have learnt.

Check up!

- Ask a learner/pair to think of (or pick from a bag without looking) a 2D shape. The rest of the class asks them questions where the answer can be only 'yes' or 'no'. For example:
  - *"Does the shape have straight sides?"*
  - *"Does the shape have three equal sides?"*
  - *"Does the shape have one straight side and one curved side?"*
- The learner/pair who correctly guess the shape after their question choose a new shape of their own.
- This allows the teacher to hear correct mathematical vocabulary and language in order to find the shapes.

More activities

Shape matching (pairs)

You will need the *Shape cards* photocopy master (p53), one set per pair, and scissors.

Cut out the *Shape cards*, shuffle them and place a set face down in front of each pair. Learners take it in turns to take and turn over a card until all of the cards have gone. They then match the shape, the properties and the name from the cards they have picked. Any cards that are left from each player are shuffled and put back face down. Play as before, shuffling and placing in the centre until all of the cards have gone. The player with the most cards is the winner.

Geoboard investigations (individual or pair)

Each individual or pair will need a 5×5 pin board and elastic bands (or spotty paper and a ruler). Investigate:
1. The number of ways of forming a square surrounding five pins/dots.
2. The number of ways of forming a symmetric cross, each of which surrounds five pins/dots.
3. The number of ways of forming a square which surrounds nine pins/dots.

Carroll diagram (individual or pair)

You will need paper and pens/pencils.

Use a Carroll diagram to sort shapes according to sets of criteria such as right angle/not right angle, more than four sides/four sides or less.

Games Book (ISBN 9781107694019)

Shape sort and cover (p35) is a game for two players. This is designed to reinforce the names and properties of 2D shapes.

Resources: Polydron shapes (alternatively, both pages of the *Card shapes* photocopy master (CD-ROM), one set per learner, and scissors). (Optional: square shapes; paper, pens/pencils and sticky tape.)

Note: this activity may take two sessions if there is no additional help.

Give learners a supply of polydron shapes (squares and triangles); if polydron shapes are not available, hand out copies of the two sheets of *Card shapes* and ask learners to cut the sheets along the lines to form the squares and triangles. These are an excellent way to explore properties of 3D shapes. Ask the learners to work in pairs to make some squares. How many different squares are made? Ask learners to show the square that they have made and, as a class, discuss similarities and differences.

"Have all of the squares been made with the same number of pieces? How many different totals of shapes do we have in each square?"

Sort and classify the number of pieces used to make the square.

Ask pairs of learners to make five more squares the same size as the one they have just made. *"You can make it in the same way or a different way. Join your six squares together so that you make a cross."* This may need to be modelled so that the learners are clear about the task. Ask the learners to fold the pieces up. *"What shape have you made?"* (**cube**)

Now say, *"I wonder what would happen if you used triangles? Join four equilateral triangles together and fold them up. What shape have you made?"* (**a pyramid**) Ask, *"Can you make a pyramid in a different way? Is there a way where you use four equilateral triangles and another shape?"*

Give time for pairs to discuss and discover. Take feedback. (**four triangles and a square**)

Vocabulary

cube: a 3D shape with six square faces.

prism: a solid object that has two identical ends and all flat sides. The cross section is the same all along its length. The shape of the ends give the prism a name, such as 'triangular prism'. Regular prisms are shapes with equal edge lengths, and equal angles.

polydron: geometric plastic shapes that can be clipped together.

equilateral triangles: a triangle with all three sides the same length and all three angles the same size.

pyramid: a 3D shape with a polygon base and all other faces triangles, meeting at a corner (vertex).

cuboid: a 3D shape with rectangular faces.

cylinder: a 3D shape with two circular bases.

sphere: a circular shape like a ball.

circular: in the shape of a circle.

rectangular: in the shape of a rectangle.

hexagonal: in the shape of a hexagon.

vertex: the point where two sides join, another word for corner; plural vertices.

Look out for!

- Learners experiencing difficulties. *Although this is an activity that all learners can succeed at, they will need to use fine motor skills. Working with a partner will help.*
- Learners who have completed the tasks successfully. *Give extra challenges such as:*
  - *This solid needs eight equilateral triangles. Green triangles are always joined to yellow triangles. There are four green triangles. Only two colours are used.*
  - *This solid is a cube. Only three colours are used. One blue square touches all three red squares. Another blue square touches only two red squares. A yellow square touches only one blue square.*

"Using the shapes, can you make other solids? Can you make a cuboid or a prism?"

"What solids can you make and what solids can't you make?"

As the learners are working, walk around the room to make sure that everyone understands the task.

Ask questions such as, *"Can you make that solid in a different way? How can you make it longer/wider? Can you make that solid using fewer or different shapes?"*

- *Learners make a shape and give instructions to their partner on how to make it.*

Opportunities for display!

Completed solids.

At the end of the session, ask learners to share the solids that they made, and say how they made them. Ask, *"Were you able to make all of the solids? Were you able to make a cylinder or a sphere? Why not?"* Display and label the solids that were made, discussing the different ways of making them.

Summary

By the end of this activity learners will have revised their knowledge and understanding of 3D solids and will have built on this when constructing, comparing and discussing shapes.

Notes on the Learner's Book

Exploring 3D shapes (p26): this page reinforces work done in the session, with a problem to solve followed by more closed questions which allow learners to show what they know about 3D shapes.

Check up!

Ask:
- *"How many equilateral triangles to make a square based pyramid?"*
- *"Tell me a shape that has six faces."*
- *"Tell me a shape that has six faces which are all the same size."*
- *"Tell me what a prism is."*
- *"Give me an example of a prism."*

More activities

Making pentominoes (pairs/class)

You will need five square shapes.

Put five shapes (using only square shapes) together to make a pentomino. There are 12 different ways of doing this, where each square is placed edge to edge to another square. Challenge the class to find them all.

Using the pentominoes that have been made, explore how many of them can fold up to make an open cube (a box with no lid). Ask learners to discuss with their partner which they think will and which won't before they fold them.

Nets (individual)

You will need paper, pens/pencils and sticky tape.

Ask learners to make a solid, open it out and draw the net. How many different nets of a cube can they find?

Resources: Examples of prisms and pyramids in everyday life, e.g. cereal boxes, dice, tins, drink cans. *Nets of solids* photocopy masters (pp54–58), copies of two different pages (one a prism, one a pyramid) for each learner. Scissors, glue, paper and pens/pencils. (Optional: paper, pens, coloured pencils, scissors and glue; *Net sentences* photocopy master (CD-ROM), one copy per learner; a selection of 3D solids in a bag, cubes, cuboids, square-based pyramids, triangular prisms enough for each learner to use.)

Show the class the examples of prisms and pyramids. Ask, "*What do you notice? What is the same about these shapes and what is different?*" (e.g. a prism has two bases and a pyramid only one. In a prism, the two bases are 'joined' together by rectangles or a cylinder; in a pyramid, a triangle is attached to each side of the base, with the free corners of each triangle meeting at an apex.)

Choose a cereal packet and find where it has been glued. Open it along this join. Open out the packet to see the shape of its net. Ask, "*What shapes can you see in this net? How have they been arranged? Do you think if I open another box it will look the same?*"

Open another of the boxes that will give a different net. Ask, "*What do you notice with this box? What is the same and what is different?*"

Choose a different box that is a prism. "*What can you tell me about this box? What is the same, and what is different about this box when we compare it with these others?*"
Use this as an opportunity to reinforce correct mathematical vocabulary and language.

Give each learner two copies of pages from *Nets of solids* to make their own solids, one a prism and the other a pyramid. Explain that, "*These are nets to make two different solids, one will be a prism and the other will be a pyramid. Make them both and decide which is which. Write three things about each solid which you can share with the rest of the class.*"
As the learners are working, walk round the class to make sure that they understand the task. Ask questions such as, "*How are you going to tackle this? What equipment will you need? Which do you think is which before you cut and glue it? Why? What clues can you see?*"

At the end of the session ask learners to tell you things about their solids. Record their answers so that all the class can see. How many different things did they say? Sort into two columns, Prisms and Pyramids. Leave as a reminder for future work.

Look out for!

- Learners who are unable to define the two solids. *Give a lot of practical experience in holding and feeling the shapes and talk about the similarities and differences. Place one of each in a bag and let the learner feel inside and guess which shape it is. Gradually increase the number of solids in the bag.*
- When using the nets, some learners may need the shapes enlarged.
- Learners who can use the nets to make a prism and a pyramid. *Ask them to make their own nets for a prism or pyramid that uses a different shape at the ends or the base and to write instructions for a friend to make the shape.*

Opportunities for display!

Completed models of the solids.

Summary

By the end of this activity the learners will have applied their knowledge and understanding of 3D shape by identifying, making and describing prisms and pyramids. They will be able to use correct mathematical vocabulary and language in order to describe what they did and what they found out.

Notes on the Learner's Book
More 3D shapes (p28): this activity extends what has been learnt in the core activity by using what the learners know in order to find out what they don't know when constructing a cube. This is followed by activities to show understanding and knowledge of 3D shape.

Check up!
- *What do the prism nets have in common?*
- *What do the pyramid nets have in common?*
- *What is the main difference between the prism nets and the pyramid nets?*

More activities

Nets challenge (individual)

> You will need paper, pens, colouring pencils, scissors and glue.

Challenge learners to draw the following. In each case they should check their answer by cutting out and folding the net(s).
- The net of a cube.
- The net of a cube with two red faces opposite each other, two blue faces opposite each other and two yellow faces opposite each other.
- Two *different* nets that make the *same* rectangular prism.
- Two *different* nets that make the *same* triangular pyramid.

Net sentences (individual)

> You will need the *Net sentences* photocopy master (CD-ROM) one copy per learner, pens/pencils.

For each sentence on the *Net sentences* sheet, learners make a drawing and fill in the missing words.

Roll and trace (individual)

> You will need a selection of 3D solids in a bag, enough for each learner to use, paper, pens/pencils, scissors and glue.

Learners choose a prism or pyramid and place it on a piece of paper. They trace around the face in contact with the paper. Then, along one of the edges of the solid, they roll the solid onto another face and trace around that face. They repeat the rolling and tracing process until all faces have been traced, then cut out the shape and fold along the lines to make the solid shape.

Box sort (individual/class)

Ask learners to create three new shapes from nets and divide them into two groups: 'the prisms' and 'the pyramids'. Lead a discussion, "*What do these prism nets have in common? What do the pyramid nets have in common?*"

Shape cards

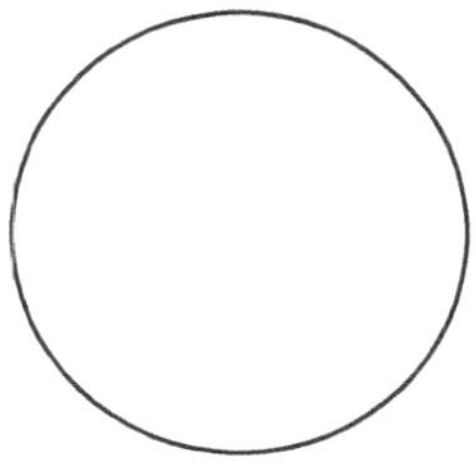

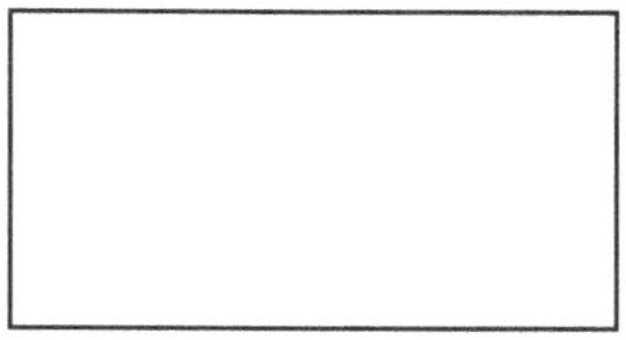

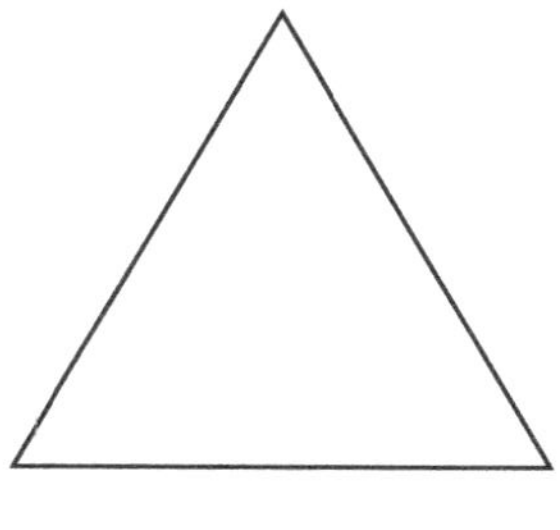

	I am a 2D shape. I have: • four edges all the same length • four right angle corners.	**SQUARE**
	I am a 2D shape. I have: • one edge • no corners.	**CIRCLE**
	I am a 2D shape. I have: • two long edges and two short edges • four right angle corners.	**RECTANGLE**
	I am a 2D shape. I have: • three edges • three corners.	**TRIANGLE**

Instructions on page 44

Nets of solids: Pentagonal prism

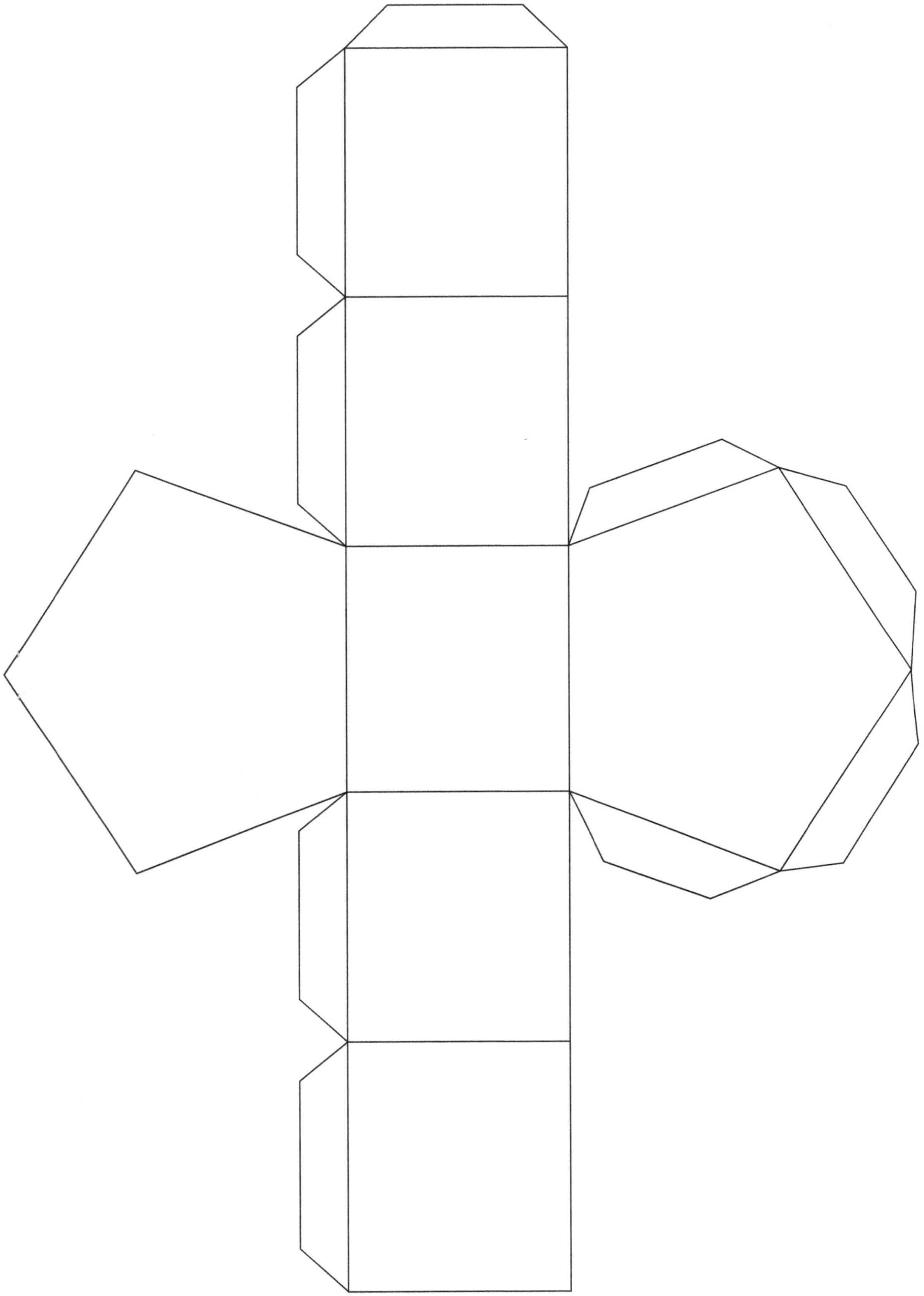

Instructions on page 50

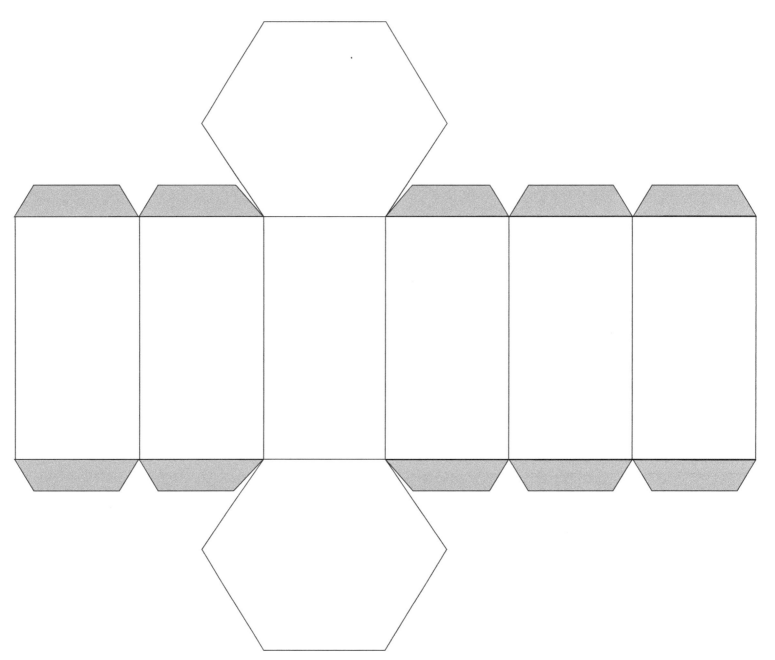

Hexagonal prism

Cuboid

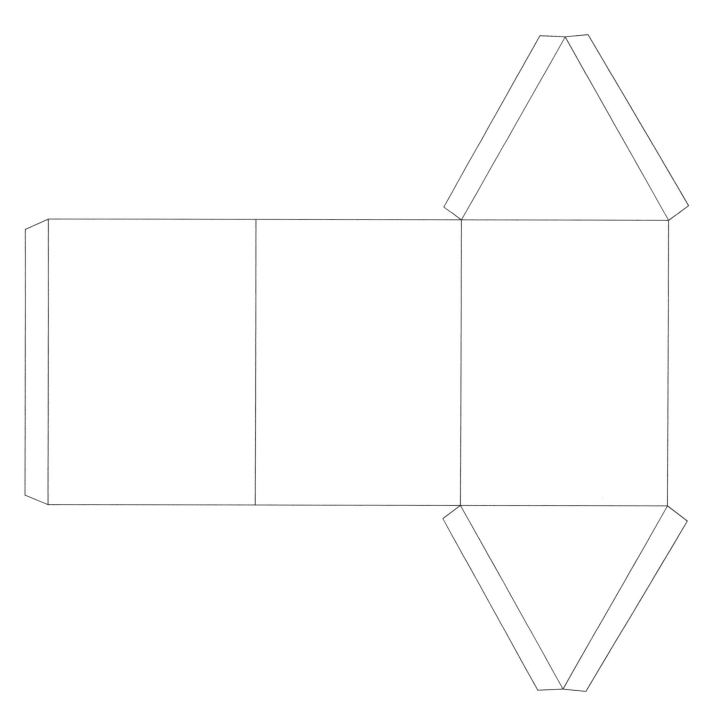

Triangular prism

Triangular-based pyramid

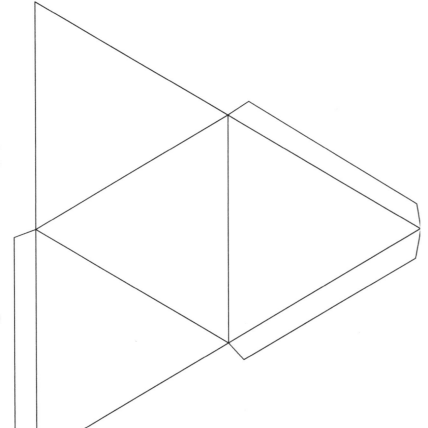

Hexagonal-based pyramid

Quick reference

Core activity 8.1: Symmetry (Learner's Book p30)

This activity examines the idea of line symmetry of regular shapes. It explores the connection between the number of sides of regular shapes and the number of lines of symmetry.

Core activity 8.2: Maze routes (Learner's Book p32)

This activity begins by looking at position in relation to a person or object, and giving and following instructions for movement that involve distances, directions and half or quarter turns, and points of the compass.

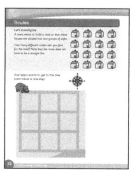

Prior learning	Objectives* – please note that listed objectives might only be partially covered within any given chapter but are covered fully across the book when taken as a whole
• Knowledge and understanding of names and properties of shape. • Some knowledge and understanding of reflective symmetry. • Beginning to understand the language of position and movement.	**1B: Geometry** 3Gs5 – Draw and complete 2D shapes with reflective symmetry, draw reflections of shapes. 3Gs7 – Identify 2D, 3D shapes, lines of symmetry and right angles in the environment. 3Gp1 – Use the language of position, direction and movement including clockwise and anti-clockwise. **1B: Problem solving** 3Ps6 – Identify simple relationships between shapes such as: these shapes all have the same number of lines of symmetry.

*for NRICH activities mapped to the Cambridge Primary objectives, please visit www.cie.org.uk/cambridgeprimarymaths

Vocabulary

(N, S, E, W) • anti-clockwise • clockwise • compass point • diagonal • equiangular • equilateral • grid • half turn • horizontal • line of symmetry • mirror line • plan • quarter turn • reflection pattern • regular shape • repeating pattern • right angle • row • symmetrical • vertical • whole turn

Resources: *Regular shapes for symmetry* photocopy master (p67), one copy per pair. A mirror (per pair) A4 paper, scissors and pencils. (Optional: peg boards and pegs and a sheet of paper; interlocking cubes and a mirror for each learner; a sheet of squared paper for each learner or pair; kaleidoscopes and items with shiny surfaces for each pair; a sheet of squared paper, coloured pencils and a mirror for each learner; a sheet of paper and a pencil/pen for each learner.)

Give each pair of learners a mirror and a *Regular shapes for symmetry* sheet. Explain the task. *"Work with a partner and find the lines of symmetry on the shapes. If the mirror is in the right place you will be able to see the whole shape by looking in the mirror. It should look exactly the same as it does without the mirror. Draw the lines of symmetry that you find on each shape."* Give time for the pairs to work together.

Then ask, *"What did you notice about the shapes and the number of lines of symmetry that each had?"* (**Regular shapes have the same number of lines of symmetry as their number of sides e.g. a square (four sides) has four lines of symmetry**.) *"Did that happen with all of your shapes? Which one was the odd one out? Why do you think that was?"*

Give time for pairs to talk together, then ask, *"Has anyone worked out why this happened?"* If there are no responses ask questions such as, *"What do you notice about the length of the sides on the other shapes? What do you notice about the length of sides for the odd one out shape? Do you think that makes a difference?"*
"What do we call shapes that have all sides and angles the same?"

Explain the next part of the task. *"Work with your partner and move around the room (or outside) and look for objects that have one or more lines of symmetry. They can be 2D or 3D. Draw what you find. Mark the line of symmetry."*
You may want to give some examples, such as capital letters, windows, electricity pylons – symmetry is all around us.

Vocabulary

regular shape: a polygon that is **equiangular** (all angles are equal in measure) and **equilateral** (all sides have the same length).

symmetrical: when two halves of a shape or pattern are mirror images of each other, they have reflective symmetry.

line of symmetry: a straight line that splits a shape/pattern into two halves that are mirror images of each other.

mirror line: a line where the two sides are reflective.

Look out for!

- Learners who may not be confident with the concept of symmetry. *Suggest that before using the mirror they fold a piece of paper in half and, with it still folded, cut random shapes. As the paper is unfolded the line of symmetry is obvious.*
- *They could do paint blob patterns where they fold a piece of paper in half, open it up and put blobs of paint on one side. Fold the paper over again and press down. Open the paper and the line of symmetry is the fold line, with the paint making a symmetrical design.*
- Learners who have grasped the simple concept of symmetry. *Encourage them to investigate different types of symmetry. Try folding paper in different ways to get different symmetrical patterns. For example, using A4 paper, try folding it so that the shorter sides end up together every time you fold. What type of symmetry do you have this time? Draw and cut a shape making sure the folds aren't cut. Open carefully.*

At the end of the session ask learners to share what they have found and to show where the lines of symmetry are.

Collect the drawings to make a class collage of symmetry.

- Use as a discussion with the rest of the class. What do you notice?
- Challenge learners to identify shapes with more than one line of symmetry.

Opportunities for display!

Collage of learners' drawings of line symmetry in the environment.

Summary

At the end of this activity learners will have explored line and reflective symmetry in 2D shapes and related it to real life examples in the environment.

Notes on the Learner's Book

Symmetry (p30): this page takes the core activity into a more practical context which allows learners to explore, as well as make, symmetrical shapes through the series of questions.

Check up!

- Show learners different cut patterns and ask if they have a line of symmetry and ask how they can prove it.
- Show both regular and irregular shapes and ask learners to tell you which will have line symmetry and which will not.

More activities

Peg boards (pairs)

> Each pair of learners will need a peg board and pegs and a sheet of paper.

Learners investigate different symmetrical shapes that can be made on a peg board, working with a partner. One of the pair makes a symmetrical pattern, then removes a number of pegs before giving it to their partner and challenging them to complete it and find the line of symmetry.

Alternatively, learners mark a line of symmetry on a pegboard (e.g. using a strip of paper) and make one half of a symmetrical pattern, then challenge their partner to complete it.

Using cubes (individual)

> You will need a set of interlocking cubes and a mirror for each learner.

Learners use interlocking cubes to make shapes. They then use a mirror to find a mirror image of the shape and try to make this mirror image with cubes.

Squared paper (individual/pair)

> You will need a sheet of squared paper for each learner or pair.

Learners fold a piece of squared paper in half to make a line of symmetry. They choose one of the shapes they or their partner made in a previous activity and draw it on the squared paper along the line of symmetry before drawing its symmetrical mirror image.

Kaleidoscopes (pairs)

> You will need kaleidoscopes, mirrors and objects with shiny surfaces.

Provide a selection of kaleidoscopes, mirrors and shiny surfaces and ask the learners, in pairs, to investigate them and talk about what they see. Introduce the fact that they all produce **reflections**.

Colour symmetry (individual)

> You will need a sheet of squared paper, coloured pencils and a mirror for each learner.

Learners draw a coloured pattern on squared paper and then reflect it.

Carroll diagram (individual)

> You will need a sheet of paper and a pencil/pen.

Make a Carroll diagram with labels 'symmetrical'/ 'not symmetrical', 'one line of symmetry'/'two lines symmetry'. Looking at objects both inside and outside, mark the position in which they belong on the sorting diagram.

Resources: *Mazes and grids* photocopy master (CD-ROM). A copy of *Easy maze 1* (CD-ROM) and a copy of *Easy maze 2* (CD-ROM) for the board (either enlarged or for projection). A *maze* and a matching (*easy* or *hard*) *maze grid* per pair and a counter, or one copy of a *maze grid* (*easy* or *hard*) per learner. (Optional: chalk or skipping ropes or other obstacles and a blindfold; *Mazes and grids* photocopy master (CD-ROM) a copy of a *Maze grid* (*easy* or *hard*) (CD-ROM) per pair, pen/pencil.)

Begin by asking learners if they know what a maze is. Ask, *"Where have you seen a maze? How many of you have ever been to a maze? Tell us what it was like."*

Project or copy *Easy maze 1* onto the board. Ask the learners to work in pairs to find the path to follow to get them through it. Some learners may need their own copy to refer to and possibly draw on.

After a few minutes choose a learner to come to the front of the class and draw the path through the maze. Ask, *"Is that the only way through the maze? Did anyone find a different way?"*

Ask learners how they could explain to someone who can't see it where the line has been drawn. Encourage the use of accurate vocabulary such as 'up', 'down', 'left', 'right', 'half turn', 'clockwise' and 'anti-clockwise'. Follow the line through the maze as learners describe it. Allow time for any alterations that need to be made to the instructions or the drawing.

Show *Easy maze 2*. This time, ask learners to find the path through the maze and then tell their partner the route.

Invite learners to describe the route through the maze to the class, with individuals giving only one direction at a time. Draw the route as it is described. If an unspecified instruction is given (go round the corner) draw the line incorrectly to help them describe the route accurately.

Explain the next activity to the class. *"You are now going to work with a partner to play Maze pairs."* Give one learner in each pair a *maze* and the other a matching *maze grid* (choosing either the *Easy* or *Hard* mazes and grids to match the ability of the learners). The learner with the maze has to solve it and give their partner instructions for the route to follow on their grid. The partner with the grid should draw a line to show the route described to them. When the person following the instructions has completed a line

Vocabulary

clockwise: in the direction in which the hands of a clock turn.

anti-clockwise: in the direction opposite to clockwise.

compass: equipment that indicates direction in terms of North, South, East and West.

N, S, E, W: the directions North (N), South (S), East (E) and West (W).

full turn: turning once in a circle; 360°.

half turn: turning half a circle; 180°.

quarter turn: turning by a right angle 90°.

compass points: are N, S, E and W.

Look out for!

Learners who may need more support. *Give them simple mazes to start with. Always allow them their own copy when working with the whole class.*

Look out for!

- Learners having difficulty remembering the points of the compass in the right order. *Use clues to help: starting with North and travelling*

or path on their grid, pairs can check the answer by comparing the mazes and see if they match. They then change roles and the one who received the instructions now gives them. Say, *"Make sure you start in the right place."*

When each learner has had a turn, draw a compass on the board and make sure that all of the class understands the meaning of N, S, E and W.

Learners repeat the activity, this time using the points of the compass in their descriptions of the route rather than using up, down, left and right.

Alternatively, this could also be done as a whole class activity, with all learners having a blank grid and the teacher giving instructions. Then a learner could be given the opportunity to give instructions to the class, or learners could then work in pairs.

At the end of the session ask questions such as, *"How did you tackle this? Did you need to ask any questions? Why? What were they?"*

Emphasise the importance of using correct and precise vocabulary.

clockwise use Naughty Elephants Squirt Water or any mnemonic the learners make for themselves.

- Learners who need more of a challenge. *Play 'Put Yourself in the Maze'. For this extension to Maze Pairs tell learners that they have to imagine that they are actually in the maze themselves, and that the only things they can do are to move forward or to turn left or right. This makes the activity much more challenging, as they now need to keep track of the direction they are facing as well as where in the maze they are. Counters with an arrow drawn on to indicate direction faced would be a useful aid.*

Opportunities for display!
Any 3D mazes made by the class.
Pictures of well-known mazes.

Summary

At the end of this activity, learners will be able to use the language of position, giving and following instructions using the language of position and movement.

Notes on the Learner's Book
Routes (p32): this activity asks learners to find the shortest route for the hippo to travel to the river. There are extension questions which use different size grids. Learners will need to be systematic in their recording in order to find all the routes.

Check up!
- Give instructions during class routines or PE sessions such as, *"Turn left out of the door; if north is where the clock is, turn to face south/east/west."*
- Ask learners to describe the movements they made when following such instructions.

More activities

Outdoor maze (class/pairs)

You will need chalk or skipping ropes or other obstacles and a blindfold.

In this activity learners take the skills they have used in the classroom outside and onto a larger scale. Draw a large but fairly simple maze on the playground with chalk, or using skipping ropes to create the 'hedges'. Get learners to take it in turns to be blindfolded and directed through the maze by a partner who is not allowed to touch them, but who has to give instructions about direction and distance. The challenge is to get through the maze with as few instructions as possible and without touching or crossing the lines. Alternatively, create an outdoor obstacle course and challenge learners to guide a blindfolded partner as before.

Reflecting (pair)

> You will need a copy of a *Maze grid* (*easy* or *hard*) per pair from the *Mazes and grids* photocopy master (CD-ROM) and a pen/pencil.

Let learners draw their own mazes on a *Maze grid*, and challenge a friend to first solve it, and then give instructions for how to get through it. You may need to give some guidance in drawing mazes – ensure that they are solvable, but try to have plenty of false paths and dead ends. Learners could take their mazes to another class and show them how they have learned to give accurate directions through the maze.

Routes to school (individual/class)

> You will need paper, pen/pencil.

Ask, "*What's your favourite way to school? Is it the shortest route? Is it the quickest route? Which is the safest route? Draw a map of your journey to school. Put in what you pass and when you turn a corner. Put in what you see.*"

Imaginary island (pair)

> You will need paper, pen/pencil.

Learners draw a map of an imaginary island and put in the compass to show North, South, East and West. They then ask a friend a question about the map, such as, "*Is the house east of the tree or west? Is it north of the tree or south?*"

Magic carpet (individual)

> You will need paper, pen/pencil.

Learners plan a journey on a magic carpet. Where would they visit? They should make a map to show their journey, putting in the compass points and writing directions.

Games Book (ISBN 9781107694019)

Across the swamp (p37) is a game for two players. This game uses position, direction, movement and points of the compass in order to cross the swamp.

Regular shapes for symmetry

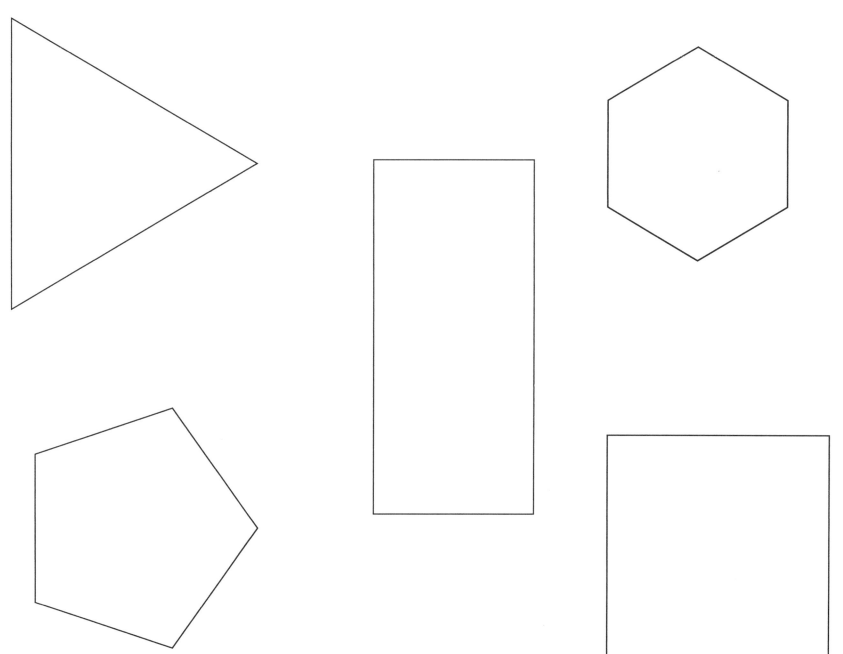

Blank page

Quick reference

Core activity 9.1: Dollars and cents (Learner's Book p34)

This activity introduces American currency: dollars and cents.

Prior learning
• Counting to 100 in 5's and 10's. • Familiarity with 100 square.

Objectives* – please note that listed objectives might only be partially covered within any given chapter but are covered fully across the book when taken as a whole

1C: Measures
3Mm1 – Consolidate using money notation.
1C: Problem solving
3Pt11 – Make a sensible estimate of the answer to a calculation.
3Ps1 – Make up number story to go with a calculation, including in the context of money.

*for NRICH activities mapped to the Cambridge Primary objectives, please visit www.cie.org.uk/cambridgeprimarymaths

Vocabulary

cent • dollar

Core activity 9.1: Dollars and cents

Resources: 100×1c coins, 20×5c coins, 10×10c coins, 4×25c coins, 2×50c coins, 1×$1 coin (or two copies of the *Coins* photocopy master (CD-ROM), ideally copied onto card, cut into separate 'coins'). Sticky tack. Large 100 square. *100 square* photocopy master (chapter 1, p12), one copy per pair. Tubs containing a mixture of 1c, 5c and 10c coins, one 25c and one 50c coin (per pair). Pen/pencil and paper. (Optional: A selection of 1c, 5c and 10c coins, paper, pen/pencil; *Coin tic tac toe* photocopy master (CD-ROM), one copy per pair, counters (two colours), scissors; masking tape, a marker pen and a collection of coins.) Learner's Book: 1c and 5c coins, paper clip (per pair)

Show the class a 1c, 5c, 10c, 25c, 50c and $1 coins (or hold up the shapes cut from the *Coins* photocopy master). Ask, "*Do you recognise any of these? What can you tell me about this one?*" Pick each one separately and find out what the class already knows. As they tell you information, write it on a board and stick the coin next to it. Make sure that each coin is named.

Then ask, "*Does anyone know how many cents are in a dollar?*" (**100**) "*Look at this 100 square. How many squares are on it? Look at the last number to help you.*" As you are talking, stick a 1c coin on each of the squares of the 100 square. "*How many cents would I need in order to cover each of the numbers on the 100 square?*" (**100**). "*So, if each of these squares has a cent in it, how much would the whole square be worth?*" (**1 dollar**)

"*What if I took 5 cents away?*" Remove the five cents from the end of the square (100, 99, 98, 97, 96). "*How much do I have left on the square? How do you know?*" (**The last number covered is 95**) "*What if I took another five cents away, how much would be left?*" (**90 cents**) "*How do you know?*"

Take all the cents off the 100 square.
Turn back to the 100 square. Ask, "*If each of these squares is worth 1 cent, which square would be worth 5 cents.*" (If necessary count from 1 stopping at 5). Stick the 5 cents coin on the 5. "*Where would the next 5 cent coin go?*" Count on five pointing to the numbers as you count. Put the next coin on 10. "*What about the next one?*" Count on five again and put the next coin on 15. "*Who can tell me where the next one will go, without counting?*" (**20**) "*What are all of the numbers where we would put these 5 cent coins?*" Class count in 5's, stopping at 100. Point to each number as the class count.

Take all the coins off the 100 square.
Show the 10 cents coin and ask, "*How much is this worth?*"

Look out for!

- Learners who struggle to total four coins. *Present them with only two coins at a time. Ask and reinforce correct responses: "give me a cent", "give me 5 cents". Point to the correct coin if the learner selects the wrong one. Move on to sorting coins and matching them to a base board.*

- *Instead of using a 100 square, use a number line to 20 or 50.*

- Learners who find adding four coins easy. *Ask them to find change for a dollar, again using a 100 square. For example, they place a counter on the price of an object (e.g. 57 cents). They place cents on each square to get to the nearest multiple of five, and then use cents to get to $1.00 (100). Learners can use whatever combinations of coins they choose, but challenge them to find the smallest amount of coins possible.*

Turn back to the 100 square. Ask, "*What numbers would I cover for every 10 cent coin I put on the square?*" (**multiples of 10**) "*How do you know?*"

Repeat for the 25c and 50c coins.

Tell the class that they are going to find the total of some coins using the *100 square*. Model the task for them first: ask a learner to choose four coins from a tub of coins. Say, for example, "*I have three 10 cent coins and a 5 cent coin. I put one on 10. Where would the next one go?*" (**20**) "*and the next?*" (**30**) "*Now we have to count on five more cents. I'll count on 5 – 31, 32, 33, 34, 35. How much money do I have all together?*" (**35 cents**).

Divide the learners into pairs and ask them to take turns to choose four coins from the tub on their table and work out how much they have using the *100 square*. They should keep a record of the coins they picked and their total.

As the class are working, walk round the room making sure that everyone understands the task and deal with any misconceptions.

Opportunities for display!

Large coins and the facts about them.

At the end of the session, choose some learners to feedback about what they did and what they found out. Ask questions such as, "*Was there anything that you already knew that helped you? Do you think this would work if you made more than a dollar? How?*"
"*I have 50 cents and 20 cents. I want to go shopping for fruit. A bag of apples will cost 80 cents. Do I have enough money?*"
"*I have $1. I spend 45 cents. How much do I have left?*"

Ask learners to work in pairs and make a number story to go with a calculation. It can be addition or subtraction. The rule: They must know the answer!
Use their number stories as part of a display.

Summary

By the end of the session learners will have consolidated using money notation and some will have used addition and subtraction facts with a total of 100 to find change.

Notes on the Learner's Book
Money (p34): you will need 1c and 5 c coins and a paper clip per pair. This page gives learners opportunities to practise what has been taught in the session and answer other questions related to money. For Question 2, remind learners that there are 100 cents in a dollar so the amounts of money can be converted to cents before they are added.

Check up!
- Use 'I have' … statements.
- "*I have 40 cents and 2 × 5 cent coins How much do I have?*"
- "*I have 10 cents. I spend 5 cents. How much do I have left?*"
- "*I have 95 cents. How much more do I need to make 1 dollar?*"

More activities

Many coins, many ways (individual)

> You will need a selection of 1c, 5c and 10c coins, paper, pen/pencil.

Challenge learners to find all of the different ways to use coins to show the day and month of today's date; for example, 26th April would be 26 cents made in various different ways (e.g. 20 + 5 + 1) and 4 cents. They may start the activity with no system or order, but with experience they will begin to have a systematic approach. This may be a chart or table. Learners should be asked to talk about the different methods they used.

Coin tic tac toe (pairs)

> You will need the *Coin tic tac toe* photocopy master (CD-ROM), one copy per pair, counters (two colours) and scissors.

Learners cut out the coins below the *Coin tic tac toe* board and each take a handful of counters in their chosen colour. The first player chooses any four of the coins and finds their total value. They cover that value on the board with a counter. The second player then puts one of the four coins back in the pile and chooses a different one. They find the new total value and cover that value on the board with a counter. Players continue to take it in turns to play, each time putting back one coin and choosing a different one, until one player gets three (or four) counters in a row.

Money ladder (small groups)

> You will need masking tape, a marker pen and a collection of coins.

Use masking tape to create a large ladder on the floor; it should have at least 11 rungs and each should have a different question written on it. Learners answer the problems by putting the right amount of money in the space above the relevant rung, working their way up the ladder one step at a time. The questions could get harder as they get higher up the ladder.

Games Book (ISBN 9781107694019)

Bank (p44) is a game for two to four players. This game consolidates the addition of money, using different coins. It examines the idea of equivalence between coins to make specific amounts.

Quick reference

Core activity 10.1: Clock times (Learner's Book p36)

This activity revises days of the week and months of the year before going on to look at specific time using both analogue and digital clocks.

Core activity 10.2: Time to grow (Learner's Book p38)

This activity puts the concept of time into a practical concept where learners can begin to understand why we need to know about the measurements of different time intervals.

Prior learning	Objectives* – please note that listed objectives might only be partially covered within any given chapter but are covered fully across the book when taken as a whole
• Some knowledge of time using an analogue clock. • Beginning to understand working with a digital clock. • Knowledge of the order of days of the week and months of the year.	**1C: Measures** 3Ml5 – Solve word problems involving measures. 3Mt1 – Suggest and use suitable units to measure time and know the relationships between them. 3Mt2 – Read the time on analogue and digital clocks to the nearest five minutes on an analogue clock and to the nearest minute on a digital clock. **1C: Problem solving** 3Pt1 – Choose appropriate mental strategies to carry out calculations. 3Pt10 – Estimate and approximate when calculating and check their working. 3Pt12 – Consider whether an answer is reasonable.

*for NRICH activities mapped to the Cambridge Primary objectives, please visit www.cie.org.uk/cambridgeprimarymaths

Vocabulary

century

Resources: Classroom calendar. Analogue clock. Digital clock. (Optional: paper and pens/pencils; *3×3 grid* photocopy master (CD-ROM), one sheet per pair, and a 1–6 dice (CD-ROM) per pair.) Learner's Book: *Blank clocks* photocopy master (CD-ROM) one copy per learner. Before the session, prepare large labels for 'second', 'minute', 'hour', 'day', 'week', 'year', 'century'.

Ask the learners to talk to a partner about what they know about time. Give some suggestions such as: do they know anything about clocks, calendars, dates, and the times when things happen in a day or week or year? What about a century?
Give five minutes for their discussions.

Show the class the labels and read them. Ask questions such as, "*What do you know about a week?*" (**7 days**) "*What do you know about a year?*" (**52 weeks, 12 months**) "*Tell me something about a century.*" (**100 years**) Look for gaps in their knowledge.
Stick the labels on a board and ask for ideas, writing them under the appropriate label.

Ask the class to chant the months of the year, the days of the week. Look at the class calendar. Ask, "*What month is showing on our calendar? How many days does this month have? How do you know that?*"

Ask different learners to find today's date, yesterday's date, a date when we are not in school.

Use the calendar as a focus for class discussion on a daily basis, changing the questions as appropriate.

Explain that, "*Today we are going to look at different ways of showing time. We will use an analogue clock*" (show the class the example) "*and a digital clock*" (show example).

Count round the class in tens, as a chant, stopping at 60 each time. Repeat the activity counting in fives. Explain that counting in fives and tens will help in counting seconds and minutes because there are 60 seconds in a minute and 60 minutes in an hour.

Show the class the analogue clock and point out that the hour is split into five minute intervals. Count in fives round the clock.

Vocabulary

century: a period of one hundred years.

Look out for!

- Learners who struggle to remember the order of the days or the number of days in a month.
  Encourage them to use rhymes to help consolidate these facts:
  – *Monday's child is full of grace, Tuesday's child is fair of face …*
  – *Thirty days has September, April, June and November, …*
  – *Solomon Grundy, born on Monday, … and so on.*
- Learners who are confident with days and dates.
  Challenge them with questions such as:
  – "*On the second Tuesday of each month a comic is issued. If the first Tuesday is the fifth of April, what are the dates of every other Tuesday for the next year?*"
  – "*Three days after the first Monday of every month, the youth club meets. What is the latest date in each month that can happen if the first of January is a Tuesday? Work it out for a whole year.*"

Ask, "*If the minute hand starts at twelve and moves half way round the clock, which number will it point to? How many minutes to half way round? If the minute hand moves a quarter way round the clock, which number will it point to? How many minutes to quarter way round? How many minutes to three quarters of the way round? Which number will the hand point to?*"

Using the demonstration analogue and digital clocks, show time passing in blocks of five minutes. Compare the two representations of the time. Ask, "*What do you notice about the analogue clock? What happens to the short (hour) hand as each set of five minutes is added? Does it stay in the same place or does it move?*"

Then ask, "*What do you notice about the digital clock? Tell me some things that are the same and some things that are different between the two clocks.*"

Show times (o'clock, half past, quarter to and past) on both clocks and ask the class to tell you the time.

Choose some learners and ask them to make the clocks say particular times such as five o'clock, half past two. Ask the rest of the class what they think: "*Are the clocks saying the right time? How do you know?* "Ask the learners, "*Do you want to change one or both of the clocks?*"

Summary

- By the end of this activity the class will have read the time to the nearest five minutes on an analogue clock and to the nearest minute on a digital clock
- They will also have had opportunities to suggest and use suitable units to measure time and know the relationships between them.

Notes on the Learner's Book

Time (p36): you will need the *Blank clocks* photocopy master (CD-ROM) one copy per learner. This page looks at different activities that can be performed within a specified time limit. It involves decision making and reasoning. Some learners may need to work with the left hand column of times rather than the whole table.

Check up!

Ask questions such as :
- "*What number will the minute hand point to if it is 10 minutes past o'clock?*"
- "*What number will the minute hand point to if it is 10 minutes to o'clock?*"
- "*What numbers will show on a digital clock if the time is half past 10?*"

More activities

Make an hour (class)

> You will need paper and pens/pencils.

Combine blocks of five, 10 and 20 minutes in different ways to make an hour. Discuss different things that can be done in five minutes, 10 minutes or 20 minutes. Record the options. Use combinations of these to make up an hour of activities.

Using a timetable (class)

> You will need paper and pens/pencils.

Working in blocks of multiples of five minutes, make a timetable for a morning in school. Record the activities in a table, for example:

Time	What I did	How long it took
9 o'clock	Started school, hung up my coat, changed my shoes.	10 minutes
9:10	Told our news.	20 minutes
9:30		

Filling fives (pairs)

> You will need *3×3 grid* photocopy master (CD-ROM), one sheet per pair, pens/pencils and a 1–6 dice per pair.

Learners write the following numbers in a 3×3 grid: 5, 10, 15, 20, 25, 30, 40, 50, 60. They take turns with a partner to throw a dice, and multiply the numbers thrown by five or 10. They cross out the answers on their grids. The winner is the first player to cross out all nine numbers.

Games Book (ISBN 9781107694019)

Time flies (p46) is a game for two to four players. Players show the time to the nearest five minutes on an analogue clock and to the nearest minute on a digital clock, choosing appropriate mental strategies to carry out calculations

Resources: *Seed packets* photocopy master (p81), one copy per pair) or empty seed packets brought from home. *Planter's plan* photocopy master (p82), one copy of sheet per learner). *Seed information* photocopy master (p82), one copy per pair). Small plant pots (one per learner), compost and sunflower seeds (or other fast-growing seeds), one per learner. *Plant recording sheet* photocopy master (CD-ROM), one copy per learner. Plastic plates (one per learner). Water. (Optional: different seeds, pots, compost, and instructions on how to care for the plants, paper, pens/pencils; bean seeds for each learner; *Life cycle of a plant* photocopy master (CD-ROM), one copy per learner, two paper plates and a split pin per learner, coloured pencils and scissors; *Make a grass head* photocopy master (CD-ROM), one copy per learner, a few grams of grass seed, an old stocking, sand, a cardboard tube, plastic plate, scissors and modelling clay per learner.)

Give each pair a collection of seed packets (from the *Seed packets* sheet, or empty ones you have brought in). Give time for learners to look at them and discover what information they show. Then ask, *"What information can you find on a packet of seeds?"* (For example, what month to plant, when to harvest, number of seeds.) *"Why do you think we need this information?"*

Give time for learners to feed back. Make a list of what they found out.

Then ask, *"When you have planted the seed, what do you think will happen next? How can you make sure that the seed will grow?"* Discuss conditions needed for growth. (**light, warmth, water**)

Give each learner a copy of the *Planter's plan* (both grids from the sheet). Give time for learners to read through and then ask, *"What could we write in the top space?"* Work through each of the sections and give time for the learners to write in each.

Give each pair a *Seed information* sheet. Ask, *"What can you tell me about these different seeds? What is the same and what is different? Do they all take the same time to grow? Are they all planted in the same month?"* Lead a discussion using the language and vocabulary of time (months, seasons).

Explain that, *"Some seeds grow very quickly and some grow a lot slower. Each of you is going to plant a sunflower seed. You will need a pot and some compost and a seed. Remember the important things about planting."* Ask learners to tell you what the important things are (**food, soil, water, light**). *"Make another Planter's plan to help you remember what to do."* Give time for planting the seeds.

Look out for!

- Learners who are having problems. *Although this is a practical activity and most learners will be able to achieve, some may need reminding about the care of a plant or how to write the date.*
  - Use picture clues for all written instructions and use the class calendar as a reference for the date.
- Learners who are confident about time. *Challenge them to measure the rate of growth of their seed and record their findings. Ask questions such as, "How long was it before it could be seen? How tall was it after one day, two days?" Ask them to graph the growth.*
- You could also plant two or three different seeds in different pots and, as they grow, ask the learners to compare and contrast the growing rates. Use a graph or chart to record time passing and the growth rates of each seed.

Tell the learners that, *"Each of you will keep a picture diary of your seed growing."* Show them the *Plant recording sheet. "Each day that you write, use the time, day, date and month. You only need to start recording when your plant starts to grow."* (It will be useful to have a few spare pots planted in case some don't grow.)

Make sure that each pot is on a plastic plate and the seeds have been watered.

Summary

By the end of this session learners will have used measurements of time in a practical way, and consolidated their knowledge and understanding of the passage of time.

Notes on the Learner's Book
Time and growth (p38): this page uses the knowledge that learners learnt in the previous sessions and puts it into a real life problem solving context involving the growth of plants.

Check up!

Ask questions such as:
- *"If I planted seeds on 5th April, and they take two months to grow, when can I pick them?"*
- *"If you sow Seed C in February what is the earliest month you could harvest it?"*
- *"Which seeds can be sown outdoors in May?"*

More activities

Planting seeds (individual)

You will need different seeds, pots, compost, and instructions on how to care for the plants, paper, pens/pencils.

Plant seeds in small pots. Each learner has a seed and instructions on how to care for the plant. Time how long it is before the first shoot appears. Is it the same for all seeds? Collect the data and represent it.

Growing and measuring seeds (individual)

You will need bean seeds, pots, compost, paper, pens/pencils.

Use beans as they grow rapidly. Use drawings, diagrams or photos to chart the growth of the plant.

Plant seeds at home (individual)

You will need seeds, pots, compost, paper, pens/pencils for each learner.

Send a seed or bean home for planting. Ask learners to keep it warm, in the light and water when dry. Ask learners to keep a time line or diary of the growth.

Life cycle of a plant (individual)

> You will need *Life cycle of a plant* photocopy master (CD-ROM) one copy per learner, two paper plates and a split pin per learner, coloured pencils and scissors.

Using two paper plates, make a continuous life cycle of a plant (see *Life cycle of a plant* for reference). Draw the cycle on one plate. Cut a section out of the other and place that one on top of the other. Secure in the middle with a split pin. Or cut the radius of them both and slot them together so that they slide round.

Make a grass head (individual)

> You will need: *Make a grass head* photocopy master (CD-ROM) one copy per learner, a few grams of grass seed, an old stocking, sand, a cardboard tube, plastic plate, scissors, modelling clay per learner.

Learners follow the flow chart on the *Make a grass head* sheet to make a head with grass hair. The grass head can then be used for collecting data, measuring time and measuring length.

Seed packets

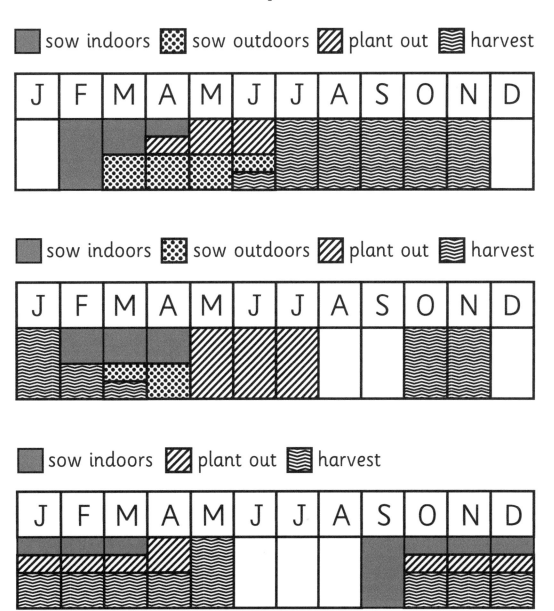

Planter's plan

Gardener's name: _____
First,
Next,
Then,
Last,

Gardener's name: _____
First,
Next,
Then,
Last,

Seed information

■ = Sow indoors

▨ = Plant out

▧ = Sow outdoors

〰 = Harvest

■ = Sow indoors

▨ = Plant out

▧ = Sow outdoors

〰 = Harvest

Seed A

Seed B

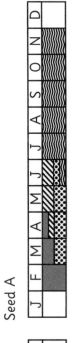

Seed C
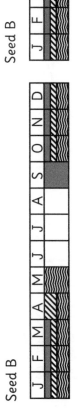

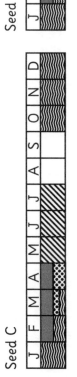

Seed A

Seed B

Seed C

Quick reference

Core activity 11.1: Growing things (Learner's Book p39)

This activity cover everyday systems of measurement in length and capacity, how to make sensible estimations and provides experience of using a table.

Core activity 11.2: Growth and harvest (Learner's Book p40)

This activity puts the concept of units into a practical concept by estimating, measuring and recording.

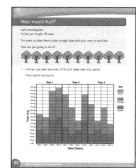

Prior learning	Objectives* – please note that listed objectives might only be partially covered within any given chapter but are covered fully across the book when taken as a whole
• Knowledge of standard ways to measure height: metres, centimetres. • Knowledge of standard terms for capacity: litre, half-litre. • Knowledge of how to set out a table for systematic recording. • Being aware of problem solving strategies and the vocabulary and language to be used. • Know about the relationship between doubling and halving.	**1C: Measures** 3MI1 – Choose and use appropriate units and equipment to estimate, measure and record measurements. 3MI2 – Know the relationship between kilometres and metres, metres and centimetres, kilograms and grams, litres and millilitres. 3MI3 – Read to the nearest division or half division, use scales that are numbered or partially numbered. **1C: Problem solving** 3Pt2 – Begin to understand everyday systems of measurement in length, weight, capacity, time and use these to make measurements as appropriate. 3Pt11 – Make a sensible estimate of the answer to a calculation. 3Ps2 – Explain a choice of calculation strategy and how the answer was worked out. Use ordered lists and tables to help solve problems systematically.

*for NRICH activities mapped to the Cambridge Primary objectives, please visit www.cie.org.uk/cambridgeprimarymaths

Vocabulary

distance apart/between • distance to... from... kilometre (km)
• metre (m) • centimetre (cm) • litre (l) • half-litre • container

---

Resources: *Planting trees* photocopy master (p88), one copy per learner. Empty 1 litre and 2 litre plant pots. Canes or strips of paper of 45cm and 1 metre length plus the depth of the pot. (Optional: a collection of coins; seeds, plant pots, compost, water, ruler, paper, pens/pencils; fruit trees.)

Begin by asking, "*Who likes to eat fruit? What is your favourite fruit? How does the fruit grow? On a tree or on a bush?*" Explain that the session today is about growing fruit trees. They come in 1 litre or 2 litre pots ready to be planted in the soil.

Tell the learners, "*There is a choice of buying a tree in a 1 litre pot*" (Show the empty pot) "*or a 2 litre pot*" (show it). "*The tree in the 1 litre pot is 45 cm high, and the tree in the 2 litre pot is 1 metre high.*" Ask, "*How many centimetres are there in a metre?*" Stand the canes or hold the paper so that the base is at the bottom of the pot and the part showing is either 45 cm or 1 metre.

Ask, "*If we wanted to plant these trees, how big would the hole for each need to be? Could they be the same size as the pot? Why/not?*" Give time for discussion between pairs. Then say, "*Tell us what you thought.*" Allow time for feedback.

Now explain that, "*When we plant trees we need to make sure that they grow well, so we add compost to the planting hole, so the hole needs to be big enough to allow us to put the compost in as well. Compost comes in 60 litre bags. We need 1 litre of compost for 2 litre pot trees and 500 ml, or $\frac{1}{2}$ litre, for 1 litre pots.*"

Then ask, "*How many different ways can we use the bag of compost? If we planted only the trees in the 2 litre pot, how many trees can we plant?*" (**60**) "*If we planted trees only from the 1 litre pots, how many could we plant?*" (**120**) "*How did you work that out?*"

Hand out a copy of the *Planting trees* sheet to each learner and explain the task. Learners work in pairs to complete (and extend) the table.

Walk around, as the class is working, to make sure that they all understand the task. For those having difficulty ask questions, such as, "*Can you explain what you have done so far? What information do you have, and what do you need to find out? Is there something you know already that can help you?*" (**doubling and halving**)

At the end of the session ask some of the pairs to feed back. Record the different ways as they are offered. Ask, "*Do you think that we have found all of the different ways? How can we make sure?*" Being systematic with the recording needs to be emphasised. Model this for the learners so that they have an understanding of what is needed.

Look out for!

- Learners who are having difficulties. *Supply a 'double and half' table as a reference, or use practical equipment such as strips of paper of interlocking cubes to reinforce the idea of whole and half and the connections between them.*

- Learners who are finding the core activity easy. *Challenge them to design a field of trees, using graph paper and a scale. The trees are planted three metres apart in every direction. What is the smallest area for planting 20 trees? 50 trees? Does the field have to be regular? Investigate irregular shapes.*

Summary

- By the end of this activity learners will have reinforced their knowledge of relationships: metres and centimetres, litres and millilitres.
- They will begin to understand everyday systems of measurement in length and capacity, and be able to use measurements in calculations.
- They will be making sensible estimations of the answer to a calculation and explaining a choice of calculation strategy and how the answer was worked out.
- They will have had experience of using a table to help solve problems systematically.

Notes on the Learner's Book

The orchard (p39): this page uses a table to show information about different styles of fruit trees and asks the learners to answer questions and then choose which tree they would choose and give reasons for their choice. Some learners may need more diagrams to explain the spacing.

Check up!

Ask questions such as
- *"If I had a full bag of compost and I planted 20 × two litre trees, how much compost would be left?"* (**40 litres**)
- *"How many one litre trees could I plant using what was left?"* (**80 trees**)

More activities

Buying trees (individual)

> You will need a collection of coins for the learners to 'spend'.

Display a list pricing trees (priced in relation to the coins available) so that the larger one costs double the smaller one. Give each learner a set amount of money. How many of each tree could be bought? How many different ways of spending the money? What would be the best buy?

Plant seeds in the classroom (individual/class)

> You will need seeds, plant pots, compost, water, paper, ruler, paper, pens/pencils.

Monitor the growth of the seeds over a number of days or weeks. Graph the growth or use rulers for precise measures and make scale drawings.

Container-grown fruit trees (class)

> You will need to buy a selection of fruit trees.

Plant the trees outside and encourage the learners to care for them (water when dry and keep weed free). Observe flowers then fruit.

Resources: Graph paper, rulers and pencils. (Optional: various fruits, weighing and measuring equipment; bar charts and tables from newspapers and magazines, sheets of graph paper and pens/pencils.)

Explain that, once a tree has been planted, you have to look after it so that it will grow. Tell the learners that, *"The tree from the 1 litre pot grows 5 cm in the first year. If it is 45 cm high when it is planted it, how tall will it be after a year? How did you work that out? So now the tree is 50cm tall. The tree grows 7 cm in the second year so how tall is the tree after two years?"* (**57 cm**). *"In the third year it grows 10 cm. How tall will the tree be after three years?"* (**67 cm**). *"It grows 10 cm every year from now on. If it is 67 cm after three years and it grows at 10 cm a year, how many years will it be when it measures 97 cm?"* (**six years**) *"How did you work that out?"*

Now tell the learners that, *"The tree in the 2 litre pot grows double the amount of the other tree each year. If the 1 litre tree grows 5 cm in the first year how much will the 2 litre pot tree grow?"* Tell the learners that they are going to draw a bar chart to show the growth of the tree from the 2 litre pot for six years. *"You will first have to work out how much it grows each year from the information about the smaller tree."* Make sure learners realise that they need to convert the original height of the taller tree (1 m) into centimetres.

As the class work in pairs, walk around to make sure that they all understand the task. For those having difficulty ask questions such as, *"Can you explain what you have done so far? What information do you have, and what do you need to find out? Is there something you know already that can help you?"* (**doubling and halving**)

When learners have drawn the graphs, tell them that, *"Both fruit trees start producing fruit when they are 2 metres tall. Using the two graphs for each of the trees to help you, tell me how long it will be when they each produce fruit. How did you work that out?"*

Then explain that once the trees start to produce fruit, they each produce 1 kg 500 g, or $1\frac{1}{2}$ kilos, in their first year and 2 kg 500 g, or $2\frac{1}{2}$ kilos, each in their second year. Every year after that they produce an additional kilo per year. *"Talk to your partner and tell me as many facts as you can about the fruit on these trees. For instance you could tell me, 'After … years the 1 litre tree produces $1\frac{1}{2}$ kilos of fruit'. What else can you find out?"* Allow some time for discussion, then take feedback.

Look out for!

- Learners who may need help to produce a graph or table. *Revise some of the basic points and remind them of previous work on graphs.*
- Learners who complete the task quickly. *Ask them to extend the graph to seven years, then ten years. Some learners can use graph paper.*
- You could also set further problems for them to solve. Ask, for example:
  - *"One in ten trees die in the first year. If you want 100 trees at the end of the first year, how many do you need to plant?"* Ask them to show how they worked out the answer.
  - *"After five years you want to produce more than 50 kilos of fruit. How many trees do you need to plant? How many different ways are there to make 50 kilos?"*

Summary

- By the end of this activity learners will be able to choose and use appropriate units and equipment to estimate, measure and record measurements.
- They will use their knowledge of relationships between metres and centimetres and kilograms and grams.
- They will have begun to understand everyday systems of measurement in length, weight, capacity and use these in calculations.
- They will have had opportunities to explain a choice of calculation strategy and how the answer was worked out, using ordered lists and tables to help solve problems systematically and making a sensible estimate of the answer to a calculation.

Notes on the Learner's Book

How much fruit? (p40): this page gives learners the opportunity to work with a bar chart to interpret the data in order to answer questions.

Check up!

Ask questions such as:
- *"Which is more, 200 cm or $1\frac{1}{2}$ metres? How do you know?"*
- *"Which is more 1 kilogram or 500 grams? How do you know?"*
- *"Would you prefer $\frac{1}{2}$ kilo or 500 grams of fruit?"*

More activities

Best value? (individual/class)

> You will need various fruits, weighing and measuring equipment.

Ask learners to bring in different fruits, then weigh and measure them. Use the information (cost, weight, size) to find the best value.

Real data (individual/class)

> You will need graphs and tables from newspapers and magazines, sheets of graph paper and pens/pencils.

Use graphs and tables from real world sources (newspaper, magazine) and extract the data. Represent it in a different way.

Planting trees

45 cm

1 metre

1 metre

COMPOST

60 litres

½ litre compost

1 litre compost

How many 45cm trees can you grow with 1 bag of compost? [ ]

How many 1 metre trees can you grow with 1 bag of compost? [ ]

Make a table to show other ways of using the compost. The first one is done for you

1 litre pots	Total compost	2 litre pots	Total compost	Total compost for both pots
20	10 litres	50	50 litres	60 litres

12 Place value (2)

Quick reference

Core activity 12.1: Three-digit numbers (Learner's Book p44)

Learners explore reading, writing and ordering three-digit numbers.

Core activity 12.2: Comparing numbers (Learner's Book p45)

Learners compare and order numbers using < and >, and find numbers in between.

Core activity 12.3: Multiplying by 10 (Learner's Book p46)

Learners explore the effect of multiplying by 10.

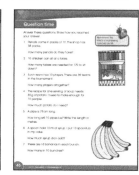

Prior learning	Objectives* – please note that listed objectives might only be partially covered within any given chapter but are covered fully across the book when taken as a whole
• Counting forward and back in ones, tens and hundreds from any number. • Experience of making three-digit numbers with place value cards. • Ordering two-digit numbers. • Some experience of using < and >.	**2A: Numbers and the number system** 3Nn3 – Count on and back in ones, tens and hundreds from two- and three-digit numbers. 3Nn5 – Understand what each digit represents in three-digit numbers and partition into hundreds, tens and units. 3Nn6 – Find 1, 10, 100 more/less than two- and three-digit numbers. 3Nn9 – Place a three-digit number on a number line marked off in multiples of 100. 3Nn10 – Place a three-digit number on a number line marked off in multiples of 10. 3Nn11 – Compare three-digit numbers, use < and > signs, and find a number in between. 3Nn12 – Order two- and three-digit numbers. 3Nn7 – Multiply two-digit numbers by 10 and understand the effect. **2A: Problem solving** (*Using techniques and skills in solving mathematical problems*) 3Pt1 – Choose appropriate mental strategies to carry out calculations. 3Pt3 – Make sense of and solve word problems, single (all four operations) and two-step (addition and subtraction), and begin to represent them, e.g. with drawings or on a number line. **2A: Using understanding and strategies in solving problems** 3Ps9 – Explain methods and reasoning orally, including initial thoughts about possible answers to a problem.

*for NRICH activities mapped to the Cambridge Primary objectives, please visit www.cie.org.uk/cambridgeprimarymaths

Vocabulary

order • hundreds • tens • ones • multiply • ten times table • is greater than • is less than • inequality

Draw or display an enlarged copy of *Place value chart 1* where everyone can see it. Ask the learners to talk to their partner about what they notice. Share the learners' ideas, making sure they have noticed that all the digits are listed in order and that each row shows ones, tens or hundreds. The chart is like the *Place value cards,* but arranged in a different way. Explain that you are going to read some numbers on the chart, all you have to do is say the number that is being pointed to when it is being pointed to, with the word 'and' after the hundreds number. Using a stick or other pointer, so that your hand does not hide any of the chart, point to 200, then 50, then 7 so that the learners read '200 AND 50 7 (257)'. Practise reading several three-digit numbers, avoiding using 10. Explain that there are two ways you might trick the learners by saying, "*I might not point to any tens, so if I point to 200 and then 9, you should say 209, and if I point to 200 then 10 then 6, it would not be right to say 200 and ten six. What should you say?*" The learners should recognise that this would be 216, so that whenever you point to the ten, they can say '200 and', but must pause until you have pointed to a number in the bottom row as well before they can complete the number. Point to several more three-digit numbers, including numbers without any tens and those with only one ten in the middle row.

Give each pair of learners a copy of *Place value chart 1* and some blank paper. One learner must point to any ten three-digit numbers while the second learner says what the number is and quickly writes the number down. The learners then swap over.

Once both learners have a list of ten three-digit numbers, ask the learners how they could put these numbers in order, starting from the smallest to the largest. Talk through looking for the number of hundreds first, then the tens, then the ones. Model this with a list of ten numbers, for example 257, 472, 836, 699, 543, 216, 764, 426, 298, 315. "*There are no one hundred numbers, but there are three 200 numbers, 257, 216 and 298. 216 has only one ten, so that comes first, then 257 with five tens, then 298 because it has nine tens. There's only one 300 number, 315, so that comes next. There are two 400 numbers, 472 and 426. Which number comes next? How do you know?*"

Vocabulary

order: to arrange according to size. This could be from smallest to largest: 237, 564, 832, 956 or largest to smallest: 956, 832, 564, 237.

Look out for!

- Learners who may need to go at a slower pace. *Encourage them to use place value cards to help them 'read' the three-digit numbers created using the place value chart.*
- Some learners may be able to explore thousands using the *Place value chart 2*. *Challenge them to read, write and order numbers to 9999.*

Once the ordering is complete, ask each pair of learners to work together to order all 20 of their numbers. Then give each pair a copy of a *Number line 0 to 1000* to mark their numbers on.

Finish the session by asking some learners to read out their list of numbers while the rest of the class listens to check the order is correct. You could also read out a list of numbers, claiming they are correct. Will learners spot your mistakes? Finally, ask the learners what they noticed when they marked the numbers on the number line. They should have noticed that they could mark their numbers on the number line in order, because they had already ordered them.

Summary

Learners know what each digit in a three-digit number represents and can use this information to order three-digit numbers.

Notes on the Learner's Book
They then create three-digit numbers from five digits and order them. *Number jars* (p44): learners put numbers in order, starting with either the smallest or the largest.

Check up!
Show learners a list of four or five numbers.
- Ask them to tell you which is the lowest (or highest) number and how they know.
- You could also ask them to order the numbers, or tell you the number closest to 500 or something else.

More activities

Snake numbers (individual)

> You will need the *Snake numbers* photocopy master (CD-ROM) one copy per learner and coloured pencils.

Learners colour in the number which 10 more or 100 more than the number at the beginning of each snake.

Number words (individual)

> You will need the *Number words* photocopy master (CD-ROM) one copy per learner) and pens/pencils.

Learners write numbers in words and read words to write a number.

Games Book (ISBN 9781107694019)

Adding 10 and 100 (p11) is a game for two to four players. Players find 10 and 100 more than two- and three-digit numbers. Other more challenging versions are also suggested.

Subtracting 10 and 100 (p12) is a game for two to four players. Players find 10 and 100 less than two- and three-digit numbers. Other more challenging versions are also suggested.

Resources: Enlarged *Place value chart 1* photocopy master (97). Stick pointer. *Number line 0 to 100 (marked in 10s)* constructed in *Core activity 1.3*, one per learner. (Optional: *Inequalities puzzle 1* and *Inequalities Puzzle 2* photocopy masters (CD-ROM), one copy per learner; *Make your own puzzle* photocopy master (CD-ROM); pens/pencils; scissors.)

Read three-digit numbers together using the enlarged *Place value chart 1*. As the learners become more confident, ask one of them to take a turn at pointing to the numbers and another to record the numbers said where everyone can see them. It does not matter if the pace becomes too fast for the learner to record every number. After about ten numbers, invite two different learners to have a go. For each list, ask questions such as *"Which is the smallest number? Which is the largest number? If we put these numbers in order from smallest to largest (or largest to smallest), what would be the second (or third or next to last) number in the list?"*

Choose two numbers from a list, say 367 and 842, and ask which is the larger of the two and which is the smaller. Revise the meaning of < (is less than) and > (is greater than) with the learners, writing 376 < 842 and 842 > 376. It may be useful to tell them that the open side of the sign always points to the larger number, like the mouth of a crocodile or lion always wanting the largest meal. Choose a third number between the other two, for example 529, and write 376 < 529 < 842 and 842 > 529 > 376. Challenge the learners to read these aloud. Explain that we call these **inequalities**. We are comparing the numbers, but since they are not equal, we cannot use the equals sign =.

Ask the learners to work with their partner to write an inequality using three numbers. After a few moments, share some of the inequalities, checking that they are true. Some learners may suggest inequalities using both < and >, for example 842 >376 < 524.

Ask each pair of learners to write at least 10 inequalities using any two or three numbers from the lists written earlier and < and >. Some learners may find it useful to have a *Number line 0 to 1000 (marked in 10s)* for support.

Finish the session with some learners reading their inequalities with two numbers and others naming a number in between. If there is time, return to the *Place value chart* and give more learners the opportunity to point to numbers while the rest of the class read them.

Vocabulary

less than: uses the symbol <.

greater than: uses the symbol >.

inequality: not equal. A number sentence using < and/or > but not =.

Look out for!

- Learners who confuse the < is less than and > is greater than signs. *Give them a card of each sign, similar to those below, to help them remember which is which.*

<	>
is less than	is greater than
17 < 23	23 > 17

They may also find it useful to have a *Number line 0 to 1000 (marked in 10s)* for support when writing inequalities.

Look out for!

- Learners who are confident about using the less than and more than signs. *Challenge them to use < and > in the same number sentence. Ask them to use 3, 4, 5 or even more numbers in the same inequality.*

Summary

Learners can use the < and > signs to write inequalities comparing at least two numbers. They can also name a number in between.

Notes on the Learner's Book

Comparing measures (p45): learners write inequalities using the weights and capacities illustrated. Challenge learners to use addition or subtraction either side of the less than and greater than signs. They could also use the less than and greater than signs two or three times in the same number sentence.

Check up!
- Say an inequality using two numbers and ask learners to tell you a number in between.
- Alternatively, say an inequality using two numbers and ask the learners to extend it by using a third number and either < or >.

More activities

Inequalities puzzles

You will need *Inequalities puzzle 1* and *Inequalities Puzzle 2* photocopy masters (CD-ROM), one copy per learner, *Make your own puzzle* photocopy master (CD-ROM), one copy per learner, pens/pencils and scissors.

Using sheet 1 or sheet 2, cut out the nine puzzle pieces and reassemble them to make a square where every number sentence is correct. Challenge learners to make their own inequality puzzle for a friend to solve. The middle piece of each puzzle has a dot (•) at the centre. Some learners will benefit from working with a partner on this activity. More confident learners may wish to construct their own puzzles using the blank *Make your own puzzle* sheets.

Puzzle 1

Current layout

4	6	8
7	3	1
5	2	9

Correct layout

1	2	3
4	5	6
7	8	9

Puzzle 2

Current layout

4	5	8
2	3	1
7	9	6

Correct layout

1	2	3
4	5	6
7	8	9

Games Book (ISBN 9781107694019)

Greater than or less than (p12) is a game for two players. This game involves quick recognition of a three-digit number and comparison of it with another number, then quickly recognising which is greater.

Resources: Enlarged *Place value chart 1* photocopy master (p97). *Multiplier* photocopy master (p98), one copy per learner. Scissors and glue, pencils and erasers. A4 paper. (Optional: *Multiplying by 10* photocopy master (CD-ROM), one copy per learner, pens/pencils; *Make your own Puzzle* photocopy master (CD-ROM), one copy per pair, coloured pencils and a 1–6 dice (CD-ROM).)

Draw a simple picture of a milometer, showing the number of miles (or kilometres) a car has been driven.

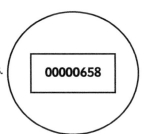

00000658

Explain that a friend has a new car and this is what the milometer shows. Ask the learners how far the car has been driven. Ask questions such as, *"What will the milometer show after another mile (or kilometre)? Another 10 miles? Another 30 miles? Another 100 miles? 200 miles?"* Change the milometer and ask similar questions. Display the *Place value chart* for support.

Write a row of ten crosses where everyone can see them. Write 1 × 10 = 10 next to it. Write a further row of 10 crosses underneath and 2 × 10 = 20 next to it. Ask the learners to write the ten times table. Read the 10 times table together. Explain that when you multiply a number by 10, it becomes ten times bigger, so 4 × 10 is 40, forty is ten times bigger than four. 8 × 10 is 80, eighty is ten times bigger than eight and so on. Call out a few × 10 questions for the learners to answer. Alongside the 10 times table, begin to write the following:

1 × 10 = 10   10 × 10 = 100
2 × 10 = 20   20 × 10 =
3 × 10 = 30   30 × 10 =   and so on.
Explain that we know that 10 times 10 is 100, and ask, *"So what could 20 × 10 be?"*
Ask the learners to complete this new table alongside the ten times table.

Once the learners have completed the table, remind them that when we calculate, it is often useful to split the number into tens and ones. *"If I wanted to multiply 32 by 10, I could do 30 × 10 and 2 × 10 and then add both parts together."* Ask the learners to do this and then tell you what they notice. 32 × 10 = 320.

Ask the learners to work with a partner and multiply 47, 96, 71, 56 and 85 by 10. Ask the learners what they have noticed. They should be able to tell you that the tens become hundreds and the ones become tens, so there are always zero ones.

Vocabulary

ten times table:
0 × 10 = 0
1 × 10 = 10
2 × 10 = 20
3 × 10 = 30
4 × 10 = 40
5 × 10 = 50
6 × 10 = 60
7 × 10 = 70
8 × 10 = 80
9 × 10 = 90
10 × 10 = 100

multiply: carry out the process of multiplication.

Look out for!

- Learners who quickly see the effect of multiplying by 10. *They will not need to use the multiplier.*
- Learners who have problems seeing the effect of multiplying by 10. *They will need to use the multiplier for support for some time.*
- Learners who find multiplying by 10 straightforward. *Ask them to explore what happens when they multiply by 100. Ask them to redesign the multiplier so that they can use it to explain multiplying by 100 to other learners.*

Give each learner a copy of the *Multiplier* sheet, scissors and glue.

Learners need to cut around the outside of both pieces and fold each along the central line, gluing the folded paper together for increased strength. They then carefully cut along the six dotted lines to create three windows. The other piece can then be threaded through the three windows and positioned so that the hundreds window is blank and two shaded squares show through the tens and ones windows. To multiply by ten, learners write the two-digit number in pencil in the shaded squares, then pull the sliding piece along until the first two windows have the two shaded squares showing and the shaded zero shows in the ones space – thus revealing the answer. The numbers can then be rubbed out and another number multiplied. The multiplier strip is double sided so that the strip can be turned over when it becomes worn.

Give the learners time to make and experiment with their multiplier.

Opportunities for display!

Display the multipliers with a heading such as 'Can you multiply by 10? We can!' The ten times table could also be part of the display.

When it is time to clear up, ask the learners if they can describe what happens to a number when it is multiplied by ten. They should be able to tell you that ones become tens and tens become hundreds, so the number moves one space to the left, with a zero in the now empty ones space.

H	T	O
	2	3
2	3	0

Explain that zero is being used to hold the hundreds and tens in their new places. Try to avoid learners saying 'just add a zero' as this only works for whole numbers, not decimals and could cause misconceptions in future.

Finish the session by asking the learners to fold a piece of A4 paper in half and half again and a third time. When opened out, the paper should have eight rectangles. Learners write a three-digit number between 100 and 500 with zero ones in each space. Call out random two-digit numbers (keep a list of the numbers used for checking) for learners to multiply by 10. If a learner has written that number on their paper, they can cross it out. The first learner to cross out all eight numbers and call out 'times 10' is the winner.

Summary

Learners can multiply two-digit numbers by 10 and understand the effect on the number.

Notes on the Learner's Book
Question time (p46): learners solve questions which involve multiplying by 10 or working out what must be multiplied by 10 to get the right number.

Check up!
- Give the learners a two-digit number and ask them to multiply it by 10.
- You could also give them a three-digit number with 0 ones and ask what number must have been multiplied by 10 to give that number.
- Challenge some learners to multiply a three-digit number by 10.

More activities

Multiplying by 10

> You will need a copy of the *Multiplying by 10* photocopy master (CD-ROM) per learner, pens/pencils.

This activity will help learners who need more experience at multiplying by 10. A copy of the *Multiplier* constructed earlier in the session might be useful.

Make 100

> You will need a copy of the *Make you own Puzzle* photocopy master (CD-ROM), one copy per pair, coloured pencils and a 1–6 dice.

Pairs of learners play using the 3 × 3 grid. They each choose a different colour to write in. They take turns to roll a dice, multiply the number thrown by 10 and write the result in one of the squares. The aim is for the numbers in each square to total 100. So if a player rolls a five, the number to enter is 50; it can be entered in any square that does not already have a total of more than 50 and has not already been written in by their opponent. When a player 'fills' a square (so that the numbers total 100), they tick it. The winner is the first player to get three ticks in a row, column or diagonally. For a more challenging game, allow scores to be split into tens and added to different squares.

Place value chart 1

100	200	300	400	500	600	700	800	900
10	20	30	40	50	60	70	80	90
1	2	3	4	5	6	7	8	9

Multiplier

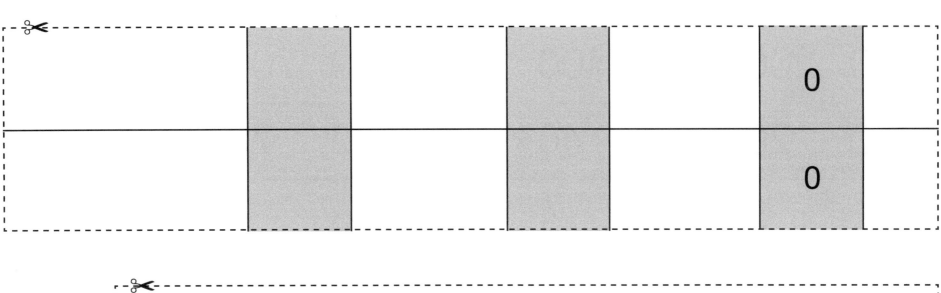

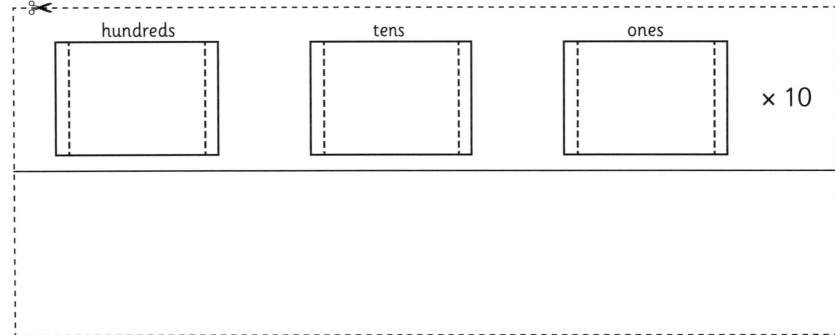

Quick reference

Core activity 13.1: Rounding to the nearest 10 and 100 (Learner's Book p48)

Learners round numbers to the nearest 10 and 100, exploring how to know whether to round up or down.

Core activity 13.2: Estimating (Learner's Book p50)

Learners explore giving estimates in the format of a range.

Prior learning	Objectives* – *please note that listed objectives might only be partially covered within any given chapter but are covered fully across the book when taken as a whole*

- Rounding to the nearest 10.
- Estimating amounts and estimating by choosing between 20, 50 and 100 (or other numbers as appropriate).

2A: Numbers and the number system

3Nn3 – Count on and back in ones, tens and hundreds from two- and three-digit numbers.

3Nn6 – Find 1, 10, 100 more/less than two- and three-digit numbers.

3Nn8 – Round two-digit numbers to the nearest 10 and round three-digit numbers to the nearest 100.

3Nc18 – Find 20, 30, … 90, 100, 200, 300 more/less than three-digit numbers.

2A: Problem solving (*Using techniques and skills in solving mathematical problems*)

3Pt1 – Choose appropriate mental strategies to carry out calculations.

3Pt3 – Make sense of and solve word problems, single (all four operations) and two-step (addition and subtraction), and begin to represent them, e.g. with drawings or on a number line.

3Pt10 – Estimate and approximate when calculating, and check working.

3Pt11 – Make a sensible estimate for the answer to a calculation e.g. using rounding.

3Pt12 – Consider whether an answer is reasonable.

2A: Using understanding and strategies in solving problems

3Ps1 – Make up a number story to go with a calculation.

3Ps2 – Explain a choice of calculation strategy and show how the answer was worked out.

3Ps3 – Explore and solve number problems and puzzles.

3Ps6 – Identify simple relationships between numbers.

3Ps8 – Investigate a simple general statement by finding examples which do or do not satisfy it, e.g. when adding 10 to a number, the first digit remains the same.

3Ps9 – Explain methods and reasoning orally, including initial thoughts about possible answers to a problem.

Vocabulary

Rounding • estimate • estimating • range

*for NRICH activities mapped to the Cambridge Primary objectives, please visit www.cie.org.uk/cambridgeprimarymaths

> **Resources:** 1–6 dice (CD-ROM); three per pair of learners, paper and pens/pencils. (Optional: *Rounding to the nearest 10* photocopy master (CD-ROM), one copy per learner, pens/pencils; *Rounding 10 and 100* photocopy master (CD-ROM), one copy per learner, pens/pencils; *Rounding problems* photocopy master (CD-ROM), one copy per learner.)

Begin the session by counting on and back in ones, twos, fives, tens and hundreds from two- and three-digit numbers. Occasionally pause a count and ask questions such as, "*What is one (or 10 or 100) more (or less) than that?*" Begin to ask questions involving 20, 30, 40 and so on more or less.

Ask the learners what they can recall about rounding numbers. If necessary, remind them that numbers with five or more ones are rounded up to the next 10, numbers with less than five ones are rounded down to the previous tens number. Draw a reminder where everyone can see it, like the one shown.

Call out a few numbers such as 27, 56, 72, 93, 124, 149, 171, 215 for learners to round to the nearest 10.

Remind the learners that they were thinking about the numbers within each ten and rounding to the nearest 10. Ask them to talk to their partner about what they might need to do to round to the nearest hundred. After a few moments, ask the learners to share their ideas. Use the ideas to suggest multiplying each of the numbers in the drawn model by 10, so that it now clearly shows that numbers from 50 to 99 are rounded up to the next hundred, while numbers from 1 to 49 are rounded down to the previous hundred.

Call out some random numbers such as 127, 256, 272, 393, 500, 424, 571, 615 for the learners to round to the nearest hundred.

Give three dice to each pair of learners and ask them to roll the dice and create a three-digit number. They record the three-digit number and round it to the nearest 100.

After a while, check some numbers together. Choose a number such as 346 and ask learners which hundred it rounds to **(300)**. Then ask them to round 346 to the nearest

Vocabulary

rounding: rounding to the nearest 10 means giving the closest tens number.

- If there are less than five ones, round down to the previous tens number.
- If there are five or more ones, round up to the next tens number.

Look out for!

- Learners who find rounding to the nearest 10 difficult. *They may also find rounding to the nearest 100 difficult. Support them with a number line marked in ones or tens, so that they can count how many to the next and previous 10 or 100 to help them decide which way to go.*
- Learners with a good grasp of the number system who find rounding straightforward. *They may be interested in exploring the errors that occur with repeated rounding, identifying which numbers are likely to be affected.*

10 **(350)**. Now which hundred does it round to **(400)**. Explain that repeated rounding can lead to inaccuracies, so we usually only round a number once. We should think carefully about rounding lengths because we may end up with something that is too short for what we need. If we round amounts for a recipe, the food might be ruined.

Talk about how rounding is useful when we only need to know roughly how many, but stress that we still need to be careful. If there are 29 learners in the class and pencils come in packs of 10, I can order three packs and have a spare pencil. But if there are 24 learners in the class and I round down to 20 and get two packs, then four learners would be without a pencil! If there is time, ask the learners to talk to a partner about when rounding would be useful and when it would not, then share ideas.

Summary

Learners can round numbers to the nearest 10 and 100.

Notes on the Learner's Book

Rounding to the nearest 10 and 100 (p48): learners round numbers and explore the inaccuracies that can occur with repeated rounding.

Check up!

- Say a number and ask learners to round it to the nearest 10 (or 100).
- Ask them to explain how they knew whether to round up or down.

More activities

Rounding 10

You will need the *Rounding to the nearest 10* photocopy master (CD-ROM), one copy per learner, pens/pencils.

This exercise gives practice in rounding numbers, money and lengths to the nearest 10.

Rounding 10 or 100

You will need the *Rounding 10 and 100* photocopy master (CD-ROM) one copy per learner, pens/pencils.

This sheet has six wheels containing numbers for learners to round to the nearest 10 or 100 as instructed by the centre of the wheel.

Rounding problems

You will need the *Rounding problems* photocopy master (CD-ROM) one copy per learner, pens/pencils.

Learners solve problem by considering how useful rounded numbers are.

Resources: Three identical see-through jars, one containing 260 small items (similar buttons, counters, cubes, marbles etc; it does not have to be full), two empty. A 0 to 1000 number line with no other markings on it except five random points (one per pair). (Optional: strips of card, a ruler and a stapler; string, scissors, sticky labels, pens/pencils and rulers or tape measures.)

Begin the session by counting on and back in ones, twos, fives, tens and hundreds from two- and three-digit numbers. Occasionally pause a count and ask questions such as, "*What is 20, 30, 40, 50 etc more or less?*"

Show the learners the jar containing the small items and ask them to estimate how many are in the jar. Accept the initial estimates, then remind them that when they last looked at estimating, they thought about whether their estimate should be 20, 50 or 100. Explain that when estimating, people often think of a range. This means a 'chunk of numbers', so we might say 1 to 50, 51 to 100, 101 to 150, 151 to 200, 201 to 250, 251 to 300 and so on. Write these ranges where everyone can see them. Explain that no number can appear in more than one range, so we could not have 1 to 50, 50 to 100, 100 to 150 and so on, because if you thought it was 100, which estimate would you choose? If you chose the range 51 to 100, it means you think the smallest number it is likely to be is 51 and the largest 100.

Ask some learners to pick which range they think is right for the jar. Now pour half the amount into a second jar identical to the first one. Ask the learners what portion of items is in each jar. If they say 'half', ask if half their original estimate still feels about right. Pour half of one of the halves into the third jar and then ask the learners what portion of the whole collection is in the third jar. If necessary, tell them that you tried to pour half of the previous jar in. Suggest that the ranges listed before are now too big and draw up a new list of ranges. This could be in tens or twenties up to 100.

Ask each pair of learners to write their estimate range for the first, second and third jar. Each pair should then check with another pair to see if they agree. If they disagree, they should try to convince the other pair that their estimate is more accurate.

After a few moments, tell the learners that you counted 260 items into the jar, so 251 to 300 would be the best estimate, but 200 to 250 is very close. The second jar should contain about 130, so the estimate 101 to 150 would be the best one. The third jar should contain about 65 so an estimate of 60 to 70 would be a good one.

Vocabulary

estimate: a sensible guess of 'how many' there are of something.

range: the spread of numbers concerned, for example 30 to 50.

Look out for!

- Learners who find estimating very difficult because they want to be correct. *Give them wide ranges to consider at first, then gradually reduce the range.*
- Learners who can give very accurate estimates. *They could use the ranges suggested as a stepping stone to identifying a single number if they prefer.*

Opportunities for display!

A table top display of jars of objects with a sheet to record estimates is interactive and will encourage discussion.

If there is time, give pairs of learners a copy of a 0 to 1000 number line with no other markings on it except five random points. Each pair should decide on a suitable range for each point and then discuss their ideas with another pair.

Summary

Learners will be able to provide a suitable range of numbers as an estimate. Their estimates are becoming more accurate.

Notes on the Learner's Book:

Marble estimates (p50): learners estimate the number of marbles in a jar and the length of some lines.

Check up!

- Ask learners to estimate how many of something they can see but to give a range rather than a single number.
- Ask them to explain why they think the range they have chosen is suitable.

More activities

How many blades of grass?

> You will need four strips of card, a ruler or tape measure and a stapler.

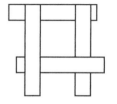

Make a 1 cm² window by stapling together four pieces of card as shown. Learners can use this to count the number of blades of grass within 1 cm² and use this to estimate how many blades of grass there are in 1 m². The same approach can be used for scaling up other estimates, for example words on a page, tufts in a carpet and so on.

String estimates

> You will need string, scissors, sticky labels, pens/pencils and rulers or tape measures.

Either cut some lengths of string without measuring them or ask the learners to do this. Use a sticky label folded over the string at some point to label the pieces a, b, c, d, e, etc. Ask learners to give an estimate with a 10 cm range, them measure the string to see how close they were. They could score a point if the length is within their 10 cm range. Which pair of learners can get the most points?

Games Book (ISBN 9781107694019)

Ranges (p15) is a game for two players. Learners estimate the total of four numbers and check the total against a range.

Blank page

Quick reference

Core activity 14.1: Doubling and halving (Learner's Book p52)

Learners explore doubling, halving and the relationship between them.

Prior learning	Objectives* – please note that listed objectives might only be partially covered within any given chapter but are covered fully across the book when taken as a whole
• Doubles to 10 and beyond. • Counting in fives. • Some experience of finding half of a shape and number.	**2A: Calculation** (*Mental strategies*) 3Nc6 – Work out quickly the doubles of numbers 1 to 20 and derive the related halves. 3Nc7 – Work out quickly the doubles of multiples of 5 (< 100) and derive the related halves. **2A: Calculation** (*Multiplication and division*) 3Nc19 – Understand the relationship between halving and doubling. **2A: Problem solving** (*Using techniques and skills in solving mathematical problems*) 3Pt1 – Choose appropriate mental strategies to carry out calculations. 3Pt3 – Make sense of and solve word problems, single (all four operations) and two-step (addition and subtraction), and begin to represent them, e.g. with drawings or on a number line. **2A: Using understanding and strategies in solving problems** 3Ps2 – Explain a choice of calculation strategy and show how the answer was worked out. 3Ps3 – Explore and solve number problems and puzzles. 3Ps6 – Identify simple relationships between numbers. 3Ps8 – Investigate a simple general statement by finding examples which do or do not satisfy it, e.g. when adding 10 to a number, the first digit remains the same. 3Ps9 – Explain methods and reasoning orally, including initial thoughts about possible answers to a problem.

*for NRICH activities mapped to the Cambridge Primary objectives, please visit www.cie.org.uk/cambridgeprimarymaths

Vocabulary

double • half • inverse

Resources: *Doubles and halves* photocopy master (CD-ROM), one copy per learner. Counters or cubes. Modelling clay or dough. Pens/pencils. Paper. (Optional: A4 coloured paper, scissors; *Place value cards* (from *core activity 1.1*), one set per pair, pens/pencils, paper; *Windows* photocopy master (CD-ROM), one copy per learner.)

Begin the session by counting on and back in ones, twos, fives, tens and hundreds from two- and three-digit numbers. Occasionally pause a count and ask questions such as, "*What is '10/20/30 etc. more or' '10/20/30 etc. less' than 20, 30, 40, 50…90, 100, 200, 300 etc.?*"

Ask the learners to remind you what we mean by 'double'. Draw a 'doubles grid' where everyone can see it.

1	2	3	4	5	6	7	8	9	10
	4			10					20

 double

Fill in some of the doubles together, then ask the learners to quickly copy and complete the grid. Once complete, talk with the learners about the patterns they notice.

Ask the learners how they could work out double 23. Talk through doubling 20 and 3 and then adding the numbers together. Also point out that double 2 is 4, so double 2 tens would be 4 tens, 40. Double 3 is 6, so double 23 is 40 + 6, 46.

List five numbers where everyone can see them for the learners to double – 17, 29, 35, 47 and 50. Check the doubles together. Now ask the learners to look at double 5, double 10, double 35 and double 50. Ask them what they notice. They should notice that all the doubles have zero ones, they are tens numbers.

> Ask the learners to talk to their partners about why that is. After a few moments, share ideas.

Look out for!

- Learners who find it useful to make the amount with counters or cubes and then get a second amount to count how many altogether. *Encourage them to organise counters in tens so that they can count in tens rather than ones.*
- Learners who find this task very straightforward. *Encourage them to look at the Doubles and halves sheet. Tell them that they have doubled every number to 20, but they have only halved some of them. Ask them to halve the numbers in between the numbers in the right hand column. If necessary, use modelling clay or dough to show that half of 3 is $1\frac{1}{2}$ by making three equal shapes and cutting all three in half. Put two pieces together to show one whole one and the other half makes $1\frac{1}{2}$.*

Check that the learners have realised that because double 5 is 10, each 5 becomes two fives (a ten) when doubling. You may find it useful to illustrate this with a ten frame cut into two fives.

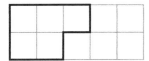

Since each 5 becomes a 10 when doubling, double any multiple of 5 must be a tens number.

Tell the learners that they are now going to look at halves, but really, they have already done that. Go back to the doubles grid and read from bottom to top, half of 2 is 1, half of 4 is 2 and so on. Ask the learners what 'half' means and what they notice about the grid. Share ideas and draw in the reverse arrow, labelling it 'half'. Check that the learners have remembered that 'half' is one of two **equal** parts of a whole. Make sure the learners have noticed that halving and doubling are **inverses** of each other. Halving reverses doubling and doubling reverses halving. Call out the doubles that they had before and ask them to find half of that number to help them to recognise the link.

Give the learners the *Doubles and halves* sheet to complete.

If there is time, call out questions such as, "*What is double 13? What is half of 26?*"

Summary

Learners can find double and half of an increasing range of numbers and are beginning to generalise. They understand that doubling and halving are inverses.

Notes on the Learner's Book

What number am I? (p52): learners use the double and half clues to identify the original number. They identify where they have heard the words 'double' and 'half'.

Check up!

Say a number and ask the learners to quickly tell you half (or double).

Opportunities for display!

Display the halves and doubles grid, labelled with the two arrows. Add a caption saying 'Doubling is the inverse of halving and halving is the inverse of doubling.'

More activities

Half of a half (individual)

> You will need A4 coloured paper, one sheet per learner, scissors.

Ask learners to fold and cut the sheet of coloured paper in half. Check that they have two equal pieces by putting them on top of each other to compare. They keep one half and swap the other half for a different colour. They fold and cut the new piece in half, then check in the same way as before. They can look at each piece and see that they have $\frac{1}{2}$, $\frac{1}{4}$ and $\frac{1}{4}$ of the original paper, and that $\frac{1}{2} = \frac{1}{4} + \frac{1}{4}$. Learners keep $\frac{1}{4}$ and again swap for a different colour. They fold, cut and compare again. They also look at what fraction of the whole their smallest piece is. Continue until the paper is too small to fold in half or until you feel you have gone far enough. Learners can put the pieces in size order and label them. Stuck to a strip of paper, this makes a good fraction display. Alternatively, they can use them to make a picture.

Place value halves (pairs)

> You will need *Place value cards* (from *core activity 1.1*) one set per pair, pens/pencils, paper. A sheet of paper or mini whiteboards for recording.

Using a set of tens *Place value cards* and even ones cards, learners create a two-digit number. One learner halves the tens, the other halves the ones. They add the two halves together to find half of the original number and record it, for example, as: 'Half of 48 is 20 + 4 = 24 or Half of 36 is 15 + 3 = 18'.

Windows (individual)

> You will need the *Windows* photocopy master (CD-ROM), one copy per learner, pens/pencils.

Write a range of even numbers in the central window. Learners write double the number in the matching right hand window and the half the number in the matching left hand window.

Quick reference

Core activity 15.1: Investigating addition (Learner's Book p55)

Learners explore adding two two-digit numbers by choosing a number, reversing the digits and adding.

Core activity 15.2: Investigating subtraction (Learner's Book p57)

Learners explore subtraction by choosing a two-digit number, reversing the digits and subtracting the smaller number from the larger number.

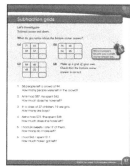

Core activity 15.3: Adding and subtracting with three-digit numbers (Learner's Book p59)

Learners explore adding and subtracting a single digit from two- or three-digit numbers. They also begin to explore adding three-digit numbers to two-digit numbers.

Prior learning	Objectives* – please note that listed objectives might only be partially covered within any given chapter but are covered fully across the book when taken as a whole	Vocabulary
• Adding and subtracting with a range of single- and two-digit numbers. • Using a number line to calculate. • Place value.	**2A: Calculation** (*Addition and subtraction*) 3Nc14 – Add and subtract pairs of two-digit numbers. 3Nc15 – Add three-digit and two-digit numbers using notes to support. 3Nc17 – Add/subtract single-digit numbers to/from three-digit numbers. **2A: Problem solving** (*Using techniques and skills in solving mathematical problems*) 3Pt5 – Check subtraction by adding the answer to the smaller number in the original calculation. 3Pt4 – Check the results of adding two numbers using subtraction, and several numbers by adding in a different order. 3Pt1 – Choose appropriate mental strategies to carry out calculations. 3Pt3 – Make sense of and solve word problems, single (all four operations) and two-step (addition and subtraction), and begin to represent them, e.g. with drawings or on a number line. 3Pt10 – Estimate and approximate when calculating, and check working. 3Pt11 – Make a sensible estimate for the answer to a calculation e.g. using rounding. 3Pt12 – Consider whether an answer is reasonable. **2A: Using understanding and strategies in solving problems** 3Ps2 – Explain a choice of calculation strategy and show how the answer was worked out. 3Ps3 – Explore and solve number problems and puzzles. 3Ps8 – Investigate a simple general statement by finding examples which do or do not satisfy it, e.g. when adding 10 to a number, the first digit remains the same. 3Ps9 – Explain methods and reasoning orally, including initial thoughts about possible answers to a problem.	addition • adding • subtraction • subtract • find the difference • pattern • multiple 

*for NRICH activities mapped to the Cambridge Primary objectives, please visit www.cie.org.uk/cambridgeprimarymaths

Core activity 15.1: Investigating addition

LB: p55

> **Resources:** Enlarged copy of *Place value chart 1* photocopy master (chapter 12, p97). Stick pointer. *100 square* photocopy master (chapter 1, p12); large version for class display and one copy per learner. Colouring pencils. Calculators. (Optional: *0 to 9 digit cards* photocopy master (CD-ROM), one copy per learner; pens/pencils, paper; *Addition walls* photocopy master (CD-ROM), one copy per learner.)

Read three-digit numbers together using the large copy of *Place value chart 1* as in *core activity 12.1*. Speed up and try to trick the learners by pointing to 10 or missing out either the tens digit or the ones digit. Ask different learners to take over the pointing. As you finish the activity, ask questions such as, *"What is the smallest number I could point to if I used all three rows? Which is the largest number if I used all three rows? I think there must be some numbers in between that we cannot make, what do you think?"* Discuss your statement with the learners until they can say that you cannot make numbers with zero ones or zero tens if you are using all three rows.

Tell the learners that you have not done any adding or subtracting for a while and ask them to talk with their partner about different ways of doing these. You could choose to focus on addition only in this session and use a second session for subtraction. After the learners have had sufficient time for discussion, draw up a list of ways. These might include:

<table>
<tr><td>

Addition:

Counting on.

Using a number line.

Looking for number pairs for ten.

Adding too much and adjusting.

Looking for doubles.

Splitting the numbers into hundreds, tens and ones.

…

Check by:

Adding in a different order.

Take one of the two numbers away from the total.
</td><td>

Subtraction:

Counting on (finding the difference).

Counting back.

Using a number line.

Using number pairs for 10.

Taking away too much and adjusting.

Splitting the numbers into hundreds, tens and ones.

…

Check by:

Adding the answer to the smaller number.
</td></tr>
</table>

Vocabulary

subtraction: 'take away'; remaining something from a group.

difference: how many more is needed to make the smaller amount the same as the larger amount, for example, the difference between 6 and 4 is 2.

110 **Unit 2A** 15 Addition and subtraction

If the learners do not suggest some of the methods given above, suggest some of them and ask if they remember how to use that particular method. If necessary, model that method.

Ask the learners how they could check if their answers were right and give them another few minutes to talk to their partner.

Extend the lists to include their ideas. Remind them that they have done some estimating and they could also **estimate** their answers. So for 123 + 56, you could round both numbers and say that the total is roughly 120 + 60, which is 180. You could say, *"When we estimate, we don't know the exact number that we want, but it gives you a good idea. So if I wrote 123 + 56 = 679 I should realise something wasn't right as that total is not reasonable. It is too high for the numbers involved."*

Tell the learners that you would like them to investigate addition. You would like them to choose any two-digit number, swap the digits over and then add the two numbers together. So if you chose 34 and reversed the digits to get 43, 34 + 43 = 77. They should do this several times before talking to their partner about anything they notice. Ask the learners, *"Do you think there is going to be a pattern in the totals? What sort of pattern might it be?"* Record the ideas and let the learners explore.

Circulate around the room, as the learners work, asking how they reached a particular total and how they could check they were right. Suggest that they try a different method. Remind the learners to look for a pattern in the answers and ask pairs what they have noticed so far.

After the learners have had plenty of time to explore, ask one of them to tell you one of their totals. Ask if anyone else got the same total. Check if they did the same calculation. Mark the numbers on the large 100 square to help the learners to recognise the pattern. All the totals are a multiple of 11. Learners are likely to notice that below 100, both digits are the same. They may need to count from one recorded total to another to discover that each total is 11 more than the one before. Although the pattern continues beyond 100, the digits are no longer the same making it harder for learners to recognise the pattern. If the learners are interested, explain why this happens.

32 + 23 = 55

Call 3: a and 2: b

Therefore, 30 is 10 lots of a and 20 is 10 lots of b; 32 is (10a) and b, while 23 is (10b) and a.

So $32 + 23 = (10a) + b + (10b) + a = 11a + 11b$. There is probably no need to go as far as $11(a+b)$.

Look out for!

- Learners who need help to see the pattern of numbers. *They will find it useful to colour in the totals on a 100 square as they add the numbers to help them see the pattern. They may also benefit from using a calculator, either for all the additions or to check them.*
- Learners who are finding the task straightforward. *Challenge them to see what happens when they do the same with three-digit numbers. Let them decide on how they approach the challenge. For example, should they swap the hundreds and ones digits or do something else?*

Summary

Learners have explored adding two two-digit numbers, using a variety of methods and looking for patterns.

Notes on the Learner's Book

Addition walls (p55): learners explore finding the highest and lowest totals after a series of additions. They solve some addition problems. Some learners could go on to predict and explore the totals made with bigger walls. Learners will need a copy of the *Addition walls* photocopy master.

Check up!

- Ask the learners what the answer could be if you had a two-digit number, swapped the digits and added. "*Could it be 23? Or 45?*"
- Ask them to explain how they know.

More activities

Target 100 (individual)

> You will need the *0 to 9 digit cards* photocopy master (CD-ROM), one set per learner.

Using the digit cards, learners find as many ways as they can to add two two-digit numbers to make 100. Remind them that they know that 50 + 50 = 100, but they only have one 5 and one zero, so they cannot make that calculation. So they could start with 51 + 49 and continue from there. Encourage learners to work systematically.

What's my line? (individual)

> You will need pens/pencils, paper.

Draw a number line where everyone can see it. Do not label the line, but draw and label the jumps on it. Ask the learners to write a matching addition calculation.

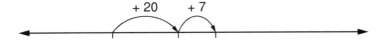

Partners (individual)

Give every learner in the class a two-digit number. Learners move around the room, finding a series of different partners to add their number with. Name two learners you have seen working together and ask if they know their total. Ask questions to find out the highest total and who made it.

Resources: Timer. *True or False cards* photocopy master (CD-ROM), one copy for every five learners. *100 square* photocopy master (chapter 1, p12); large version for class display and one copy per learner. Scissors. Glue. Colouring pencils. Calculators. (Optional: *Place value cards* photocopy master (CD-ROM) (or from *core activity 1.1*), one per learner; *100 square* photocopy master (CD-ROM), one copy per learner and colouring pencils; pens/pencils and paper.) Before the session, print out the *True or False cards* photocopy master (CD-ROM) – each row is a card. Fold each row along the middle and glue the two plain backs together (or ask learners to do this at the beginning of the session).

Play 'True or False' with the learners. Each learner needs one *True or false* card. Make a statement such as, "*A triangle has four sides* (**false**). *This number is four hundred and ten*" (write 4010 on the board) (**false**). "*10 000 metres is the same as 1 kilometre*" (**false**). "*All numbers in the five times table have either five or zero ones*" (**true**), and so on. For each statement, give learners just one minute to talk with their partner about their answer. After the minute, ask everyone to show their answer with their *True/False* card. Whatever the response, ask a few learners to explain their answer. The statements can be about any area of mathematics and will help to check and reinforce understanding. If you did not revise methods of subtracting in the previous session, you need to do that before continuing.

Remind the learners that when they reversed the digits in a two-digit number and then added the numbers together, the total was always a multiple of 11. Ask them to talk to their partner about what might happen when they reverse the digits in a two-digit number and then subtract the smaller number from the bigger number. After a few minutes, ask the learners if they think the answers will make a pattern and if so, what that pattern might be. Record some of their ideas where the learners can see them. Ask them to explore, just as they did with adding two numbers. They should look at their results and see if there is a pattern. At the same time, they could check if their results match any of the patterns already suggested.

Remind the learners of the different methods of subtraction they suggested and the ways of checking a subtraction (see the lists from *core activity 15.1*). Circulate around the room, as the learners work, asking how they reached a particular total and how they could check they were right. Suggest that they try a different method. Remind the learners to look for a pattern in the answers and ask pairs what they have noticed so far.

After the learners have had plenty of time to explore, ask one of them to tell you one of their totals. Ask if anyone else got the same total. Check if they did the same calculation. Mark the numbers on the large 100 square to help the learners to recognise the pattern. All the totals are a multiple of nine. Learners are likely to notice that for totals up to 90, the digits add up to nine. Higher numbers may need the digits to be added together a second time before nine is reached. Learners may need to count from one recorded total to another to discover that each total is nine more than the one before. Alternatively, they may recognise the numbers from the nine times table.

Look out for!

- Learners who are having difficulties. *They will find it useful to colour in the totals on a 100 square as they subtract the numbers, as this will help them see the pattern. They may also benefit from using a calculator, either for all the subtractions or to check them.*

- Learners who are performing the task with confidence. *Challenge them to see what happens when they do the same with three-digit numbers. Let them decide on how they approach the challenge. For example, should they swap the hundreds and ones digit or do something else?*

If the learners are interested, explain why this happens. $41 - 14 = 27$

Call 4: a and 1: b

Therefore 40 is 10 lots of a and 10 is 10 lots of b; 41 is (10a) and b, while 14 is (10b) and a. So $41 - 14 = (10a) + b - (10b) - a = 9a - 9b$. There is probably no need to go as far as $9(a - b)$.

Summary

Learners have explored subtracting two-digit numbers, using a variety of methods and looking for patterns.

Notes on the Learner's Book

Subtraction grids (p57): learners subtract across and down a grid. They make up their own grids and solve some subtraction problems.

Check up!
- Ask the learners what the answer could be if you had a two-digit number, swapped the digits and subtracted the smaller number from the larger number. *"Could it be 22? Or 27?"*
- Ask them to explain how they know.

More activities

High and low differences (individual)

> You will need a set of *Place value cards*, the *100 square* photocopy master (CD-ROM), one copy per learner, and colouring pencils.

Using the *Place value cards*, learners explore which numbers they can find by subtracting a two-digit number from another two-digit number. Suggest $91 - 87 = 4$ as a starting point. Can they find a smaller difference? What is the largest difference they can find? Encourage the learners to work systematically. They could colour in the differences they have found on a 100 square to help them keep track of what they have found.

What's my line? (individual)

> You will need pens/pencils, paper.

Draw a number line as in *core activity 15.1* More activities, but this time ask the learners for a subtraction calculation.

Partners again (individual)

> Give every learner in the class a two-digit number.

Learners move around the room, finding a series of different partners to subtract their number from or be subtracted from. Name two learners you have seen working together and ask what is the difference between them. Ask questions to find out the largest and smallest difference and who made them.

Games Book (ISBN 9781107694019)

Add and subtract game (p15) is a game for two players. Adding and subtracting numbers on the game board to match a particular total.

Resources: (Optional: pens/pencils, paper; the *0 to 9 digit cards* photocopy master (CD-ROM), one per individual or pair; the *Place value cards* photocopy master (CD-ROM), one per learner.)

Play, *What's in the box?* Draw a box where everyone can see it. Invite learners to give you a number. Write the number in the box if it agrees with your rule (multiples of five, odd numbers, even numbers, numbers where the digits add up to seven and so on) and outside the box if it does not. Once three numbers are in the box, learners can either give you another number or tell you what the rule is. After a few games, ask a learner to be the leader.

Remind the learners that they have worked on addition and subtraction, but they have mostly explored two-digits. Tell them they are going to explore three-digit numbers. Draw a number line and mark on 137. Explore adding single digit numbers. Talk through how they might do it. Tell the learners you want to add one and ask what they know about adding one. They should be able to tell you that adding one is just the next counting number. Now add two, focusing on $7 + 2 = 9$. Some learners will need to count on two, most should know that $7 + 2 = 9$. Now add three. This time the learners should tell you that this a number bond for 10. Continue until you have added nine.

Now ask the learners to work with their partner to work through subtraction of single digits (1 to 9). Ask them to record briefly how they would do it, for example for '–1' they might write 'count back one', 'one less' or something else. For example, for subtracting seven from 137, they might write 'cross out the 7 to leave 130'. After giving the learners sufficient time to discuss, share ideas.

Call out some 'three-digit add or subtract one- digit' calculations for the learners to quickly solve. Remind them that they can check by adding the smaller number to the answer.

Explain that they have been good at adding and subtracting a single digit from a three-digit number, so now you are going to move on to adding a three-digit and a two-digit number. Tell the learners that you know they can do this, because they can add two-digit numbers. Ask one learner to give you a two-digit number and another to give you a three-digit number, say 57 and 239. Tell the learners that you know they can add 57 and 39 and ask them to do the calculation quickly. They should now add 200 to what they had and get 296.

Look out for!

- Learners who will find it hard to recognise the rule in the game, What's in the box? *Work with these learners in a small group, talking through what to look for. Use rules they have recently explored.*
- Learners who find subtracting a single digit number from a three-digit number straightforward. *Challenge them to find as many (sensible) different ways as they can to carry out such a subtraction. They could then highlight their preferred method and explain why they prefer it.*

Explain that what you did was remove the hundreds so that they were left with two-digits + two-digits, then put the hundreds back at the end! Illustrate this as follows:

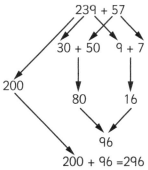

Draw two large circles where everyone can see them. Write three-digit numbers in the first one and two-digit numbers in the second one. Ask the learners to choose a number from each circle to add together.

After the learners have had added three sets of numbers, talk about what they noticed. They should find this straightforward as they can add two two-digit numbers. Adding on hundreds at the end should also be straightforward because of their understanding of place value. The highest number they can make is 198 (if both two-digit numbers were 99), so they will never be adding the removed hundreds number to more than one hundred.

Summary

Learners can add and subtract a single digit from a two- or three-digit number. They are beginning to add three-digit and two-digit numbers by using what they already know.

Notes on the Learner's Book
Rope lengths (p59): learners explore how to make particular lengths by adding and finding the difference. They then answer some addition and subtraction problems. Some learners could explore which lengths could be made with three ropes.

Check up!
- Give the learners a three-digit number and ask them to quickly add (or subtract) seven (or any other single digit number).
- Ask them how they could check their answer.

More activities

What's my line? (individual)

> You will need pens/pencils, paper.

Draw a number line as before but with just one jump labelled with a single digit. Challenge learners to write matching additions and subtractions, using two-digit and three-digit starting numbers.

Digit addition and subtraction (individuals or pairs)

> You will need the *0 to 9 digit cards* photocopy master (CD-ROM), one per individual or pair.

Shuffle a set of digit cards (excluding zero) and turn over the top four cards. Use the cards to make two-digit additions and subtractions, and three-digit add or subtract a single digit calculations. How many different calculations can the learners make and solve from each set of four cards?

HTO add and subtract (individual)

> You will need the *Place value cards* photocopy master (CD-ROM), one per learner.

Using a set of *Place value cards*, learners choose two single digit cards, one tens card and one hundreds card. They make a three-digit number and then add and subtract the single digit number. They swap the two single digits over and repeat. What can they say about their totals? In each case, the additions will be the same but the subtractions will not be. They could also explore adding and subtracting a three-digit and a two-digit number this way, choosing one hundreds number, two tens numbers and two single digit numbers.

Quick reference

Core activity 16.1: Multiples of 5 and 10 (Learner's Book p61)

Learners use a number line marked in fives to help them explore the 5 times table and the matching division facts.

Core activity 16.2: Multiples of 2 and 4 (Learner's Book p63)

Learners double the 2 times table to find the 4 times table and matching division facts.

Core activity 16.3: Multiples of 3, 6 and 9 (Learner's Book p64)

Learners use the 3 times table to find the 6 and 9 times table.

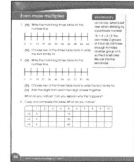

Prior learning	Objectives* – *please note that listed objectives might only be partially covered within any given chapter but are covered fully across the book when taken as a whole*
• Number patterns such as odd, even and counting in multiples of 2, 3, 4 and 5. • Number pairs for 10. • Fact families for addition and subtraction. • Doubling.	**2A: Numbers and the number system** 3Nn4 – Count on and back in steps of 2, 3, 4 and 5 to at least 50. **2A: Calculation** (*Mental strategies*) 3Nc2 – Know the following addition and subtraction facts: Multiples of 100 with a total of 1000. Multiples of 5 with a total of 100. 3Nc3 – Know multiplication/division facts for 2×, 3×, 5×, and 10× tables. 3Nc4 – Begin to know 4× table. **2A: Calculation** (*Multiplication and division*) 3Nc21 – Multiply single-digit numbers and divide two-digit numbers by 2, 3, 4, 5, 6, 9 and 10. 3Nc24 – Understand that division can leave a remainder (initially as 'some left over'). 3Nc26 – Understand the relationship between multiplication and division and write connected facts. **2A: Problem solving** (*Using techniques and skills in solving mathematical problems*) 3Pt6 – Check multiplication by reversing the order, e.g. checking that 6 × 4 = 24 by doing 4 × 6. 3Pt7 – Check a division using multiplication, e.g. check 12 ÷ 4 = 3 by doing 4 × 3. 3Pt1 – Choose appropriate mental strategies to carry out calculations. 3Pt3 – Make sense of and solve word problems, single (all four operations) and two-step (addition and subtraction), and begin to represent them, e.g. with drawings or on a number line. **2A: Using understanding and strategies in solving problems** 3Ps1 – Make up a number story to go with a calculation. 3Ps2 – Explain a choice of calculation strategy and show how the answer was worked out. 3Ps3 – Explore and solve number problems and puzzles. 3Ps5 – Describe and continue patterns which count on or back in steps of 2, 3, 4, 5, 10 or 100. 3Ps8 – Investigate a simple general statement by finding examples which do or do not satisfy it, e.g. when adding 10 to a number, the first digit remains the same. 3Ps9 – Explain methods and reasoning orally, including initial thoughts about possible answers to a problem.

Vocabulary

commutative • fact family • multiple • remainder • times table

*for NRICH activities mapped to the Cambridge Primary objectives, please visit www.cie.org.uk/cambridgeprimarymaths

Resources: Large 100 square (chapter 1, p12). Counters. (Optional: the *Multiples of 5* photocopy master (CD-ROM) and *Multiples of 10* photocopy master (CD-ROM), one per learner; A4 paper, one sheet per learner, pens/pencils.)

Count on and back in steps of two, three, four and five to at least 50 using a large 100 square for support. Ask the learners to describe the patterns for counting in each multiple, extending the questioning to include questions such as, *"How is counting in twos and in fours the same? How is it different?"* Help the learners to recognise that when counting in fours, they are saying every other number from when they counted in twos.

Tell the learners that they have used the 100 square to help them to count in fives, but you are going to show them the same counting on a number line. Draw or reveal the number line below and ask the learners to tell you pairs of numbers on the line that make 100 (e.g. 5 and 95).

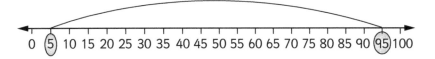

Draw lines to link the number pairs. After the learners have given you several pairs, choose a number pair and ask the learners, *"If you know 35 + 65 = 100, what else do you know?"* Check that the learners can tell you the other three facts in the fact family.

> Ask each learner to choose one of the number pairs to 100, then turn to their partner and tell them the fact family for that number pair. Learners can help each other if they get stuck.

Remind the learners that the numbers they have been using are called 'multiples', multiples of five because each number is five more than the one before. Tell the learners that times tables arrange the multiples in order. Begin to write the five times table where the learners can see it, drawing in the jumps of five on the number line and counting them to write the next fact.

Vocabulary

fact family: the set of four addition and subtraction facts that can be found from one set of numbers. For example, if we know that 35 + 65 = 100, we can work out the other three facts,

65 + 35 = 100,

100 − 35 = 65,

100 − 65 = 35.

times table: arranging the multiplication facts for a particular number in order. So for multiples of five, the five times table is:

$0 \times 5 = 0$

$1 \times 5 = 5$

$2 \times 5 = 10$

$3 \times 5 = 15$

$4 \times 5 = 20$

$5 \times 5 = 25$

$6 \times 5 = 30$

$7 \times 5 = 35$

$8 \times 5 = 40$

$9 \times 5 = 45$

$10 \times 5 = 50$

commutative: we can add or multiply two or more numbers in any order and the total will be the same. Both multiplication and addition are commutative.

$0 \times 5 = 0$
$1 \times 5 = 5$ (show the learners one jump of five)
$2 \times 5 = 10$ (show the learners two jumps of five)

Ask the learners to write the rest of the 5 times table, up to 10 times 5.

When the learners have finished, ask a few questions to check, for example, *"What is 7×5?"* Tell the learners that, just like addition, they can multiply in any order, so $7 \times 5 = 35$ and $5 \times 7 = 35$. Ask if they can remember the mathematical word for this, and if not remind them of 'commutative'. Circle a fact from the five times table, say $4 \times 5 = 20$. Find 20 on the number line and say, *"$4 \times 5 = 20$, there are four fives in 20, so 20 divided by five is four. That's two of the facts in the fact family, what are the other two facts?"* If necessary, remind the learners that they have done this before for facts in the ten times table.

Return to your fives number line and cross out the numbers with five ones on the number line and draw in jumps of 10. Ask the learners to write the 10 times table, up to 10×10.

Again, when the learners have finished, ask a few questions to check, for example, *"What is 10×7?"* If necessary, remind the learners that they can multiply in any order, so 10×7 is the same as 7×10.

Choose a multiplication fact such as $7 \times 10 = 70$ and tell the learners a matching story. For example, there are 10 biscuits in a packet, the shop has seven packets, so there are 70 biscuits altogether.

Ask the learners to choose a fact from the five or 10 times table and tell their partner a story about it. It might be useful to discuss some things that come in fives (fingers, toes, the number of sides on a pentagon, 5c coins and so on) and tens (10c coins, packs of different foods or pencils and so on) to give the learners some ideas.

End the session by returning to number pairs, but this time multiples of 100 with a total of 1000. Draw a 0 to 1000 number line marked in hundreds. Ask the learners to talk to their partner, taking it in turns to name a pair of multiples of 100 to make 1000 and saying the fact family. If there is time, ask the learners to use the same number line to help them write the 100 times table.

Look out for!

- Learners have counted in fives and tens many times.
- Learners who find it hard to realise that counting in fives and tens is the same as the times table, although they will be familiar with this counting sequence. *Lay out counters in rows of five and count them, 5, 10, 15, 20, 25. Then ask the learner to count again slowly as you say "1 times 5" – the learner says 5, "2 times 5" – the learner says 10, "3 times 5" – the learner says 15 and so on. Tell the learner that you were both saying the same thing. Repeat until the learner can say what you say and then tell the learner they have said the five times table, explaining that it is just counting in fives.*
- Learners who find the five and 10 times tables straightforward. *Give them challenging calculations like: 17×5, 23×5, and multiplying three-digit numbers by 10.*

Summary

Learners can write the five and 10 times tables and the related division facts. They can also write the fact families for multiples of five with a total of 100 and multiples of 100 with a total of 1000.

Notes on the Learner's Book

Multiples of 5 and 10 (p61): learners write out the 5 and 10 times table. They write fact families, draw and interpret arrays, draw number lines and solve calculations for both tables. They also write their own story for some calculations. Give some learners higher multiples of 5 and 10 to calculate and write a story for.

Check up!

- Say a fact in the five or 10 times table without saying the answer, ask the learner to finish that fact for you and to say the next fact in the table.
- Some learners will also be able to tell you the four facts in the fact family.

More activities

Multiples of 5, multiples of 10 (individual)

> You will need the the *Multiples of 5* photocopy master (CD-ROM) and the *Multiples of 10* photocopy master (CD-ROM), one per learner.

These two activities are for learners who need more practice in recognising multiples of five or 10.

Multiplication bingo (individual/class)

> Each learner will need a sheet of A4 paper and a pen/pencil.

Ask learners to fold a sheet of paper in half, then half again and a third time. When they open it up, they will have eight spaces. They choose numbers that are multiples of five up to 50 and 10 up to 100 and write one number in each space. Call out a multiplication fact. Learners work out the total and cross it out if they have it. The winner is the first person to cross out all their numbers.

Games Book (ISBN 9781107694019)

Making tens (p18) is a game for two to six players. Learners use any or all of the four operations to make a multiple of 10.

Resources: One *True/False* card from *core activity 15.2* per learner, paper, pens/pencils. (Optional: A4 paper, one sheet per learner, pens/pencils.)

Write $0 \times 10 = 0$ where everyone can see it and ask learners to say the rest of the ten times table up to 10×10. Ask the learners several questions about the ten times table, including the fact family for particular times tables facts. Repeat for the five times table, then the two times table.

Ask the learners to write out the two times table

$0 \times 2 = 0$	$0 \times 4 = 0$	
$1 \times 2 = 2$	$1 \times 4 = 4$	$4 \div 4 = 1$
$2 \times 2 = 4$	$2 \times 4 = 8$	$8 \div 4 = 2$
$3 \times 2 = 6$	....	....
$4 \times 2 = 8$		
$5 \times 2 = 10$		
$6 \times 2 = 12$		
$7 \times 2 = 14$		
$8 \times 2 = 16$		
$9 \times 2 = 18$		
$10 \times 2 = 20$		

When they have completed the table, remind them that double two is four, so an easy way to work out the four times table is to double the two times table.

Talk through the first few lines of the table and ask the learners to use their own two times table to write the four times table. When they have done so, tell them that you are going to say some statements about the numbers in the two and four times table and you would like them to use their *True/False* cards to tell you if they agree or not. Explain that you will ask some learners to explain why they have chosen their answer. Include statements such as:
- Answers to the four times table are double those in the two times table.
- Answers in the four times table can be divided by two with none left over.
- Answers to the two times table are always odd.
- Answers to the two times table are double those in the four times table.
- Answers to the four times table are always even.
- Answers in the four times table can be divided by three with none left over.

Look out for!

- Learners who may be confused over which numbers to double and why. *Ask them to write out the two times table, then highlight all the × 2. Explain that double two is four, so when we double a two, we will get four. Ask the learners to write out the 4 × table without the answers. Then highlight the answers in the two times table and explain that because we doubled the twos to get fours, we can now double each answer in the two times table to get the answers in the four times table. Work through the first few with the learners, linking the times tables. So you might say, "3 × 2 = 6, so 3 × 4 is double that, because double 2 is 4. Double 6 is 12, 3 × 4 = 12. We can check this by adding three fours, 4 + 4 + 4 = 12."*

- Learners who find the two and four times tables straightforward. *Challenge them to work out facts like 13 × 4, 23 × 2. They could also predict, and then find out, what happens when they double the four times table.*

Tell the learners that they are very good at multiplication but are they as good at dividing? Ask them to look at their two and four times tables and remind them that just as addition and subtraction undo each other, so do multiplication and division. Read the two times table from right to left, starting with 1 × 2 = 2 but saying 2 divided by 2 is 1, pointing along the table fact as you do it. Ask the learners to join in with you when they are ready.
Start to do the same with the four times table, writing the division fact alongside the multiplication fact and ask the learners to write the division fact next to each of their 4× times table facts.

Remind the learners that when they added two numbers together, they could check by adding in a different order, and when they subtracted, they could check by adding one of the numbers to the answer. Ask the learners to talk to their partner about how they could check a multiplication and how they could check a division. After giving the learners a few moments to discuss, share their ideas. Check that the learners understand that just like adding, they can multiply in any order, and just like subtracting, they can check a division using a multiplication. Talk through a few examples of this, for example they could check $12 \div 3 = 4$ by multiplying 3×4.

Summary

Learners can find the four times table facts by doubling the two times table facts. They are beginning to find the matching division facts. Learners can give examples which satisfy or disprove a general statement.

Notes on the Learner's Book
More multiples (p63) learners explore the 2 and 4 times tables, looking for patterns. They solve word problems and write a story to go with a calculation. Give some learners higher multiples of 2 and 4 to calculate and write a story for.

Check up!
- Say a fact in the two or four times table without saying the answer.
- Ask the learner to finish that fact for you and to say the next fact in the table.
- Some learners will also be able to tell you the four facts in the fact family.

More activities

2, 4 bingo (individual/class)

> Each learner will need a sheet of A4 paper and a pen/pencil.

Ask learners to fold a piece of paper in half, then half again and a third time. When they open it up, they will have eight spaces. They choose numbers that are multiples of two up to 20 and 4 up to 40 and write one number in each space. Call out a multiplication fact. Learners work out the total and cross it out if they have it. The winner is the first person to cross out all their numbers.

Resources: *3, 6, 9!* photocopy master (p129), one copy per learner). Coloured pencils. Pots of counters (per pair). (Optional: counters or cubes, paper, pens/pencils; A4 paper, one sheet per learner.)

Write $0 \times 2 = 0$ where everyone can see it and ask learners to say the rest of the two times table up to 10×2. Ask the learners several questions about the two times table, including the fact family for particular times tables facts. Remind the learners that they found the four times table by doubling the two times table, because when we double something we get two lots of it and two lots of two is four. Explain that you are going to ask them some four times table questions and they will find it helpful to double two times to find the answer. So if you asked them to tell you what 6×4 is, they could do 6×2 and double it. Ask questions such as, *"What is 3×4? How do you know? What is 5×4? How do you know? What is 8×4? How do you know?"*

Tell the learners that they are doing so well with their times tables that today you are going to look at the three, six and nine times tables. Give each learner a copy of the *3, 6, 9!* sheet. Talk through the number line on the sheet, counting to 30 in threes. Then explain that the learners can draw jumps from one number to another along the line to help them write the three times table.

Give the learners sufficient time to write the three times table, then draw them back together again.

Ask them to take a coloured pencil and draw a ring around every other number, starting with six, then 12 and so on up to 60. Ask the learners what they can tell you about the ringed numbers. Ensure that they realise they have highlighted every other three, and two lots of three are six so these are the numbers in the six times table. Ask learners to use the same coloured pencil to draw in the matching jumps of six. Now ask the learners to take a different coloured pencil and ring every third number, starting with nine, 18 and so on up to 90. Ask the learners what they can tell you about these ringed numbers. Ensure that they realise they have highlighted every third three, and three lots of three are nine so these are the numbers in the nine times table. Ask learners to use the same coloured pencil to draw in the matching jumps of nine.

Give the learners sufficient time to draw in the jumps on the number line for the six and nine times table and to write all three tables.

Vocabulary

remainder: what is left over when dividing by a particular number.

$15 \div 4 = 3$ r 3. You can make three groups of four but do not have enough to make another group of four, so the three is left over. We call this the remainder.

Look out for!

- Learners who may be getting confused when seeing patterns of number in the times tables. *Having doubled the two times table to get the four times table, learners may link changing the three times table to get the six times table to doubling. While this is fine, they may want to double again, believing this will give them the nine times table. Explain that they are right, double three is six so we can double the three times table to get the six times table, but double six is 12, so if we double the six times table we will get the 12 times table, not the nine times table.*

- Learners who are confident in finding patterns of numbers. *They may want to continue the process: highlighting every fourth multiple of three to get the 12 times table or even every fifth multiple to get the 15 times table. These are useful patterns for learners to explore but there is no need for them to try and memorise them.*

When the learners have completed all three tables, give each pair of learners a pot of counters. Ask the learners to take 12 counters and lay them out in a 3 by 4 grid. Ask four different learners to write one of the facts from the fact family for the array, $4 \times 3 = 12$, $3 \times 4 = 12$, $12 \div 3 = 4$ and $12 \div 4 = 3$. Ask the learners to move the counters into a 2 by 6 grid and invite four more learners to write one of the facts from the matching fact family, $2 \times 6 = 12$, $6 \times 2 = 12$, $12 \div 2 = 6$ and $12 \div 6 = 2$. Tell the learners that they have seen all these numbers in the times tables that they looked at recently, but they haven't seen 13. Ask them to take another counter so that they have 13. When they had 12, they divided by two, three, four and six and each number went into 12 exactly, with none left over, but what about 13? Can they divide 13 by two? Make sure the learners realise that they can make six groups of two but there is one left over. Show the learners how to write $13 \div 2 = 6$ r1, six groups of two and a remainder of one. Ask the learners to use the counters to help them to do $13 \div 3$, 4 and 6. They should then get four more counters and divide 17 by two, three, four, five, six and nine, writing the matching number sentence each time.

Share the results, making sure the learners have realised that 17 cannot be divided exactly by two, three, four, five, six or nine, there is always a remainder. Explain that there will often be some left over, a remainder, when we divide.

Summary

Learners can find the six and nine times table from the three times table. They recognise that division can leave some left over and that we call this the **remainder**.

Notes on the Learner's Book

Even more multiples (p64): learners explore the 6 and 9 times table, looking for patterns. They solve word problems and write a story to go with a calculation.

Check up!
- Say a number fact from the three, six or nine times table without saying the total.
- Ask the learner to finish that fact for you and to say the next fact in the table.
- Some learners will also be able to tell you the four facts in the fact family.
- Ask learners if a particular number can be divided exactly by 2, 3, 4, 5, 6, 9 or 10 and how they know.

More activities

Explore division (pairs)

You will need some counters or cubes, paper and pens/pencils.

Give each pair of learners a number to investigate. Using cubes or counters to help them, can their number be divided by two, three, four, five, six and nine? Ask them to record what happened each time, as they did with 13 ($13 \div 2 = 6$ r1) and 17.

3, 6, 9 bingo (individual/class)

> Each learner will need a sheet of A4 paper and a pen/pencil.

Ask learners to fold a piece of A4 paper in half, then half again and a third time. When they open it up, they will have eight spaces. They choose numbers that are multiples of three up to 30, multiples of six up to 60 and multiples of nine up to 90 and write one number in each space. Call out a multiplication fact. Learners work out the total and cross it out if they have it. The winner is the first person to cross out all their numbers.

Clap times (class)

Divide the class into three groups. One group is the threes, one group is the sixes and one group is the nines. Count in ones from one. Each learner claps on the multiples from their table. Ask the learners what they notice.

Games Book (ISBN 9781107694019)

Multiple mayhem (p18) is a game for two or three players. Multiplying single digit numbers by 2, 3, 4, 5, 9 and 10.

3, 6, 9!

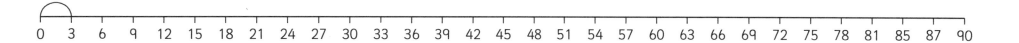

0 3 6 9 12 15 18 21 24 27 30 33 36 39 42 45 48 51 54 57 60 63 66 69 72 75 78 81 85 87 90

Blank page

Quick reference

Core activity 17.1: Digital clocks (Learner's Book p66)

This activity gives students the opportunity to construct digital numbers and arrange them on a digital clock face. It also involves changing time on a digital to an analogue clock.

Core activity 17.2: Time intervals (Learner's Book p67)

Learners are asked here to solve a problem involving the calculation of time intervals in hours and minutes using a simple timetable.

Core activity 17.3: The calendar (Learner's Book p68)

This activity uses what students already know about months on a calendar in order to solve number problems and puzzles.

Prior learning	Objectives* – please note that listed objectives might only be partially covered within any given chapter but are covered fully across the book when taken as a whole
• Being able to read an analogue and digital clock. • Know the names of the different units of time: second, minutes, hour, day, week, month, year and the differences between them. • Know the construction and purpose of a calendar.	**2B: Measures** 3Mt1 – Suggest and use suitable units to measure time and know the relationships between them. 3Mt2 – Read the time on analogue and digital clocks to the nearest five minutes on an analogue clock and to the nearest minute on a digital clock. 3Mt3 – Begin to calculate simple time intervals in hours and minutes. 3Mt4 – Read a calendar and calculate time intervals in weeks or days. **2B: Problem solving** 3Pt2 – Begin to understand everyday systems of measurement in length, weight, capacity, time and use these to make measurements as appropriate.

*for NRICH activities mapped to the Cambridge Primary objectives, please visit www.cie.org.uk/cambridgeprimarymaths

Vocabulary

time • intervals • minutes • analogue clock • digital clock

Resources: *Digital display* photocopy master (CD-ROM), one copy per learner and an enlarged copy. Colouring pencils. Art straws or lolly sticks. Glue. Blank paper. *Blank clocks* photocopy master (CD-ROM), one or two copies per learner). Mirrors. (Optional: digital and analogue clocks for demonstration.)

Explain that this session will be examining digital clocks and times, and linking them to analogue time. (Learners need constant reminders of reading analogue and digital clocks.)

Give each student an empty *Digital display* and tell them that when we look at a digital number we can see that it is made up of different light bars: we can make any number we want to by lighting the bars. Demonstrate what you mean on an enlarged copy of *Digital display*. For example, to make 6, colour two light bars down on the left, one across the bottom, one up the right side and one across the middle. Explain that to make numbers higher than 9 we put two or three or more digits together.

Say, "*Choose a number between 0 and 9 and colour the light bars to make that number.*" Give some time for students to complete the task.

Now explain that you are going to play a game called 'What's my rule'. Say, "*I have a rule in my head and if your number fits my rule you can come through my gate. If it doesn't you have to sit down. Everyone stand up and show me your number.*" Choose students to come and stand next to you if they have numbers 4, 5, or 6. The rule is that the number of light bars showing is the same as the number itself. Ask, "*Who can tell me my rule? Talk to your friend.*" Give short time for discussion and take feedback.

Now draw or display the ten digits of a digital clock – this is a digital number line:

0 1 2 3 4 5 6 7 8 9

Look out for!

- Learners who are having difficulties. *They may need the support of a digital number line on their table.*
- Learners who are already familiar with digital and analogue times. *Challenge them to explore the digits showing on an digital clock by setting challenges:*
  - "*I have a 12 hour digital clock which shows the time, using four digits, on a piece of glass, so it can be seen from both sides. At what time between 4 o'clock and 11 o'clock does the time look the same from both sides?*"
  - "*Look at the symmetry of digit times. Place a mirror where the dots are and students will see symmetry. How many times within 12 hours do the digits show symmetry?*"

Opportunities for display!

- Digital number line (a number line with the digits written as on a digital clock).
- The digital numbers made with art straws or lolly sticks.

Ask the learners to work with a partner to make all of these numbers, using art straws or lolly sticks (some of the times made can be glued onto paper for display later). Give each learner a copy of *Blank clocks* and have some spares available. Tell them to, *"Make as many different times as you can where the digits total 10. Record each of the times on a digital clock and on an analogue clock. How many different times can you make?"*

Share some of the times made and show the analogue recording the students have done. Play the gatekeeper game again, choosing a student to think of the rule.

Summary

By the end of this activity students will have had experience of digital numbers and the connection between analogue and digital times.

Notes on the Learner's Book
Time 2 (p66): investigates the light bars on a digital clock and how digital and analogue clocks show the same time.

Check up!
- Show four digital numbers to the class in a row and ask students to show you the times on an analogue clock.
- Show the time on an analogue clock and ask students to show it using digital numbers.

More activities

Special times 1 (individual)

> You will need paper and pens/pencils.

On a digital 24 hour clock, at certain times, all the digits are consecutive. How many times like this are there between midnight and 7 am? Choose other times from midnight. Is the answer still the same? Find all of the times within the 24 hours?

Special times 2 (class)

> You will need digital and analogue clocks for demonstration.

Compare digital and analogue clocks. On a digital clock showing 24 hour time over a whole day, how many times does a five (substitute a different number to continue the investigation) appear? Is it the same amount for an analogue clock over 24 hours? Is there a quick way to work this out?

Light bars (individual)

> You will need the *Digital display* photocopy master (CD-ROM), one copy per learner, and colouring pencils.

What times on a digital clock could be made using up to 30 light bars? Investigate other totals of light bars. What time uses the least number and what time uses the most? Could you make a time that uses exactly 30 light bars?

Resources: *Bus schedule* photocopy master (p139), one sheet per pair or small group. Pens/pencils. (Optional: two analogue demonstration clocks; *Matching time* photocopy master (CD-ROM), one copy per learner, scissors; a digital or analogue clock (if not available, you can make your own analogue clock using the Analogue clock photocopy master on the CD-ROM).)

Explain that this session is about time, but that you need their help to solve a crime (fictional). *"I have heard about a theft of a diamond ring. It happened at a theatre while the play was being acted on the stage. The ring was in a dressing room at 3 o'clock in the afternoon, but when the actress got back to her room at 4 o'clock, it had gone."* Write the times on the board as a reference for later.

"The police have three suspects, people who may have taken the ring. They were all in a town a bus journey from the theatre."

"Number 1 says he had a meeting at 2:15 pm and was there for at least an hour." (Write the information on the board.)

"Number 2 says she was at a restaurant until 3:30 pm" (Write the information on the board.)

"Number 3 says he went to the dentist at about 1:00 pm and was there for two hours." (Write the information on the board.)

"What the suspects have said is true. But only one of them could have made it to the theatre in time to steal the ring."

"Use this bus schedule to find who the thief was."

Explain the timings on the timetable and give each pair a copy.

Remind the learners to keep a record of what they are doing and what they find out to share at the end of the session.

As the class is working, walk round and answer any queries or deal with misconceptions.

When learners think they know the answers, ask, *"Who do you think stole the diamond ring? Tell us why. What proof do you have?"*

Look out for!

- Learners who find this activity challenging. *They may benefit from working in a small group rather than a pair. They will see and hear others using the strategies needed to solve the mystery.*
- Learners who finish the task early. *Ask them to write their own story where they will need to produce a timetable in order to solve a problem. It can be a mystery, a journey or a real life experience.*

Summary

By the end of this session learners will have begun to calculate simple time intervals to solve a problem and recorded their thinking and working.

Notes on the Learner's Book

Timetables (p67): this page develops the idea of using timetables and looking at the importance of time.

More activities

Using a television schedule (class)

> You will need two analogue clocks for demonstration.

Ask students about their favourite TV shows. Make a table to record the show, the start time and the end time. Use a 4th column to state how long the show lasts. (Elapsed time). Use two clocks, one set at the start time and the other at the end time. Model how to count hours or minutes (in 5's or 1's) by moving the hour hand round the clock until it matches the end time.

Matching time (individual)

> You will need the *Matching time* photocopy master (CD-ROM), one copy per learner, scissors.

The learners cut the times and statements and match them.

Number line (class)

> You will need a digital or analogue clock for demonstration.

Draw a number line marked with regular times (e.g. every quarter of an hour) instead of numbers to show how elapsed time can be shown. Use alongside a digital or analogue clock. Ask questions such as, *"How many $\frac{1}{4}$ hours is it from 2 o'clock to 3 o'clock? How many quarter hours from 5 o'clock to half past 5?"*

Games Book (ISBN 9781107694019)

How long will it take? (p48) is a game for two to four players. Players begin to calculate simple time intervals in hours and minutes.

Resources: Calendar; a calendar sheet (page copied from a calendar) per learner. *Calendar puzzles* photocopy master (p140), one puzzle per learner. *Calendar puzzles answers* photocopy master (CD-ROM) one copy. Calculator. *Time rhymes* photocopy master (CD-ROM), one copy per pair. (Optional: the *Time problems* photocopy master (CD-ROM), one copy per group, a bag, a calendar sheet and some counters per group; paper and pen/pencil per learner.)

Explain to the class that this session is all about using the dates and months on a calendar and involves solving problems. Show a page from a calendar to the class. Ask, *"What can you tell me about this page?"* (the month, the number of days, how many weeks) *"Are all the months the same?"*

Show a different month and ask, *"What month is this? How many days does it have? How many Mondays? What is the first day of the month and what is the last day?"*

Point out how the days are arranged on the page. *"Some of them have seven days in a row, but others have fewer. Why is this?"*

Now explain that you are going to use the numbers on the page to solve some puzzles. Show the class the *Calendar puzzles. "Each of these is a separate puzzle and you will choose just one to work on. You will need your calendar sheets."*

Choose one of the puzzles, read it to the class and work through it in small steps, making sure that everyone understands. (You can check the answers using the *Calendar puzzles answers*.)

Divide learners into pairs and ask them to choose a puzzle to work on. *"Talk to each other about ways to solve the puzzle. Keep a record of what you are doing so that you can share it with the rest of the class at the end of the session."*

As the class is working, walk round giving support to those who need it. If some students have completed a puzzle, suggest that they chose another one.

At the end of the session ask, *"What have you found out? Why do you think that happened?"* Choose different students to tell the class which puzzle they chose, what they found out and why they think that happened.

Look out for!

- Learners who find the calculations difficult. *Encourage them to use a calculator so they can see the patterns that emerge without incorrect calculations stopping it happening.*
- Learners who have completed the task easily. *Challenge them to find other patterns from a month on a calendar sheet. They could investigate dates in rectangles rather than squares, for example, 3 × 2 (or 2 × 3), 3 × 4 (or 4 × 3) and 4 × 2 (or 2 × 4) rectangles.*

Summary

By the end of this activity learners will have consolidated their knowledge and understanding of the format and content of a calendar and used it to solve number puzzles.

Notes on the Learner's Book

Days and weeks (p68): this page looks at problems using a page from a calendar. Learners are asked to work forwards and backwards to find days and dates. Discuss possible strategies for answering the initial problem with learners. If necessary, suggest that they draw a table, on lined paper, with seven columns headed Monday to Sunday to help them.

Check up!

- Ask questions such as, "*How many months are there in a year? How many days in a week? How many weeks in a year?*"
- If the 1st of May is on Monday, which day will be the 31st?
- Chant time rhymes such as, "*30 days has September*"… and "*Monday's learner is*" and "*Solomon Grundy*".

More activities

About today's date (individual)

Visit www.richardphillips.org.uk/number/index.htm. This website contains facts about every day of the month from a maths perspective.

Time problems (groups)

> You will need the *Time problems* photocopy master (CD-ROM), one copy per group, a bag, a calendar sheet, some counters and scissors per group.

Cut out the individual *Time problems* cards and put in the bag. When you say, "*Go!*" each team takes all the problems from the bag. As the learners solve the problems, they place a counter on the matching numbered calendar square. When the entire page is covered, the team stand up. Clear the calendar sheets, mix up the problems and play again.

Time problems, pass and pick (group)

> You will need the *Time problems* photocopy master (CD-ROM), one copy per group, a bag, a calendar sheet, some counters and scissors per group; paper and pen/pencil per learner.

Cut out the individual *Time problems* cards and put in the bag. Students pass the bag clockwise around the group. The first student takes a problem from the bag, calculates the answer and finds that day on the calendar, covering it with a counter. They each keep note of the number they have covered as they play. As the game continues each student keeps a running total of their score. When the last problem is taken, play stops and the winner is the player with the highest total.

The empty maths calendar (class)

Draw a blank calendar grid and mark two dates on it. Circle another day on the grid and ask the students to work out what the date of the circled square is. Students explain how they worked out the answer.

Games Book (ISBN 9781107694019)

Calendar game (p51) is a game for two to four players. Write number sentences using all four operations; read a calendar and calculate time intervals in weeks or days.

Bus schedule

Left town	Arrived at theatre
1:10 pm	1:40 pm
2:00 pm	2:40 pm
2:30 pm	3:10 pm
3:10 pm	3:50 pm
3:40 pm	4:10 pm
4:00 pm	4:30 pm

Blank page

Quick reference

Core activity 18.1: Estimating (Learner's Book p70)
This activity starts with whole class activities and discussion and moves on to group work to estimate and then measure in length, weight and capacity.

Core activity 18.2: Measuring (Learner's Book p72)
This activity looks at the use of measures in a real-life context and requires learners to make a drawing of an elephant enclosure, measuring accurately to the nearest cm.

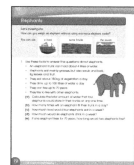

Prior learning	Objectives* – please note that listed objectives might only be partially covered within any given chapter but are covered fully across the book when taken as a whole
• Understanding of the vocabulary for measures. • Knowledge of reading scales including rulers and tape measures. • Knowledge of the relationship between measures. • Know how to use a ruler.	**2B: Measures** 3Ml1 – Choose and use appropriate units and equipment to estimate, measure and record measurements. 3Ml2 – Know the relationship between kilometres and metres, metres and centimetres, kilograms and grams, litres and millilitres. 3Ml3 – Read to the nearest division or half division, use scales that are numbered or partially numbered. 3Ml4 – Use a ruler to draw and measure lines to the nearest centimetre. 3Ml5 – Solve word problems involving measures. **2B: Problem solving** 3Pt2 – Begin to understand everyday systems of measurement in length, weight, capacity, time and use these to make measurements as appropriate. 3Pt10 – Estimate and approximate when calculating and check their working.

*for NRICH activities mapped to the Cambridge Primary objectives, please visit www.cie.org.uk/cambridgeprimarymaths

Vocabulary

approximately • compare • measuring scale • scale division • guess • estimate • about the same as • length • width • height • long • short • tall • high • low wide • narrow • longer • shorter • taller • higher • longest • shortest • tallest • highest • distance apart/between • distance to… from… • kilometre (*km*) • metre (*m*) • centimetre (*cm*) • ruler • weigh • weighs • heavy/light • heavier/lighter • heaviest/lightest • kilogram (*kg*) • half-kilogram • gram (*g*)

Resources: The room needs to be set up so that there are three work stations: one each for length, weight and capacity, with the following equipment:
Length: a selection of rulers and tape measures, copies of *How long are the lines?* photocopy master (CD-ROM).
Weight: a range of different weighing scales (including electronic scales), four bags with different weight of contents, small items such as peas, grains of rice, copies of *How heavy are the bags?* photocopy master (CD-ROM), small items such as peas, grains of rice.
Capacity: a source of liquid or dry rice/pulses; a range of different measuring jugs for pouring the contents into and four different size cups/mugs, copies of *How full are the cups?* photocopy master (CD-ROM).
What do you think? photocopy master (CD-ROM) a source of liquid or paper and pencils. (Optional: tape measure, pen/pencil, paper per pair; the *Loop cards* photocopy master (CD-ROM), one copy per group, scissors; the *Measurement problems* photocopy master (CD-ROM), one copy per learner; a matchbox and a collection of small items which will fit inside it (such as a paper clip, a button, a hair) per learner.)

Note: This activity may take more than one session.

Start the session by asking quick questions about measures, such as:

"How many centimetre in a kilometre?"
"How many grams in a kilogram?"
"How many centimetres in 2 metres?"
"How many metres in $3\frac{1}{2}$ kilometres?
"If I had 500 millilitres, what would be the equivalent in litres?"
"Tell me two different ways of saying double 250 grams."
"I have 350 kilograms. How many grams do I have?"

Tell the class that this session is all about estimating. Ask, *"Who can tell us what estimating means?"* Ask for some responses from the class. Establish that **estimation** is a guess of the actual value. *"I could estimate that we have 102 students in our class today. Would that be a close estimate?"* (**No**). *"So I could estimate again and this time say there are 68 students in our class today. Is that estimate closer?"* (**Yes**) *"An estimate does not have to be the right answer, but with practice you will get closer."*

Vocabulary
scale division: a scale division is the graduation of measure.
approximately: almost exact or correct.

Draw a line on the board and ask, "*How long do you think it is? What would be your estimation of the length of the line?*" Ask students to discuss with their partner and take feedback. Note all of the different estimations. Then ask, "*How could we find out how close our estimations are?*" (**Use a ruler/tape measure**). Ask two students to measure the line and write how long it is. "*Were our estimations close?*"

Now choose six students to come to the board and each draw a line they think is 25 cm long. Measure the lines and note the lengths. "*How close were they?*"

Divide the learners into pairs and ask them each to draw a line. They should then estimate the length of the line their partner drew and write their estimate next to the line. They then measure the line with a ruler, and see how close their estimate was.

Explain the main task to the class. Give each learner a copy of *What do you think*? and talk it through to make sure that everyone understands.

Remind them that an estimate is not about getting the right answer, although that may happen. It's about making a good guess.

Divide the class into three groups and give each their start table (length, weigh or capacity). Explain that they will have about 10 minutes at each task before they have to move to the next one. Remind them to leave the table ready for the next group before they move on.

As the class is working, walk round to check that they all understand.

At the end of the session, ask learners to discuss with a partner what they found out. Ask, "*Were your estimates close or were you surprised by some of the results? Which was the easiest to estimate? Which was the hardest? Why do you think that was?*"

Look out for!

- Learners who need practice in using and understanding the language of measures. *Put up posters or charts as a visual reminder. For example, 'capacity is the amount a container can hold'. (This does not mean that it has to be liquid.) Watch out for words that have inaccurate associations:*
  Bigger = larger, taller, longer
  Smaller = lighter
- Learners who are finding the activity easy. *Challenge them to find weights of a pea, a sheet of paper or a grain of rice. Ask how they would set about weighing such light objects. For example: to find the weight of a pea, weigh 10 peas and divide by 10. Use a calculator to help. Electronic scales can be used.*

Summary

By the end of this session learners will have had opportunities to estimate and then measure length, weight and capacity by reading scales for each.

Notes on the Learner's Book

Using units (p70): learners are asked to solve a problem involving weight and then to use their own knowledge and understanding of conversion of units.

Check up!

Ask questions such as:
- "*How heavy do you think this ball is?*"
- "*How long do you think this string is?*"
- "*Which do you think holds the most, this tall thin bottle or the short fat bottle?*"

More activities

Be a tailor (pairs)

> You will need tape measures, pen/pencil and paper per pair.

Develop the learners' estimation and practical measuring skills by asking them to estimate and then measure the length of each other's arms and legs.

Loop cards (group)

> You will need the *Loop cards* photocopy master (CD-ROM), one copy per group, and scissors.

Cut the cards along the thicker lines and give each learner a card (it is important that all the cards are handed out). The learner with the START card begins and reads out the question on the card. The other learners check their cards and if they have the answer they say what it is. If their answer is correct, they then read the question on the same card. This continues in a loop until you reach the person with the END CARD. You could also ask students to make their own set of cards using a blank set.

Measurement problems (individual)

> You will need the *Measurement problems* photocopy master (CD-ROM) one copy per learner.

Learners use their knowledge of the relationships between measures to solve the problems on the sheet. Challenge them to make up their own problem and write it in the blank space.

Fill a matchbox (individual)

> You will need a matchbox and a collection of small items which will fit inside it (such as a paper clip, a button, a hair).

Try to put as many things as possible in a matchbox to find its capacity. How many items will fit?

Games Book (ISBN 9781107694019)

Matching measures (p51) is a game for two to four players. Players choose appropriate units for measuring length, weight and capacity.

Resources: *Elephant enclosure* photocopy master (p148), one copy per pair. A3 paper. Rulers. Cm squared paper. Cm square cubes. (Optional: a collection of Lego® or other interlocking cubes; access to reference books, pens/pencils and paper; tape measure and chalk for each group.)

Say to the class, "*If I hadn't been a teacher I would have liked to have been a zoo keeper. As a zoo keeper, I would use maths every day. What do you think I would be doing that includes maths?*" Allow time for discussion in pairs. Take feedback. Make sure that the answers include the following:

- Preparing the food for the animals (for example: grouping, weighing, quantity).
- Designing new enclosures for the animals (for example: length, height, volume capacity).
- Checking the growth of the animals to make sure they are healthy (for example: weight, height, length).
- Measuring the weight of the animals if they are ill.

Ask, "*Where do you go when you feel ill? What do we call the person who would come to help the animals? Sometimes animals need medicine or an operation to make them better. Why would I need to get the weight of the animal right? When the vet comes to give an anaesthetic he works out how much to give by the weight of the animal. He would need to get the correct dose – we wouldn't want our lions waking up in the middle of an operation.*"

Now ask, "*Have you ever been to a zoo? I like the elephants best. Did you know that the elephant doesn't use its trunk to drink through? Does anyone know what the trunk is used for?*" (**The elephant uses the trunk to suck water and then sprays it into the mouth or over its body.**) "*A trunk can hold around four litres of water.*" "*What does an elephant like to eat?*" The learners talk to their partners. Give time for discussion and get feedback. Establish that elephants eat mainly grasses, but also scrub and bark, fig leaves and fruit. They eat about 150kg of vegetation and drink up to 100 litres of water a day.

Explain to the class that they are going to pretend to be zoo keepers and design an elephant enclosure with a partner. Give each pair a copy of the *Elephant enclosure* sheet and some A3 paper. Say, "*Read the information and use it to design a new elephant enclosure for the zoo. Use the scale of 1 cm = 1 metre. So every time you measure 1 cm it stands for 1 metre.*"
As the class is working, walk round and make sure that the learners understand the task. Some may be having difficulty with scale and in measuring accurately. Remind students of the things they need to remember to make a suitable enclosure for elephants.

At the end of the session, invite students to show their plan and to talk about what they did and why they did it.

Look out for!

- Learners who find the idea of scale difficult. *Allow them to work on centimetre squared paper where one square represents one metre. They can use cm square cubes to get a visual 3D image of their drawing.*
- Learners who finish quickly or find the activity easy. *Challenge them to find the cost of railings and other materials. For example:*
  - "*Each rail of 10 metres costs $150. How much will it cost to go round the enclosure (perimeter)?*"
  - "*When building the shelter you will need to think about the cost. If each panel of wood costs $400 how much will your shelter cost? Show how you worked it out.*"

Opportunities for display!

The scale drawings of the elephant enclosure.

Summary

By the end of this activity, students will have used a ruler to draw and measure lines to the nearest centimetre.

Notes on the Learner's Book

Elephants (p72): the Learner's Book page gives facts about an elephant which the learners use to answer questions.

Check up!

- If I drew a line 5 cm long and each cm represented 1 metre, how long would the actual line be?
- If I had a piece of wood $10\frac{1}{2}$ metres long how long would the wood be on a plan drawn to the scale of 1cm:1 metre?

More activities

Build a zoo (individual or group)

> You will need a collection of Lego® or other interlocking cubes to construct a 3D zoo.

Elephant facts (individual)

> You will need access to reference books, pens/pencils and paper.

Investigate other facts about elephants. Draw a time line of an elephant's life.

Life size elephant (group)

> You will need a tape measure and chalk for each group.

Draw a full size elephant on the playground using accurate measurements.

Elephant enclosure

Design an elephant enclosure for toy elephants.

Make it the same as the one pictured below for real elephants.

Use the scale 1 cm: 1 metre

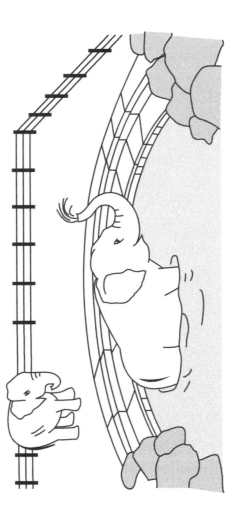

The enclosure is 900 cm long and 800 cm wide.

How many metres wide is that? How long will you draw your line?

How many metres long is that? How long will you draw your line?

Think about what you need to put inside the enclosure.

The elephants need:

• A pool of water large enough for up to five elephants to completely submerge.

• A separate source of water for drinking.

• Shade.

• Rocks, boulders and tree trunks for scratching on.

• Room for the elephants to exercise.

• An indoor space.

Quick reference

Core activity 19.1: Calculating with money (Learner's Book p74)

This activity works with giving change from $1. It uses different combinations of coins to add and then subtract from $1.

Core activity 19.2: More calculations with money (1) (Learner's Book p76)

This activity uses the theme of a café to give experience of using money in a real life context. Students are asked to budget and calculate total costs and change given.

Core activity 19.3: More calculations with money (2) (Learner's Book p78)

This activity uses what students know about money and liquid measures to solve problems about 'best buys'. It challenges students to use different amounts of liquid measures in as many different ways as possible to solve the final problem.

Prior learning	Objectives* – please note that listed objectives might only be partially covered within any given chapter but are covered fully across the book when taken as a whole
• Knowledge of numbers to 100. • Knowledge of $ and cents and the links between them. • Addition and subtraction with a total of 100. • Some knowledge of litres and millilitres and the connections between them. • Understanding of problem solving strategies.	**2B: Measures** 3Mm1 – Consolidate using money notation. 3Mm2 – Use addition and subtraction facts with a total of 100 to find change. 3Ml2 – Know the relationship between kilometres and metres, metres and centimetres, kilograms and grams, litres and millilitres. **2B: Problem solving** 3Pt1 – Choose appropriate mental strategies to carry out calculations. 3Pt11 – Make a sensible estimate of the answer to a calculation. 3Pt12 – Consider whether an answer is reasonable. 3Ps1 – Make up number story to go with a calculation, including in the context of money.

*for NRICH activities mapped to the Cambridge Primary objectives, please visit www.cie.org.uk/cambridgeprimarymaths

Vocabulary

money • coin • price • cost • buy • spent • pay • change • how much? • total • amount • more/most • expensive/cheap • costs less • cheaper • less/least expensive • spend • change price • capacity • full • half full • empty • holds • contains • litre (*l*) • half-litre • millilitre (*ml*) • container.

> **Resources:** *Gift shop price list* photocopy master (p156) and the *Calculating change* photocopy master (CD-ROM), one copy per learner. (Optional: some small items to 'sell', some money; a collection of till receipts; a supply of cakes and cookies etc., either made by the learners or bought.)

Tell the class that you are going to spend some money at the zoo gift shop. "*You will each have $1 and you can decide how much of that to spend. Each of you will have a chance to calculate the change needed from the $1.* Show the class the *Gift shop price list.* "*You can buy whatever you want as long as you spend less than $1.*"

Choose some students to tell the class what they would buy. Start with just one item then two and above. Ask, "*If you bought that how much would it cost? What if you could buy two items, how much would that total? Is that more or less than a dollar?*"

Then ask, "*If I spent 90 cents, how much change would I have?*" (**10 cents**) "*How did you work that out? If I spent 25 cents, how much change would I have?*" (**75 cents**) "*How did you work that out?*"

Remind the class that sometimes it is easier to count on to 100 to calculate change rather than subtracting the spent amount from 100. If necessary draw a 0 to 100 number line on the board and demonstrate. Learners can also use the addition and subtraction facts to 100 that they know.

Show the class the *Calculating change* sheet. "*You will need one of these each. You can spend up to 99 cents in the gift shop. Write what you bought and what you spent. Your partner needs to work out the change to give you. Take turns to each complete one row at a time.*"

As the class is working, walk round to clear any misconceptions and to make sure that all students understand the task.

At the end of the session, ask, "*How did you check that the change you were given was correct? Do you think you were given too much change, not enough or just right? Explain how you know. What was the least amount of change that you had? What was the most?*"

Look out for!

- Learners who find addition and subtraction to 100 difficult. *Give them a number line to 100 or a blank number line where they can record their own calculations.*
- Learners who are more familiar with working amounts within a dollar. *Challenge them with other problems, for example:*
  - "*Make as many different totals up to $1 using just six coins as you can. Keep a record of totals you can make and totals you can't make (e.g. can you make 5 cents with six coins? Can you make 86 cents using six coins?)*"

Summary

By the end of this activity students will have calculated costs to $1 and found change, using their knowledge and understanding of addition and subtraction to 100.

Notes on the Learner's Book

Money 2 (p74): this page begins with a money problem to solve and moves on to giving learners practice in calculating costs and finding change.

Check up!

Ask questions such as:
- *"I spend 45 cents. How much change do I have from $1?"*
- *"I buy an item for 30 cents and another for 45 cents. How much change do I get from $1?"*

More activities

Shop (group)

> You will need some small items to 'sell', some money.

Set up a role play shop where students can work with real money, in a real life situation, working on real problems.

Till receipts (individuals/groups)

> You will need a collection of till receipts.

Use till receipts to work out a daily or weekly shopping bill.

Baking (class)

> You will need a supply of cakes and cookies etc., either made by the learners or bought.

Set up a class shop and sell cakes, cookies etc. each day for a week. If students bake, they will be reinforcing measures in a practical, real-life context.

Resources: *Menus* photocopy master (p157), one copy (whole set) per group. Notes and coins (ideally real). (Optional: paper, pens/pencils.)

Tell the learners that today you are going to work with money, in the context of a zoo café. *"When I go on a visit I always want something to eat and drink. Zoos usually have a café or restaurant. There is a menu where you can choose what you would like."* Show them the *Menus*.

Tell the learners that they need to decide what to order: *"You can choose from any or all of the cards and as many items as you like, but you only have $10 to spend for the whole group. Talk to each other and see what you could buy. Keep a record of your order."* Give time for the groups to talk and discuss the menu items and their choices.

Ask the groups to tell the class what they ordered. Ask, *"Do you think that is the only way to spend $10? Is there a group who spent their money in a different way?"* As each group shows their spending, display the different ways of spending up to $10.

Repeat the activity, this time saying, *"Now I'm going to give you $20 dollars for the group, but I want $4 change. How much will that give you to spend? I don't need exactly $4 – I could have more, but I don't want less. As a group, investigate different ways to spend your money so that you have up to $4 change."*

Look out for!

- Learners who find it difficult to work with abstract ideas involving money. *Give them actual coins and notes (real would be best) so that they can relate the problem to real life.*
- Learners who find the activity easy. *Challenge them to find as many different combinations of food where there will be change of up to $4. Which order will give change closest to $4?*

Opportunities for display!

Set up a role-play area of a café and display the menus and prices.

Summary

By the end of this activity students will have worked on costing, finding totals and giving change.

Notes on the Learner's Book

At the zoo (p76): this page begins with a short problem to solve and moves on to addition and subtraction of money.

Check up!

Using the menu cards ask questions such as:

- *"What could I buy and still have change from $5?"*
- *"What would cost the most if I had one item from each menu?"*
- *"What is the cheapest/most expensive item in the café?"*
- *"I have three friends and we all want an ice cream. How much would it cost? How much change would there be from $6?"*

More activities

Virtual café (group)

Set up a virtual café for each group. Allow $100 to spend on ingredients. Set prices. Imagine what sells and what doesn't. How much profit can be made in a day? A week? Each group compare their results.

Ways to a dollar (individual)

> You will need paper and pens/pencils.

Investigate how many different ways $1 can be made. Would it be double the number of ways for $2? Set out the results in a table or chart.

Games Book (ISBN 9781107694019)

How much will you have to spend? (p58) is a game for two players. Players recognise the value of coins, exchange coins of equivalent values, and make change.

Resources: *Take away drinks menu* photocopy master (p158), one copy per learner. Pens/pencils and paper. Measuring equipment (cups, bowls, bottles, spoons). Coins and notes (ideally real). (Optional: one container holding 5 litres, another holding 8 litres (not showing any scale or other volume markings), access to water; a 150 ml and a 25 ml container.)

Tell the learners that the zoo café also has a *Take away drinks menu*. Show them the menu and say, "*The zoo café sells lots of drinks to take away. Some are in bottles, some are in cartons and some come from a machine. It also sells soup. You can have a small bowl or a large bowl.*"

Explain that all the drinks cost different amounts. The soup is charged according to whether it is a big bowl or a small bowl.

Ask, "*If I wanted 2 litres of bottle water, which would be the cheapest way to buy it? How much would 2 × 1 litre bottles cost?*" (**$2.40**) "*How many $\frac{1}{2}$ l bottles would I need to buy to make 2 litres?*" (**4**) "*How much would that cost?*" (**$3.20**) "*Which is the most expensive way to buy 2 litres of water?*" (**500 ml bottles**)

Now ask, "*How could we find out which is the cheapest and which is the most expensive way to buy 2 litres of juice. Work with the person next to you and find out.*" Leave time for discussion and feedback. Establish that the smaller cartons are more expensive in terms of how much they contain, and ask, "*Why do you think it is more expensive to buy lots of small bottles instead of one large one?*" Allow students to discuss reasons; include the cost of materials in the feedback if no-one mentions it.

Now discuss the soup with the class. "*I really like soup. I could buy a large bowl. How many small bowls would be the same as the large bowl?*" (**three**) "*Which would cost the least money?*" (**one large bowl**) "*I'm going to buy a large bowl but my friend only wants a small bowl. How much soup do we have altogether?*" (**1000 ml or 1 litre**) "*How do you know?*"

Look out for!

- Learners who find this activity difficult. *Encourage them to use practical equipment to show what each liquid measure looks like. Use cups, bowls, bottles, spoons. Use coins and notes to show money values.*
- Learners who can cover the activity quickly and competently. *Set them more problem solving strategies such as:*
  - *Plan a party for 20 guests. Each guest will drink a litre each except the five youngest who will only drink $\frac{1}{2}$ litre each. What would be the cheapest way of buying the drinks? Compare bottles, cartons and machine prices.*

Opportunities for display!

Use the ways of filling the soup container as part of a display on liquid measures.

Now tell the learners to work with a partner to solve the following problem. *"The owner has emptied the container for soup. The container holds 7.5 litres of soup. He only has a 1 litre jug, a 2 litre bottle and a 500ml mug. Find ways to fill the soup pan using all of the containers. Find as many different ways as you can."* As the class is working, walk round to answer any questions or clear misconceptions.

At the end of the session, ask, *"How many different ways have you found to fill the soup container?"* Collect responses and use the recording as a display.

Summary

- By the end of this activity students will have had experience of using their knowledge and understanding of money and liquid measures and the links between the two.
- They will also have used their problem solving skills throughout.

Notes on the Learner's Book
Liquid measures (p78): this page begins with a problem to solve and then, using learners' knowledge and understanding of liquid measure, asks questions which can be used for assessment.

Check up!
Ask questions such as:
"What are the different ways of making five and a half litres of drink using 2 litre, 1 litre and 500 ml containers?"

More activities

Measure problems (group)

Set problems for the learners to solve in pairs or small groups. Different questions can be set for different ability levels. For example:.

- Ask how you can get exactly 6 litres of water using only two containers, one holding 5 litres and the other holding 8 litres. (The containers do not have scales on them.)
- Answer: Fill the 8l container with water, pour 5l into the 5l container and throw it away. Pour the remaining 3l into the 5l container. Take another 8l of water, and fill up the rest of the 5l container, which is 2l. There should be only 6l left in the 8l container.
- I have a big bucket. I need to put 1 litre of water in it for my science enquiry but I only have a 150 ml and 25 ml containers. How can I get 1 litre of water using these containers?
- Answer: There are several different ways, including 6×150 ml $+ 4 \times 25$ ml
- Lucas and Roderigo are lost in the desert. They each have a 1 litre bottle of water. Lucas drinks half of his. How much does he have left?
Roderigo only drinks a mouthful every hour. If a mouthful is 50 ml how many hours does his water last?
- Answer: Lucas has $\frac{1}{2}$ litre/500 ml left. Roderigo's water lasts 20 hours.
Encourage students to make problems of their own to share with the rest of the class.

Gift shop price list

Item	Price	Picture
Pencil	25 cents each	
Eraser	20 cents each	
'King of the jungle' Badge	10 cents each	
Animal stickers	50 cents each	
Model panda	30 cents each	
Plastic spider	15 cents each	
Butterfly stickers	35 cents each	
Snow globe	95 cents each	
Pencil sharpener	18 cents	
Elephant badge	18 cents	
Model chimpanzee	28 cents	
Notebook	28 cents	

Menus

MENU

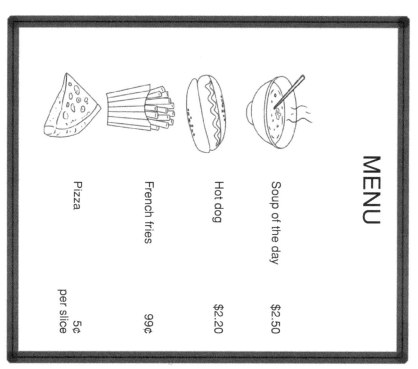

Soup of the day $2.50

Hot dog $2.20

French fries   99¢

Pizza   5¢ per slice

Drinks Menu

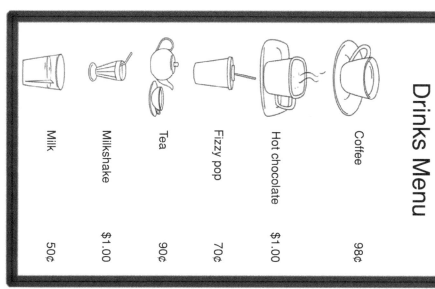

Coffee   98¢

Hot chocolate $1.00

Fizzy pop   70¢

Tea   90¢

Milkshake $1.00

Milk   50¢

Dessert Menu

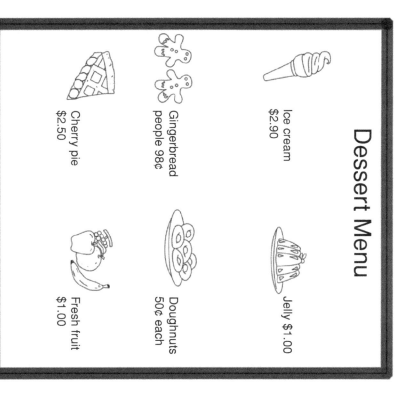

Ice cream $2.90

Jelly $1.00

Gingerbread people 98¢

Doughnuts 50¢ each

Cherry pie $2.50

Fresh fruit $1.00

Original Material © Cambridge University Press, 2014

Take away drinks menu

Juice cartons

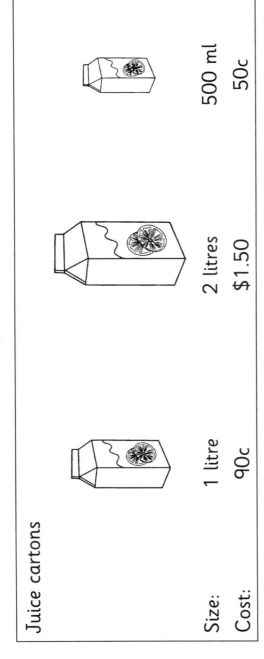

	1 litre	2 litres	500 ml
Size:			
Cost:	90c	$1.50	50c

Water bottles

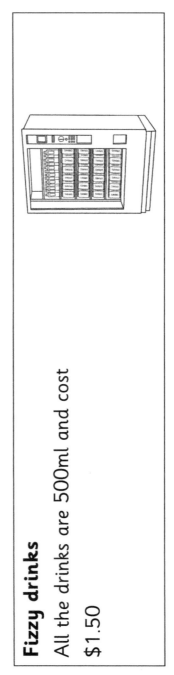

	1 litre	2 litres	½ litre
Size:			
Cost:	$1.20	$2.20	80c

Fizzy drinks

All the drinks are 500ml and cost

$1.50

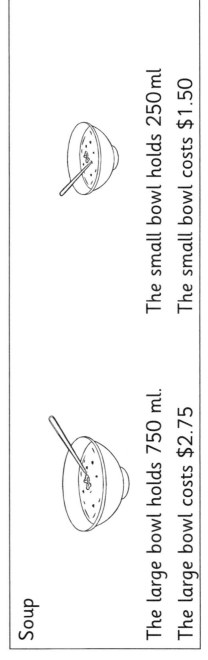

Soup

The large bowl holds 750 ml.

The large bowl costs $2.75

The small bowl holds 250ml

The small bowl costs $1.50

Quick reference

Core activity 20.1: Venn diagrams (Learner's Book p80)

This activity reviews previous work on Venn diagrams, with learners choosing their own rules for others to interpret.

Core activity 20.2: Tallying (Learner's Book p82)

This activity introduces tally charts and frequency tables in the context of a game.

Core activity 20.3: Pictograms and bar charts (Learner's Book p84)

This activity builds on previous knowledge of pictograms and bar charts and develops it into solving problems.

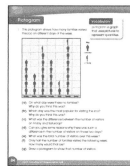

Prior learning	Objectives* – please note that listed objectives might only be partially covered within any given chapter but are covered fully across the book when taken as a whole
• Understanding the order of numbers when counting. • Know the structure of a Venn diagram. • Knowledge of block graphs will be useful and pictograms and the difference between them.	**2C: Organising, categorising and representing data** 3Dh1 – Answer a real-life question by collecting, organising and interpreting data, e.g. investigating the population of mini-beasts in different environments. 3Dh2 – Use tally charts, frequency tables, pictograms (symbol representing one or two units) and bar charts (intervals labelled in ones or twos). 3Dh3 – Use Venn or Carroll diagrams to sort data and objects using two criteria. **2C: Using understanding and strategies in solving problems** 3Ps4 – Use ordered lists and tables to help to solve problems systematically.

*for NRICH activities mapped to the Cambridge Primary objectives, please visit www.cie.org.uk/cambridgeprimarymaths

Vocabulary

axes • chart • Tally chart • bar chart • table • frequency table • Carroll diagram • Venn diagram label • title • diagram • most popular • most common • least popular • least common • sort • vote • graph • block graph • pictogram • represent • group • set • greater than • less than • axis

Resources: *1–100 number cards* photocopy master (CD-ROM); use cards 1–36 only. Large 'greater than' and large 'less than' symbols for class display. Large Venn diagram for class display. *Blank Venn diagram* photocopy master (CD-ROM), one copy per pair. (Optional: paper and pens/pencils.)

Give one number card to each learner. Ask one of the class to come and stand next to you. *"Stand next to me, look at the number on your card but don't let anyone else see it."*

Tell the rest of the class about the game you are going to play. *"We are going to play a game called, 'you can come through my gate if ….' We have chosen a rule which tells us whether you can come through the gate or not. Each of you will come up, one at a time, and show us your number. We will ask you to move to either the left or right of us, but you won't know what our rule is until the end of the game."*

Each learner shows their number as they come to the front. If the number is less than the 'gate' number, they stand to the right. If it is greater than the 'gate' number they stand to the left.

When all of the numbers have been sorted in this way ask each group to look at the numbers within the group, talk to each other and decide why their numbers are together. The students will need to see the numbers in the other group for comparison.

Say, *"We know the numbers in each of the groups, so what do you think our hidden number is? How do you know?* Point to each group in turn and ask, *"What do you think our rule for this group was?"* (**greater than**) *"and what was the rule for this group?"* (**less than**).

Explain that, *"Any pair of numbers can be put in an order of less than and greater than."*

Show the cards 'greater than' and 'less than' and read them. Choose two learners to show their numbers (e.g. 6 and 27). Ask, *"Who can make up a sentence about these two numbers that uses the words, 'greater than 'and 'less than'."* (**6 is less than 27, 27 is greater than 6**) Record the sentence on the board. Repeat with two or three more examples.

Display or draw a large Venn diagram on the board.

Vocabulary

chart: a visual representation of data.

Venn diagram: a way of sorting numbers or objects according to their different features.

Look out for!

- Learners who are having difficulties. *They may need to work with a lower range of numbers, such as 1–10, when sorting their own Venn diagram. Some will need a single or double Venn diagram with no intersection.*
- Learners who find the activity straightforward. *Set problems and challenges such as:*
  - *"I know how to describe all the numbers to make this statement true: 300 is greater than [ ]"*
  - *"I can use a Venn diagram with an intersection to sort numbers to 50 with labels 'even number' and 'multiples of 5' I can see a pattern in the numbers in the intersection and I can tell you what it is."*
  - *Use a three way intersecting set of circles to sort data, such as the students in the class, 'boy', '8 years old', 'long hair'.*

Write even numbers in the circle and odd numbers outside.

Ask, "*What's the rule? How do you know?*" Write 'even' in the circle.

Now draw two circles (not overlapping) on the board and ask students to write their number in either circle so that it fits the rule of 'even' or 'greater than 13'.

Ask questions such as, "*How do you know this is the right place for your number? Where should we put 16?*"

Work with the class to reorganise the sets so that the numbers that are both 'even' and 'more than 13' can go in the **intersection**.

Ask, "*What can we do with these two circles so that we have a third section for numbers like 16 which is both 'more than 13' and also 'even'?*" Establish that the circles need to overlap.

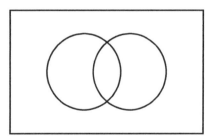

Give each pair of students a *Blank Venn diagram*. "*Choose your own rule and sort the numbers 1–36. Don't label the circles, we will try and guess your rule.*" If appropriate, suggest learners work with higher numbers, and encourage them to think of a complex rule (e.g. involving fractions).

Allow time for the class to work on the task and then choose pairs of students to show their sets and ask the rest of the class to guess the rule.

Summary

- By the end of this activity, learners will be able to read and complete number sentences for 'greater than' and 'less than' and follow the structure of a Venn diagram to sort numbers.
- They will be able to use a rule when designing their own Venn diagrams using the properties of numbers.

Notes on the Learner's Book

Venn diagram (p80): this page uses a Venn diagram as a starting point for an investigation and develops using the learners' own ideas. Learners will need a copy of the *Blank Venn diagram* photocopy master.

Check up!

Ask questions such as:
- *"Tell me a number less than 5or greater than 12."*
- *"What's my rule if I let numbers 2, 4, 6, 8 through my gate but not 1, 3, 5, 7, 9? How do you know?"*
- *"If I had a two circle Venn diagram with an intersection and the numbers on the left were 4, 2, 12 and the numbers in the intersection are 10, 20 30, 40 and the numbers on the right are 15, 45, 25, what are the labels? Explain how you know that."*

More activities

Carroll diagram (individual or pairs)

> You will need paper and pens/pencils.

Use a simple Carroll diagram for sorting numbers (e.g. even, not even). Increase to a two-attribute Carroll diagram for learners who need more of a challenge. Use labels such as 'even', 'not even', 'greater than 21', 'not greater than 21'.

Multiples and common factors (individual or pairs)

> You will need paper and pens/pencils.

Use two circles with an intersection to sort multiples of numbers e.g. multiples of 5 and multiples of 6. The intersection shows common multiples of 5 and 6.

Sort and classify (individual or pairs)

> You will need paper and pens/pencils.

Consider varieties of minibeasts (number of legs etc.), or similarities and differences between animals e.g. whales and fish. Whales have hair, give live birth to their young and breathe air. Fish lay eggs, have scales and breathe water. The intersection will show commonalities such as live in water, have fins, can swim.

Resources: The *Tally score sheet* photocopy master (CD-ROM), one copy per pair, and the *Flip game board* photocopy master (CD-ROM), one copy per pair – if preferred, the three zones can be coloured. Counters (two per learner). Pens/pencils. Colouring pencils. (Optional: newspapers, magazines or books, pens/pencils and paper.)

Explain to the class how to tally. *"Tallying is another way of recording information. It's easy to do a tally, just put marks on a piece of paper."*

"For 1, draw 1 mark, for 2, draw 2 marks, 3 needs 3 marks and 4 has 4 marks."

Draw it so that the class can see:

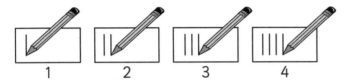

| 1 | 2 | 3 | 4 |

For the 5th mark, draw a line across the previous 4 marks:

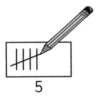

5

Show how to make 10.

Ask, *"How do you think we can write 12 using tally marks?"* Ask some students to show the class. Give several experiences of tallying by asking for different numbers (13, 15, 20). *"What do you notice about the numbers that have a line drawn through them?"* (**multiples of 5**) *"So we can easily count in 5's and then add on the extra ones."*

Explain to the class that they are going to play a game in pairs where they can use tallying. Give the learners two counters and a *Tally score sheet* each. Each pair will also need a copy of the *Flip game board*. *"Take turns to place one of your counters on the black circle. Use the other counter to flick the one on the circle towards the game board."*

Vocabulary

frequency table: a table that lists items and uses tally marks to record the number of times they occur.

tally chart: a chart that uses marks to record counting; tallies are grouped into fives. The tally chart symbol for 5 is :

Look out for!

- Learners who may be having problems with tallying. *Make sure that they are using the procedure correctly. Earlier use of jottings may lead them to think that tallying is simply putting a line to represent each item; such as:*

||||||||||||||||||||||||||||||

Watch out for the misconception that the diagonal line of a tally 'crosses out' each group of five – the diagonal line actually is the fifth item.

- Learners who are confident with tallying. *Encourage them to find displays of data in magazines, comics or papers that they or their family read. Collect these and discuss the types of data presented, how it has been displayed, how effective the presentation is. Get the learners to make a poster display about this.*

You may need to demonstrate.

"Use tallying to keep score." Show the Tally score sheet. *"If your counter lands in Zone A, make a mark for 1 in the tally column next to A."*

"If it lands in Zone B make a mark for 1 in the tally column next to B."

"If it lands in Zone C, make a tally mark for 1 in the tally column next to C."

"Record all of the flips on the same sheet. Have 10 turns each."

"When you have finished playing, total the tallying and put the answer in the 3rd column called 'frequency'." Explain that a frequency table is a table that shows the total for each category or group of data.

As the class are playing, walk round to make sure that they all understand the task and the rules. You may need to remind some learners about the 5th mark going through the other four.

When learners have finished, ask them to play the game again and see if they get the same results.

At the end of the session, invite pairs to feedback on their results. Ask questions such as, *"Tell us one thing that you noticed about the results of the two games. Were you surprised by the results? Why? If you played the game again what do you think will happen? Do you think it is possible to have two games with exactly the same results? Why/why not?"*

Summary

By the end of this activity, students will have learnt how to use tallying and a frequency table to show and interpret results.

Notes on the Learner's Book

Tallying (p82): this page asks students to use what they have learnt in the session to answer questions and solve puzzles.

Check up!

- *"Using tallying show me how to write 35, 26, 100."*
- *"Using tallying show me a number greater than 14, a number less than 56."*

More activities

Surveys (class)

Set questions, such as: how did we get to school today? What is the favourite colour of the class? The class collect and represent the data as a tally chart and frequency table.

Using texts (individual or pair)

You will need newspapers, magazines or books, pens/pencils and paper.

Give learners a manageable amount of text (a paragraph) and make a tally chart to show how many times each vowel (a, e, i, o, u) has been used. They can go on to make a bar chart to show their results. Do the same with a paragraph of German or French text to find if the pattern is the same. Make a tally chart of all of the letters in a paragraph.

Games Book (ISBN 9781107694019)

A walk in the park: what do you see? (p77) is a game for two to four players. Use pictograms to represent data.

Resources: Bag or box of counters or cubes in various colours (per group). Rulers (one per student). Squared paper. Interlocking cubes. Pens/pencils. (Optional: a 1–6 dice (CD-ROM).)

Explain to the class that in this session you are going to look at two more different ways to represent data. Ask, "*Who can tell me what a pictogram is? Have you ever seen a pictogram? Where have you seen one?*" Explain that a pictogram is a symbol or a picture which represents an idea or some data. "*We see pictograms every day in signs. Who has seen a 'no smoking' sign or a road sign? Describe what you have seen.*"

Give time for some learners' feedback.

Tell the learners that, "*When we make a pictogram there are some things that we have to remember.*" (Demonstrate these by drawing them on a board as you are saying it.) "*We need information (data) and we need to have two axes. One is vertical, which we call the y-axis, and the other is horizontal, which we call the x-axis. There also needs to be a key. The key tells the number that each picture or symbol represents. For example, if we have 10 people who like pizza, the piece of paper with 10 people drawn on it would be very large. So we can use a picture of a person for every 2 people in our survey. How many pictures would we need? How did you work that out? If we had 8 people how many pictures would we need? If we had 6 people how many would we need?*"

Give time for feedback. Establish that 35 is half way between 30 and 40, so we can use half a person to represent five. Ask, "*What would two whole people and a half a person represent?*" (**25**)

Divide the learners into groups (or pairs) and tell them they are going to make their own pictogram. "*Each of you takes a handful of counters (or cubes) and sorts them into colours. Keep a record of the colours you chose. Total all of the cubes in colour sets at the end, and represent the information as a pictogram. You might have too many to show each cube (counter) individually so make each worth two. How can you show an odd number?*" (Draw half a cube/counter) "*Make sure when you put the cubes back in the bag that you shake them up so that the person after you doesn't pick the same ones.*"

Vocabulary

axes: the plural of axis. The 'x' and 'y' lines that cross at right angles to make a graph. The 'x' axis is a horizontal line, and and 'y' axis is a vertical line. For example, $y \perp x$

pictogram: a graph that uses pictures to represent quantities.

bar chart: a graph with bars to show how large a quantity is.

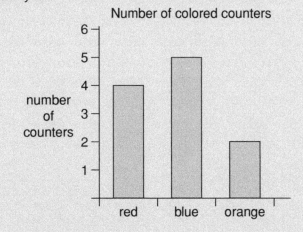

Number of colored counters

Look out for!

- Learners who are having difficulties in plotting or understanding a graph. *They need to know what the data represents and the relationship between*

As the class is working, walk around making sure that they all understand the task and have remembered the important points of the pictogram. Suggest that they refer to the one on the board if they forget.

When learners have completed their pictogram, ask them if they remember block graphs. Remind them, if appropriate, that a block graph has a horizontal line, which we now know is the *x*-axis, that is labelled with groups and each block represents one item in a group, and there are gaps between each group on the horizontal line. Explain that there is a similar graph that uses bars instead of blocks and has a vertical (y) axis that is labelled with numbers that tell us how much each bar shows. This is a bar chart. We do not need a key because the height of each bar tells us the frequency, and the number of blocks. Ask, "*How can we use a bar chart to show the same information as our pictograms?*" Demonstrate how to draw one as you give the information. "*It has two axes, the same as a pictogram. It has bars drawn from the horizontal (x) axis. These show the number of cubes/counters that are in each colour pile. Remember to leave a space between each of them.*" (The information is **discrete**. Discrete data is data that can only take certain values For example, the number of students in a class (you can't have half a student). If the gaps are removed the data will appear **continuous**). "*The vertical axis (y) has the numbers. You need to mark them in twos to match the pictogram. What happens if we have an odd number? Instead of drawing half a cube (counter) you need to make the top of the bar half way between the two numbers.*"

Choose some learners to show where 11 or 7 would go.

Remind learners that they also need to write a title, for example, 'Cubes we picked', and that both the side and the bottom of the graph need a label that tells what kind of data is shown (colours across the bottom and the numbers up the side).

Give time for students to work on the bar chart.

At the end of the session ask, "*Which do you think shows the data more clearly? Which do you like the best? Why? Tell me another time you could use a pictogram or bar chart.*"

column height and quantity. Ask students to answer simple questions about specific data in a prepared graph. Use their knowledge and understanding of vertical and horizontal number lines to make a connection to the axes of a bar chart.

- Learners who confuse the two axes of a graph or who do not leave gaps between the bars for discrete data. *Encourage them to find more examples and continue practising.*
- Learners who complete the task quickly. *Challenge them to graph the same information using different scales and to note which is the best scale and why.*
  Ask them to tell you:
  - *what the tallest bar represents,*
  - *what the shortest bar represents,*
  - *the difference in height between two bars and what this represents.*
- *You could also ask them to collect the same information every school day for a week (e.g. the number of learners absent) and comment on any increase or decrease they see in the bars across the week.*

Opportunities for display!

Display the completed examples of bar charts and pictograms which show the same data. Display examples of pictogram and bar charts from newspapers, with questions asking people what they think it is about.

Summary

By the end of this activity students will have consolidated their knowledge and understanding of bar charts and pictograms and will know the difference between them as well as knowing the significant features of both.

Notes on the Learner's Book

Pictogram (p84): this page starts by interpreting data shown in a tally chart and continues with learners interpreting, solving and developing other data.

Check up!
- Use interlocking cubes to make bar charts. Red represents cars, blue represents buses.
- Are there more cars or buses?
- How do you know?
- Change the height of the towers and the context.

More activities

Letters in our name (group)

> You will need pens/pencils and squared paper.

Learners make a pictogram to show the letters in the names of group members, where one circle represents two students, with the vertical axis from 0 to 10. For any odd number, the circle is halved.

Popular names (group)

> You will need pens/pencils and squared paper.

Learners make a bar chart to show the most popular names in the class/school. The vertical axis has the number of learners as multiples of 2, 5 or 10. The horizontal axis has the five or 10 most popular names.

Six to start (individual, pair or group)

> You will need a 1–6 dice, pens/pencils and squared paper.

In many games, players need to throw a 6 in order to start. Learners can investigate this by throwing a dice 20 times and seeing how often a 6 shows compared to the other numbers. They can use a bar chart to represent the data.

Games Book (ISBN 9781107694019)

Walk through the toy shop (p81) is a game for two to four players. They use pictograms to represent data and read data from pictograms.

Quick reference

Core activity 21.1: Comparing, ordering and rounding (Learner's Book p88)

Learners compare, order and round two- and three-digit numbers.

Core activity 21.2: Multiplying by 10 (Learner's Book p90)

Learners revise multiplying by 10 and use tens numbers to estimate a quantity as a range.

Prior learning	Objectives* – please note that listed objectives might only be partially covered within any given chapter but are covered fully across the book when taken as a whole

Prior learning

- Rounding to the nearest 10.
- Comparing numbers using less than < and greater than.
- Ordering numbers.

Objectives * – please note that listed objectives might only be partially covered within any given chapter but are covered fully across the book when taken as a whole

3A: Numbers and the number system

3Nn11 – Compare three-digit numbers, use < and > signs, and find a number in between.

3Nn7 – Multiply two-digit numbers by 10 and understand the effect.

3Nn12 – Order two- and three-digit numbers.

3Nn8 – Round two-digit numbers to the nearest 10 and round three-digit numbers to the nearest 100.

3Nn13 – Give a sensible estimate of a number as a range (e.g. 30 to 50) by grouping in tens.

3A: Problem solving (*Using techniques and skills in solving mathematical problems*)

3Pt1 – Choose appropriate mental strategies to carry out calculations.

3Pt3 – Make sense of and solve word problems, single (all four operations) and two-step (addition and subtraction), and begin to represent them, e.g. with drawings or on a number line.

3Pt10 – Estimate and approximate when calculating, and check working.

3Pt11 – Make a sensible estimate for the answer to a calculation e.g. using rounding.

3Pt12 – Consider whether an answer is reasonable.

3A: Using understanding and strategies in solving problems

3Ps1 – Make up a number story to go with a calculation.

3Ps2 – Explain a choice of calculation strategy and show how the answer was worked out.

3Ps3 – Explore and solve number problems and puzzles.

3Ps5 – Describe and continue patterns which count on or back in steps of 2, 3, 4, 5, 10 or 100.

3Ps6 – Identify simple relationships between numbers.

3Ps8 – Investigate a simple general statement by finding examples which do or do not satisfy it e.g. when adding 10 to a number, the first digit remains the same.

3Ps9 – Explain methods and reasoning orally, including initial thoughts about possible answers to a problem.

Vocabulary

rounding • ordering • less than < • greater than > • place holder

*for NRICH activities mapped to the Cambridge Primary objectives, please visit www.cie.org.uk/cambridgeprimarymaths

Resources: You will need the *Place value chart 1* photocopy master (chapter 12, p97), one copy. Cloakroom tickets (or three-digit numbers written on pieces of paper) and the *0 to 9 digit cards* photocopy master (CD-ROM), one set per pair. (Optional: the *0 to 9 digit cards* photocopy master (CD-ROM), one set per pair (remove the zero card); the *0 to 100 cards* photocopy master (CD-ROM) (sheets 1 to 6), one set per group or per pair.)

Read a range of numbers together using the *Place value chart*. After reading several numbers, ask the learners to round each number. Have a series where you round to the nearest 10 and another series where you round to the nearest 100. So, if you pointed to 327 and you are rounding to the nearest 100, the learners will say 327, 300. Fold back the top row of the *Place value chart* so you are left with tens and ones. Point to a series of two-digit numbers and ask the learners to round them to the nearest 10. So, if you pointed to 84, the learners would say 84, 80.

Ask the learners to explain how they put numbers in order. Check that they compare the number of hundreds, then the number of tens, then the ones. Write three three-digit numbers where everyone can see them and talk through ordering them from smallest to largest. So, for 453, 354 and 435, we look at the hundreds first to see that 354 is the smallest. Both of the other numbers have four hundreds, so we need to look at the tens. One has three tens so it must be smaller than the one with five tens. The order is therefore 354, 435, 453. Do the same for five numbers with some two-digit numbers included.

Give six learners a cloakroom ticket with a different three-digit number on and ask them to order themselves. Ask the learners to read out their numbers while the rest of the class check. Repeat with another six learners and different cloakroom tickets.

Give pairs of learners a set of *0 to 9 digit cards* (excluding zero). Explain that they need to shuffle the cards and turn them over three at a time to create three three-digit numbers. They then order the numbers. Each pair can then join with another pair, ordering their six numbers. The learners then record their six numbers and each learner chooses a number to write between each of the ordered numbers. This will give them a list of 11 numbers. They then write some less than < and greater than > statements about their numbers.

Vocabulary

greater than: > means greater than, for example, 453 > 250.

less than: < means less than, for example, 250 < 453.

Look out for!

- Learners who find it difficult to extend their understanding of ordering numbers to three-digits. *Explain that two-digit numbers have zero hundreds, but we don't write the zero. Give them some two- and three-digit cloakroom tickets (or numbers written on pieces of paper) to sort into no hundreds, one hundreds and two hundreds. They can then sort within each hundred.*
- Learners who find ordering straightforward. *Give them sets of numbers using the same digits and with zero tens to order since this will be more challenging.*

Opportunities for display!

Strips of paper with ordered cloakroom tickets stuck on make a good number display or border for another display.

After the learners have had sufficient time to record several statements, go round the room asking a learner to read out one of their statements. Ask for someone to read out another statement that starts with a number between (or greater than or less than) the numbers used in the previous statement.

If there is time, end the session by playing What's in the box? Draw a box where everyone can see it. Invite learners to give you a number. Write the number in the box if it agrees with your rule (multiples of 10, odd numbers, even numbers, numbers greater than 200) and outside the box if it does not. Once three numbers are in the box, learners can either give you a number or tell you what the rule is. This gives you a good opportunity to revise various properties of number. After a few games, ask a learner to be the leader.

Summary

Learners can round numbers, compare and order them. They are continuing to develop their sense of number.

Notes on the Learner's Book

Order, order (p88): learners put numbers in order, compare numbers using < and > and filling in the missing numbers.

Check up!
- Give learners a number and ask them to round it to the nearest 10 or 100.
- Ask them how they know whether to round up or down.

More activities

Rounding digits (pair)

You will need a set of the *0 to 9 digit cards* photocopy master (CD-ROM), one copy per pair, (remove the zero).

They shuffle the cards and put them face down on the table. They turn over the first four digits and use them to make as many different two-digit numbers as they can. They then round each number to the nearest 10. Using the same digits, they make as many three-digit numbers as they can and round these to the nearest 100. If there is time, they can repeat the activity with the next four digits.

Round the group (group)

You will need the *0 to 100 cards* photocopy master (CD-ROM) (sheets 1 to 6), one set per group.

Remove the tens cards from a pack of *0 to 100 cards*. Shuffle the remaining cards and give eight to each learner in the group. Shuffle the tens cards and place in a pile face down in the middle of the table. Turn over the top tens card. Learners place a card which rounds to that number next to it. When everyone has placed a card or missed a turn because they do not have a number which rounds to that tens number, the next tens number is turned over. Learners again place a card which rounds to that number next to it. Play continues in the same way. The winner is the first player to get rid of all their cards.

Shuffle order (pair)

You will need the *0 to 100 cards* photocopy master (CD-ROM) (sheets 1 to 6), one set per pair.

Shuffle a set of *0 to 100 number cards*. Give each pair of learners 10 cards. They turn over the cards one at a time, laying them out in a line. They then put them in order from smallest to largest by swapping two cards at a time.

Games Book (ISBN 9781107694019)

All round (p20) is a game for two players. Players round numbers to the nearest 10 on the first board, or 100 on the second board.

Resources: You will need the *Place value chart 1* photocopy master (chapter 12, p97), one copy. A stick pointer. Paperclips or other small items and small bowls or pots (e.g. empty yoghurt pots). Rice (or chick peas, small beans or other small items). Assorted spoons and place value apparatus. (Optional: a collection of 1c coins; the *0 to 9 digit cards* photocopy master (CD-ROM) and the *Slides* photocopy master (CD-ROM), one copy per learner; one page of text photocopied from a book, newspaper or magazine per learner.)

Read a range of numbers together using *Place value chart 1*. After reading several numbers, fold back the top row of the chart so you are left with tens and ones. Point to a series of two-digit numbers (using a stick pointer, so you do not hide any of the chart) and ask the learners to say the number then multiply it by 10. So, if you want the number 64 point to 60 then 4, the learners would say 64, and then 640. If the learners find this difficult, remind them what happens when you multiply by 10. So, for 64, each ten becomes a hundred and each one becomes a ten. 64 becomes 640. The effect is to move all the digits one place to the left and we put a zero in the ones as a 'place holder', to hold the digits in their new values.

Remind the learners that we call numbers with zero ones 'round numbers', because these are the numbers that other numbers are rounded to. These numbers are often used to estimate. We often do not need to know something exactly, so an estimate is sufficient. Sometimes we estimate by deciding if the number is likely to be within a range. Show the learners some paperclips or other small items in your hand. Allow the items to fall into a small bowl or pot to help the learners get a better look at their size and the quantity. Ask the learners to estimate how many paperclips there could be. Explain that we don't need to know exactly, so a range would be useful. Was it 10 to 20? Or 20 to 40? Discuss and agree a range. Quickly group the paperclips in tens to see if the amount is within the range suggested.

Show the learners a bag of rice and pour some into a bowl. Explain that you would like the learners to take a teaspoon of rice (roughly level, not piled) and estimate how many grains there are. They should choose a range, rather than one number. The grains are small and it would be hard to get the exact number, so a range with a difference of 20 or 30 would be fine. Give each table some small pots of rice and three or four spoons of different sizes. They should estimate then count by putting the grains into piles of 10. You could also use chick peas, small beans or something else. Use larger spoons for larger items.

Vocabulary

place holder: zero, 0, is a place holder. It is used with other digits to occupy the space where there are no ones or tens or hundreds. So in 609, the zero shows us that there are no tens. If we did not use 0 as a place holder we would have no way of knowing if 69 meant 690, 609 or simply 69.

Look out for!

- Learners who do not understand that multiplying by 10 makes a number ten times bigger. *Using place value apparatus, make some numbers such as 7, 12 and 15 with single cubes. Show the learner that when you multiply by ten, 7 becomes 70, as you change exchange each 1 for a 10. Do the same for 12, so that 12 becomes 120, then 15 becomes 150. Some learners will benefit from seeing this written as:*
  $\times 10$
  $7 \rightarrow 70$
  $12 \rightarrow 120$
  $15 \rightarrow 150$

Once the learners have had time to estimate and count the contents of around three spoons, discuss the estimates and counts for each different size of spoon. Finish the session by asking about how estimates might change as the items in the spoon change. For example, "*Would you expect there to be more or less grains of sand than grains of rice in a teaspoon? What is different about rice and sand that makes you want to change your estimate? What if it were beans instead of rice?*"

> *Encourage them to have a go for themselves, doing the exchange and recording what they did. Help them to notice what is happening to the numbers.*
> - Learners who are confident at multiplying by 10. *Challenge them to explore what happens to numbers when they are multiplied by 100 or even 1000.*

Summary

Learners can multiply two-digit numbers by 10 and estimate using a range.

Notes on the Learner's Book

Times ten (p90): learners multiply by 10 and solve a range of problems which involve multiplying by 10.

Check up!

- Give learners a number to multiply by ten.
- Ask them how they found the answer.

More activities

Exchange (individual)

You will need a number of 1c coins for each learner.

Ask learners to imagine every coin is now a 10c coin. Each coin is now worth 10 times more. Ask them to record the changed values as 7c × 10 = 70c.

Slides (individual)

You will need the *0 to 9 digit cards* photocopy master (CD-ROM) and the *Slides* photocopy master (CD-ROM), one copy per learner.

Give each learner a set of digit cards. They must keep 0 to one side as they will need it to keep the other digits in place. Learners use two digit cards to make a two-digit number, putting each digit in the correct place on the *Slides* sheet. They then slide each digit one box to the left and put zero in the ones place to keep the digits in place. They record what they did on the *Slides* sheet. There is an example to help them.

Words on a page (individual)

You will need a photocopied page of text from a book, newspaper or magazine.

Ask the learners to estimate how many words on the page using a range. They then cross out or ring words in groups of ten and count in tens to find out how many.

Quick reference

Core activity 22.1: Fractions (Learner's Book p92)

Learners explore fractions of a circle and begin to explore equivalent fractions.

Core activity 22.2: Fractions and division (Learner's Book p94)

Learners explore other fractions of a circle and an amount. They begin to relate fractions to division.

Core activity 22.3 Fractions are numbers too (Learner's Book p92)

Learners explore marking fractions and mixed numbers on a number line, focusing on halves and quarters initially. They begin to explore other fractions.

Core activity 22.4: More fractions (Learner's Book p96)

Learners find halves of odd numbers and explore fractions of shapes.

Prior learning	Objectives* – please note that listed objectives might only be partially covered within any given chapter but are covered fully across the book when taken as a whole
• Experience of halving a number and a shape. • Division as sharing.	**3A: Numbers and the number system** 3Nn14 – Find half of odd and even numbers to 40, using notation such as $13\frac{1}{2}$. 3Nn15 – Understand and use fraction notation recognising that fractions are several parts of one whole, e.g. $\frac{3}{4}$ is three quarters and $\frac{2}{3}$ is two thirds. 3Nn16 – Recognise equivalence between 1 half, 2 quarters, 4 eighths, and 5 tenths using diagrams. 3Nn17 – Recognise simple mixed fractions, e.g. $1\frac{1}{2}$ and $2\frac{1}{4}$. 3Nn18 – Order simple or mixed fractions on a number line, e.g. using the knowledge that $\frac{1}{2}$ comes half way between $\frac{1}{4}$ and $\frac{3}{4}$, and that $1\frac{1}{2}$ comes half way between 1 and 2. 3Nn19 – Begin to relate finding fractions to division. 3Nn20 – Find halves, thirds, quarters and tenths of shapes and numbers (whole number answers). **3A: Problem solving** (*Using techniques and skills in solving mathematical problems*) 3Pt1 – Choose appropriate mental strategies to carry out calculations. 3Pt3 – Make sense of and solve word problems, single (all four operations) and two-step (addition and subtraction), and begin to represent them, e.g. with drawings or on a number line. **3A: Using understanding and strategies in solving problems** 3Ps2 – Explain a choice of calculation strategy and show how the answer was worked out. 3Ps3 – Explore and solve number problems and puzzles. 3Ps5 – Describe and continue patterns which count on or back in steps of 2, 3, 4, 5, 10 or 100. 3Ps6 – Identify simple relationships between numbers. 3Ps8 – Investigate a simple general statement by finding examples which do/do not satisfy it, e.g. when adding 10 to a number, the first digit remains the same. 3Ps9 – Explain methods and reasoning orally, including initial thoughts about possible answers to a problem.

Vocabulary

fraction • half • quarter • third • eighth • tenth • mixed number

*for NRICH activities mapped to the Cambridge Primary objectives, please visit www.cie.org.uk/cambridgeprimarymaths

Resources: You will need the *Fraction circles sheets 1, 2 and 3* photocopy master (p192), one copy per pair. The *Fraction Wall* photocopy master (p191), one copy per learner. Colouring pencils. Scissors.

Begin the session by counting on and back in ones, twos, tens, fives and hundreds from any two- and three-digit numbers. Occasionally pause the count and ask the learners to tell you 20, 30, . . . 90, 100, 200, 300 more or less than any number.

Ask the learners to tell you what they can remember about a half and a quarter. Check that they recall that these are both fractions, which means parts of a whole. That whole can be something like a cake that we cut into quarters so that four people can have a quarter each, or a packet of 12 pencils where four people get three pencils each. Write $\frac{1}{2}$ and explain that we can look at it as one out of two equal pieces. So $\frac{1}{4}$ is one out of four equal pieces and $\frac{3}{4}$ is three of four equal pieces. Tell the learners that to help them find out a bit more about fractions, you have some fraction circles for them to explore.

Give each pair of learners a set of the five *Fraction circles* ($\frac{1}{10}, \frac{1}{8}, \frac{1}{4}, \frac{1}{3}, \frac{1}{2}$) but no scissors at this point. Ask them to talk to their partner about what they notice. After a few minutes, share ideas. Ensure that the learners have noticed that when the circle is marked in ten equal pieces, there are 10 of them and they are called tenths; when the circle is marked into 8 equal pieces, they are called eighths and there are 8 of them; when the circle is marked into 3 equal pieces, there are three of them and they are called thirds. Also look at how this links to how the fraction is written. Revise quarters and halves in the same way.

Give each pair of learners a pair of scissors and ask them to carefully cut out each circle and its fractions. They can then explore them in any way they wish. For example, they could mix them up and find out how many different ways they can put other fractions with $\frac{1}{2}$ to make a whole circle. Or they might like to explore in some other way.

After the learners have had plenty of time to explore, ask them to share what they found out. List the observations on the board, grouping any equivalences. For example if learners have noticed that two quarters are the same as one half, write $\frac{1}{4} + \frac{1}{4} = \frac{1}{2}$. You might then write next

Vocabulary

half: one of two equal sized parts of a whole.

quarter: one of four equal sized parts of a whole.

fraction: part of a whole.

one third, thirds: $\frac{1}{3}$, one of three equal pieces of a whole.

one eighth, eighths: $\frac{1}{8}$, one of eight equal pieces of a whole.

one tenth, tenths: $\frac{1}{10}$, one of ten equal pieces of a whole.

Look out for!

- Learners who find it hard to recognize equivalent fractions. Place two quarters on top of a half to show they are the same size. Repeat with two eighths on top of a quarter and so on. *Challenge learners who quickly grasp the idea of equivalent fractions to find further fraction for a half, such as $\frac{6}{12}$ or $\frac{9}{18}$. They could also explore equivalences for $\frac{1}{4}$ and $\frac{3}{4}$ or extend the fraction wall to include other smaller fractions. Alternatively, challenge these learners to make their own fraction circles. Using the existing fraction circles, challenge them to make $\frac{1}{5}$ and $\frac{1}{16}$ fraction circles. They could cut out their circles and look for further equivalences.*

to this, someone else's suggestion of $\frac{1}{8} + \frac{1}{8} = \frac{1}{4}$. If necessary, draw a ring around any fractions that are equivalent to half and then write the list as $\frac{1}{2} = \frac{2}{4} = \frac{4}{8} = \frac{5}{10}$.

Give each learner a copy of the *Fraction Wall* sheet. Talk through the arrangement of the fractions. Count how many thirds, tenths and eighths and check that the learners understand that there are three, eight and ten equal parts of a whole.

Show the learners how they can see 'equivalent fractions' on the fraction wall. Focus on fractions equivalent to a half at first and then those that are equivalent to a quarter. Ask the learners to colour the first half, the first third, the first quarter and so on in different colours so that they can easily identify where each of those fraction ends.

Finish the session by asking questions such as, *"Tell me a fraction that is equal to $\frac{1}{2}$ (or $\frac{1}{4}$) Tell me a fraction that is between $\frac{1}{10}$ and $\frac{1}{3}$ in size . Which is bigger, $\frac{1}{3}$ or $\frac{1}{4}$? How do you know?"* and so on.

Opportunities for display!

Display the fraction walls and an enlarged set of fraction circles as part of a display on fractions. Make sure that each of the fraction circles are the same size. Occasionally rearrange the fractions into different mixed circles, for example one circle could be made up of $\frac{1}{2}, \frac{1}{4}, \frac{1}{8}$ and $\frac{1}{8}$.

Summary

Learners understand what is meant by thirds, eighths and tenths and understand that the larger the number on the bottom of the fraction, the smaller the fraction as the whole has been cut into more pieces.

Notes on the Learner's Book

Fraction wall (p94): learners use the fraction wall to help them answer the first seven questions about fractions, including some greater than and less than statements about fractions.

Check up!

Ask questions such as:
- *"Which is bigger two halves or three quarters?"*
- *"How do you know?"*
- *"Tell me a fraction which is the same as $\frac{1}{2}$."*

More activities

Fraction cake shop (pairs or small groups)

You will need a set of *Fraction circles* as cakes, a 1–6 dice, and a dice or spinner labelled $\frac{1}{4}, \frac{1}{2}, \frac{1}{3}, \frac{1}{8}, \frac{1}{10}$ and 0.

Learners roll a 1–6 dice and a fraction dice (or spinner labelled $\frac{1}{4}, \frac{1}{2}, \frac{1}{3}, \frac{1}{8}, \frac{1}{10}$ and 0). They collect that amount from the 'cake shop'. If the shop does not have enough of that fraction, they miss that turn. When the shop is empty, the learners compare cakes to see who has the most. This is easier if only two learners are playing.

Quarters (individual)

> You will need two large, different coloured circles (e.g. one red, one blue) marked in quarters, and scissors.

Cut both circles along one of the quarter lines from the outside into the middle of the circle. Slide the circles together so that they rotate about the middle. Ask the learners to show you three red quarters and one blue quarter, or two red quarters and two blue quarters. Extend to $\frac{1}{3}$ red, $\frac{2}{3}$ blue and so on.

Games Book (ISBN 9781107694019)

Collect a fraction 1 (p23) is a game for two to four players. Players collect halves and quarters of circles, making whole circles by recognising that two quarters are equivalent to one half. Some learners may be able to express their total as a mixed number.

Quarters game (p27) is a game for two to four players. Players recognise a quarter and three-quarters of a shape, and that two quarters are equivalent to one half.

Core activity 22.2: Fractions and division

Resources: You will need the *Fraction circles* from activity 22.1 and coloured counters or cubes.

Begin the session by asking the learners to remake their fraction circles. Ask them to order the circles from largest pieces to smallest pieces, that is $\frac{1}{2}, \frac{1}{3}, \frac{1}{4}, \frac{1}{8}, \frac{1}{10}$. Explain that they are going to check the pieces with you. Begin by saying $\frac{1}{2}$ + *another* $\frac{1}{2}$ *is 2 halves = 1 whole. Move on to* $\frac{1}{3}$ + *another* $\frac{1}{3}$ + *another* $\frac{1}{3}$ *is three thirds = one whole then* $\frac{1}{4}$ + *another* $\frac{1}{4}$ + *another* $\frac{1}{4}$ + *another* $\frac{1}{4}$ *is four quarters* = *one whole* and so on for eighths and tenths. Show the learners how to write the total number of halves, two halves as $\frac{2}{2}$, three thirds as $\frac{3}{3}$ and so on. Remind the learners that each of the circles are the same size, so we can write $\frac{2}{2} = \frac{3}{3} = \frac{4}{4} = \frac{8}{8} = \frac{10}{10} = 1$. Focus on the fact that we have two equal pieces when we have halves, three equal pieces when we have thirds and so on.

Give each pair of learners some counters or cubes. Ask them to use the circle with the two half circles. Ask them to get eight counters and put half of them on one of the $\frac{1}{2}$ pieces and half of them on the other $\frac{1}{2}$ piece. Explain that they can see that half of eight is four and that another way of saying this would be eight divided by two equals 4. Link the 'divided by two' with the 'bottom part of the fraction'. Show learners how to record this as $\frac{1}{2}$ of 8 = 4 and 8 ÷ 2 = 4. Ask the learners to find $\frac{1}{4}$ of eight, or in other words, eight divided by four. If necessary, tell the learners to share the counters equally between the four quarters. Ask what eight divided by four is and what $\frac{3}{4}$ of eight is. Record as $\frac{1}{4}$ of 8 = 2 and 8 ÷ 4 = 2 and then $\frac{3}{4}$ of 8 = 6. Repeat the activity with 20 counters to find 20 divided by 10, $\frac{1}{10}$ of 20, $\frac{2}{10}$ of twenty and so on. Then move on to finding $\frac{1}{3}$ of 12, 12 divided by three.

Give the learners time to explore division by sharing with the counters, but make sure that they keep their fraction circles whole, not mixing the pieces. Give learners a mini-whiteboard or piece of paper to record some of their divisions.

Vocabulary

one third, thirds: $\frac{1}{3}$, one of three equal pieces of a whole.

one eighth, eighths: $\frac{1}{8}$, one of eight equal pieces of a whole.

one tenth, tenths: $\frac{1}{10}$, one of ten equal pieces of a whole.

Look out for!

- Learners who find it difficult to link fractions and division. Show them that 8 shared equally between two people is 4 each, so 8 ÷ 2 = 4. If we imagine the 8 as 8 sweets in a pack and two learners can have half the pack each, they would each get 4 sweets. Place 4 cubes on each half and say *half of the packet is 4 sweets, so half of 8 is 4.* Repeat with a similar calculation.
- More confident learners. *Ask them to make their own fraction circles for fifths if they did not do that in the previous session and then use it to explore dividing by 5.*

184 Unit 3A   22 Fractions

Share some of the learners' observations and recording. Pair up calculations such as $\frac{1}{2}$ of with $\div\, 2$; $\frac{1}{3}$ of with $\div\, 3$; $\frac{1}{4}$ of with $\div\, 4$ and so on. Make sure that the learners understand that these are simply two ways of saying the same thing.

Summary

- Learners begin to relate fractions to division.

Notes on the Learner's Book

Fraction wall (p94): learners use the fraction wall to help them answer questions about fractions and division. They also write some greater than and less than statements about fractions.

Check up!

Ask questions such as:
- Ask learners how they would find a quarter of 20 or a third of 18.
- Change the fractions and numbers as appropriate and ask again.

More activities

$\frac{1}{3}$ **Flags** Draw the correct flag in each box in the table.

Fraction Flags Learners colour $\frac{1}{4}$ of each flag, leaving $\frac{3}{4}$ white. How many different ways can they find to do it?

Fractions of amounts Learners work out $\frac{1}{4}$, $\frac{1}{2}$ and $\frac{3}{4}$ of sets objects. They record this as a fraction or division, with the last six left for learners to record as they wish. Some learners may find the fraction circles and cubes or counters useful.

Games Book (ISBN 9781107694019)

Collect a fraction 2 (p23) is a game for two to four players. Players collect fractions of a circle, recognising equivalent and simple mixed numbers.
Quarters game (p27) is a game for two to four players. Players recognise a quarter and three-quarters of a shape, and that two quarters are equivalent to one half.

Resources: You will need the *Number lines 0 to 10* photocopy master (CD-ROM), one per learner, ideally enlarged onto A3. Rulers. (Optional: *Halves Pelmanism sheets* 1 to 4 photocopy master (CD-ROM), one copy per learner; scissors.) (Optional: the *Quarters Pelmanism sheets* 1 to 4 photocopy master (CD-ROM); The *Halves Pelmanism*; large circles in two different colours, marked in quarters sheets 1 to 4 photocopy master (CD-ROM); scissors; a set of Fraction circles; a 1–6 dice or spinner labelled $\frac{1}{4}, \frac{1}{2}, \frac{1}{3}, \frac{1}{8}, \frac{1}{10}$ and 0.)

Begin the session by asking each learner to take one half piece from their set of fraction circles. Count around the room in halves, initially as 1 half, 2 halves, 3 halves, 4 halves, five halves and so on. Repeat the count but this time joining together each set of two halves as one whole, so the count proceeds as $\frac{1}{2}$, 1, one and half, 2, 2 and a half, 3, 3 and a half, 4 and so on. Ask the learners to help you write the numbers they said. Begin with $\frac{1}{2}$, 1..., explaining that they know how to write those, then ask how you might write 1 and a half, not in words but as a number. Learners could experiment on mini-whiteboards or paper before sharing ideas. Agree $1\frac{1}{2}$, then continue to write the sequence up to the total counted to. Go on to explain that you have written a line of numbers. 3, 4, 5 and so on are numbers, so are $3\frac{1}{2}, 4\frac{1}{2}$ and so on. Show the learners a large 0 to 10 numberline. Explain that we often think of `half `as `half of something', but it is also a number on the number line, halfway between 0 and 1. Mark and label $\frac{1}{2}$ on the enlarged number line. Talk through how you might mark the point half way between 1 and 2, and how you should write it. Ask where you should mark $5\frac{1}{2}$. Give each learner a *Number line 0 to 10*, ideally enlarged to A3. Ask them to mark on the numberline the numbers $\frac{1}{2}, 1\frac{1}{2}, 2\frac{1}{2}$ and so on, up to $9\frac{1}{2}$. Do the same with $\frac{1}{4}$ and $\frac{3}{4}$ giving learners time to think carefully about how they should be written.

When the learners have completed their line ask questions such as, *"How many halves in $3\frac{1}{2}$? How many quarters in $2\frac{1}{4}$? Where is 4 and $\frac{2}{4}$ on the number line?"* This question will enable you to check that the learners understand that a half and two quarters are the same.

Tell the learners that you are going to enlarge the 0 to 1 part of the numberline and draw another line, marked 0 to 1.Explain that there is lots more space between the numbers you have marked on your 0 to 1 number line and you are going to help the learners to discover some other fractions that they might mark on a number line. Give each learner their *Fraction Wall sheet* from *Core activity 22.1*. Ask each learner to mark $\frac{1}{4}$ and $\frac{1}{2}$ on the numberline below the fraction wall. Then ask them to mark at least three more fractions between 0 and 1 on their number line, using the fraction wall to help them. So if a learner wanted to mark $\frac{2}{3}$, they could look along the thirds section, find where the second of the three thirds ends and mark the matching place on the number line below. Learners should also be able to mark $\frac{1}{3}, \frac{1}{8}$ and $\frac{1}{10}$. After a few moments, ask each learner to show their partner which numbers they marked and how they knew where to mark them. Ask some learners to come and mark one of their fractions on the number line on the board, explaining to the rest of the class how they knew where to make the mark.

Look out for!

- Learners who find it difficult to understand $\frac{1}{3}, \frac{1}{8}$ and $\frac{1}{10}$ as numbers. *Cut out the strips from a fraction wall and remind them that each strip is 1. Use the strips to show $\frac{1}{2}$ is half way along the line. Do the same with $\frac{1}{4}, \frac{1}{3}, \frac{1}{8}$ and $\frac{1}{10}$.*
- More confident learners. *Ask them to make their own fraction circles. Using the existing fraction circles, challenge them to make $\frac{1}{5}$ and $\frac{1}{16}$ fraction circles. They could cut out their circles and look for further equivalences.*

Opportunities for display!

Display marked number lines and fraction walls as part of a display on fractions.

Summary

- Learners can mark fractions on a number line. They read and understand simple mixed numbers.

Notes on the Learner's Book

Fraction trios (p92): learners represent a mixed number in three different ways then answer questions about halves and quarters.

Check up!

Ask questions such as:
- Ask learners how they would find a quarter of 20 or a third of 18.
- Change the fractions and numbers as appropriate and ask again.

More activities

Halves Pelmanism (pair or small group) You will need the *Halves Pelmanism sheets* 1 to 4 photocopy master (CD-ROM), one copy per pair or small group, and scissors. Cut out the individual game cards before shuffling them and arranging them face down in an 8 by 5 grid. Two, three or four learners take it in turns to turn over two cards. If the two cards have the same value, the learner keeps them. If not, they turn them back face down in the same positions. The learner who collects the most cards is the winner. The same cards could be used to play halves snap.

Quarters Pelmanism (small group of 2, 3 or 4) You will need the *Quarters Pelmanism sheets* 1 to 4 photocopy master (CD-ROM) and scissors. Cut out the individual game cards before shuffling them and arranging them face down in an 8 by 5 grid. Learners take it in turns to turn over two cards. If the two cards have the same value, the learner keeps them. If not, they turn them back face down in the same positions. The learner who collects the most cards is the winner. The same cards could be used to play quarters snap. Mix with the half Pelmanism cards for a more challenging game of both Pelmanism and snap.

Halves numberline (individual) You will need the *Halves Pelmanism sheets* 1 to 4 photocopy master (CD-ROM), one copy per learner. Learners order the Halves Pelmanism number cards then match with the number of halves cards to create a halves number line. They could make their own cards to extend the number line to 20. One learner could challenge another by swapping two cards and asking the other to spot what has been changed, explaining how they know. The ordered cards could then be pegged onto a washing line back to back, sometimes showing the number card and sometimes the halves card.

Quarters number line (individual or pair) You will need a set of *Quarters Pelmanism* cards and a set of *Halves Pelmanism* cards. Learners order the *Quarters Pelmanism* number cards then match with the number of *Halves Pelmanism* cards to create a halves number line. They could make their own cards to extend the number line to 10 or 20. One learner could challenge another by swapping two cards and asking the learner to spot what has been changed, explaining how they know. The ordered cards could then be pegged onto a washing line back to back, sometimes showing the number card and sometimes the quarters card.

Games Book (ISBN 9781107694019)

Collect a fraction 2 (p23) is a game for two to four players. Players collect fractions of a circle, recognising equivalent and simple mixed numbers.

Quarters game (p27) is a game for two to four players. Players recognise a quarter and three-quarters of a shape, and that two quarters are equivalent to one half.

Resources: *Doubles and halves* photocopy master (CD-ROM), completed and ideally enlarged. *Odd halves* photocopy master (CD-ROM), per learner. *Fractions circles* photocopy master, tenths only (part of sheet 3) (p194), per pair. Selection of 2D shapes. Paper. Scissors. (Optional: large circles in two different colours, marked in quarters, per learner; 2D shapes; paper; different coloured cubes; the *Fraction flippers* photocopy master (CD-ROM), one copy per learner; colouring pencils; scissors.) Learner's Book: large sheet of paper and colouring pencils.

Count in halves, thirds, quarters, eighths and tenths to at least three. Try counting backwards too.

Ask the learners to remind you what is meant by $\frac{1}{2}, \frac{1}{3}, \frac{1}{4}, \frac{1}{8}$ and $\frac{1}{10}$, writing these on the board. Check that they recognise that each of these fractions is one part of a whole. Ask the learners to put the fractions in order of size. Remind them that sometimes we have more than one part of the whole, for example $\frac{2}{3}$ and $\frac{3}{4}$.

Remind the learners that they used their *Fraction circles* to help them find a fraction of a number. Point to the half and remind the learners that they have found half of a number before, when they were finding out about doubles and halves. Show the learners an enlarged, completed copy of the *Doubles and halves* sheet. Point out that they only found halves of even numbers.

Give each learner a copy of the *Odd halves* sheet. Check that they recognise that the even numbers are shaded and ask them to quickly fill in those halves.

Remind them that they know that half of one is $\frac{1}{2}$. Ask, *"But what about half of three?"* If necessary use three of the half fraction circles to remind the learners that half of three is $1\frac{1}{2}$. Ask them to complete the *Odd halves* grid with the halves of all the odd numbers, using the half fraction circles to help them if necessary. This would be a good place to break this Core activity into two sessions if necessary.

Remind the learners that they know a circle can be cut into halves, thirds, quarters, eighths and tenths because they have used the *Fraction circles*, but can all shapes be cut into any fraction? Give each pair of learners a *Fraction circle* in tenths, some 2D shapes, paper and scissors. Ask the learners to check that all the tenths are the same size by putting them on top of each other. Now

Look out for!

- Learners who believe that folding in half gives halves, folding in half again gives you quarters and folding again gives you thirds or sixths. *Fold a piece of A4 paper in half three times, opening after each fold to clearly show what has happened.*

  - *Some learners will need help to fold each shape accurately before cutting into fractions. Give them larger shapes to work with as these are easier to fold, particularly when smaller fractions are needed. Remind them that they can fold eighths by folding in half, half again and half again. Folding into thirds can be difficult. Show learners how to loosely roll the paper, squashing it gently as you adjust it so that it has three equal layers, then flatten. Alternatively, fold over part of the shape so that it looks like the two pieces you can see are both a half. This is easier to judge than $\frac{1}{3}$.*

- The more confident learners. *Challenge them to find half of three-digit odd numbers. They may need to split the number into hundreds, tens and ones then find half of each part and add the halves back together to find half of the number.*

ask them to draw around a 2D shape, then fold and cut it in half. They should check that the two pieces are the same by putting them on top of each other to see if they match. They then need to cut out further copies of the shape and fold it to find out if it can be cut into four quarters, three thirds, eight eighths and 10 tenths. Each time, they need to check that the pieces are equal in size.

After giving the learners plenty of time to investigate, draw up a table like the one below and use it to check what the learners have found out.

Once completed, ask the learners questions such as, *"Which shapes can be folded and cut into quarters? Which shapes cannot? Which shapes can be folded and cut into thirds? Which shapes cannot?"* Ask the learners if it is true that all shapes be cut into any fraction.

	$\frac{1}{10}$	$\frac{1}{8}$	$\frac{1}{4}$	$\frac{1}{3}$	$\frac{1}{2}$
Circle	✓	✓	✓	✓	✓
Square					
Rectangle					
Triangle					

Opportunities for display!

Reassemble some of the shapes cut into fractions. Label the fractions and include them in your fraction display.

Summary

Learners can find halves of odd numbers and a range of different fractions of shapes.

Notes on the Learner's Book

Fraction posters (p96): learners make their own posters focusing on a chosen fraction. They solve some problems using fractions.

Check up!

- Ask the learners to tell you half of seven or 17.
- Change the numbers as appropriate and ask again.
- Ask questions such as:
  - *"If I fold a square in half, what shape could the half be?"*
  - *"Can I end up with squares if I fold a rectangle into quarters?*

More activities

Quarters revisited (individual)

> You will need large circles in two different colours, marked in quarters, scissors.

Cut out two large, different coloured circles marked in quarters. Cut both circles along one of the quarter lines from the outside into the middle of the circle. Slide the circles together so that they rotate about the middle. Ask the learners to show you a blue third, a red eighth or a blue tenth. Move on to ask for $\frac{2}{3}$ blue, $\frac{4}{10}$ red, $\frac{3}{8}$ blue and so on. Turn the circles over and use the unmarked sides to ask learners to estimate fractions such as $\frac{1}{3}, \frac{5}{8}$ and so on.

Shape shifters (groups of three)

> You will need 2D shapes, paper and scissors per group.

Learners draw and cut round two copies of any 2D shape. The first learner folds the shape in half and cuts it to make two halves. They pass one half to the next learner to fold in half and cut again to make two quarters. They pass on one quarter to the next learner to fold in half and cut again to make two eighths. They then check that $\frac{2}{8} = \frac{1}{4}$ and $\frac{2}{4} = \frac{1}{2}$ by placing the fractions on top of each other. Challenge the shape shifter groups by asking each learner to fold into thirds (three equal pieces), passing on one piece to the next learner. What fractions have they made?

Fraction cubes (individual/pair)

> You will need a collection of different coloured cubes.

Give the learners instructions to make a stick of ten cubes, for example: three red cubes, two blue cubes, four black cubes and one yellow cube. The learners then make statements about the stick, for example $\frac{3}{10}$ of the stick is red or $\frac{1}{2}$ of the cubes are red and blue. Learners can make their own stick of ten cubes and challenge a partner to make the same stick from their statements. Repeat for sticks of eight cubes making statements about eighths.

Fraction flippers (individual/pair)

> You will need the *Fraction flippers* photocopy master (CD-ROM) one copy per learner, colouring pencils, scissors.

Learners colour all the squares in the same colour on their *Fraction flippers* sheet quickly, then cut them out. The learners lay out the squares in a 5 by 4 grid. Ask the learners to flip over some of the squares to show a fraction such as $\frac{1}{2}, \frac{1}{4}, \frac{3}{4}, \frac{1}{10}, \frac{3}{10}$ and so on. Learners could work in pairs, giving each other a fraction to flip. Make sure the learners understand that they cannot use this layout to flip $\frac{1}{3}$ or $\frac{1}{8}$ because 20 does not divide exactly by three or eight. With two sets they can do eighths, but they need three sets to do thirds.

Fraction wall

1									

| $\frac{1}{2}$ | | | | | $\frac{1}{2}$ | | | | |

| $\frac{1}{3}$ | | | $\frac{1}{3}$ | | | $\frac{1}{3}$ | | | |

| $\frac{1}{4}$ | | $\frac{1}{4}$ | | $\frac{1}{4}$ | | $\frac{1}{4}$ | | | |

| $\frac{1}{8}$ | $\frac{1}{8}$ | $\frac{1}{8}$ | $\frac{1}{8}$ | $\frac{1}{8}$ | $\frac{1}{8}$ | $\frac{1}{8}$ | $\frac{1}{8}$ |

| $\frac{1}{10}$ | $\frac{1}{10}$ | $\frac{1}{10}$ | $\frac{1}{10}$ | $\frac{1}{10}$ | $\frac{1}{10}$ | $\frac{1}{10}$ | $\frac{1}{10}$ | $\frac{1}{10}$ | $\frac{1}{10}$ |

0   1

Fraction circles sheet 1

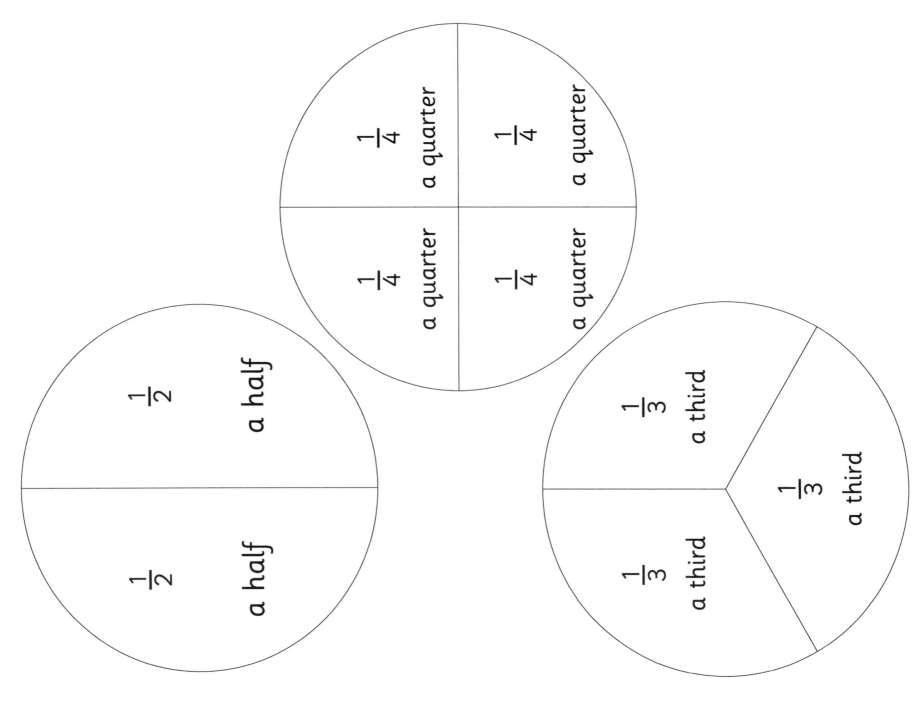

Instructions on page185

Fraction circles sheet 2

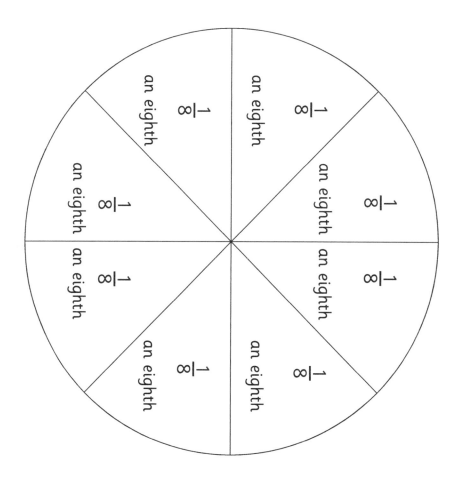

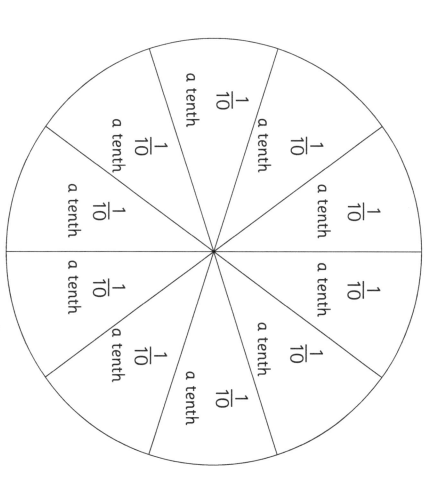

20 squares

Colour $\frac{1}{2}$ red $\frac{1}{2}$ blue.

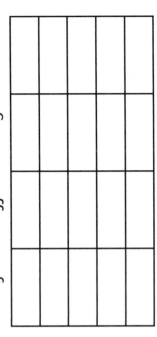

Now find a different way.

Colour $\frac{1}{4}$ red $\frac{1}{4}$ blue and $\frac{1}{2}$ yellow.

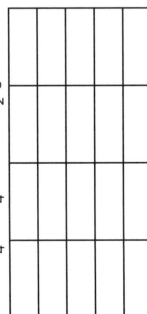

Now find a different way.

Now you have 24 squares. Find different ways to colour $\frac{1}{6}$ blue

Quick reference

<u>**Core activity 23.1: More doubles and halves**</u> (Learner's Book p97)

Learners revise doubling and halving and extend their understanding to three-digit numbers.

Prior learning	Objectives* – please note that listed objectives might only be partially covered within any given chapter but are covered fully across the book when taken as a whole
• Doubles to at least double 10 and the related halves. • Counting in multiples of 5.	**3A: Calculation** (*Mental strategies*) 3Nc6 – Work out quickly the doubles of numbers 1 to 20 and derive the related halves. 3Nc7 – Work out quickly the doubles of multiples of 5 (< 100) and derive the related halves. 3Nc8 – Work out quickly the doubles of multiples of 50 to 500. **3A: Problem solving** (*Using techniques and skills in solving mathematical problems*) 3Pt1 – Choose appropriate mental strategies to carry out calculations. 3Pt3 – Make sense of and solve word problems, single (all four operations) and two-step (addition and subtraction), and begin to represent them, e.g. with drawings or on a number line. **3A: Using understanding and strategies in solving problems** 3Ps2 – Explain a choice of calculation strategy and show how the answer was worked out. 3Ps3 – Explore and solve number problems and puzzles. 3Ps5 – Describe and continue patterns which count on or back in steps of 2, 3, 4, 5, 10 or 100. 3Ps6 – Identify simple relationships between numbers. 3Ps8 – Investigate a simple general statement by finding examples which do or do not satisfy it e.g. when adding 10 to a number, the first digit remains the same. 3Ps9 – Explain methods and reasoning orally, including initial thoughts about possible answers to a problem.

*for NRICH activities mapped to the Cambridge Primary objectives, please visit www.cie.org.uk/cambridgeprimarymaths

Vocabulary

double • half • multiple • derive

Resources: You will need the *1000 square* photocopy master (CD-ROM), one per pair. The *Place value cards* photocopy master (CD-ROM), one per pair. A calculator, per pair, and a large 100 square. (Optional: a set of the *Place value cards* photocopy master (CD-ROM) (remove the odd ones cards) per pair, calculator.
Learner Book: counters.

Draw the doubling and halving grid for 1 to 10 where the learners can see it.

1	2	3	4	5	6	7	8	9	10
2	4	6	8	10	12	14	16	18	20

Ask a few quick questions such as, "*What is double eight? What is half of 18?*" and so on. Ask the learners to quickly draw and complete an 11 to 20 doubling and halving grid. Again, ask a few quick questions such as, "*What is double 13? What is half of 36?*" Ask the learners to remind you of the link between doubling and halving, that they are the 'inverse' of each other. Tell the learners that other ways of saying double are 'multiply by two' and 'two times', so the grid is also the two times table. Read the grid as the two times table together – 1 × 2 = 2, 2 × 2 = 4, 3 × 2 = 6 and so on, pointing to the numbers as you say them. Continue to the end of the second grid, ending with 20 times 2 = 40.

Remind the learners how a ten frame shows them that the double of every five must be a 10, so the double of any multiple of five must be a tens number.

Explain that you are going to think ten times bigger and imagine that every five is a 50. Tell the learners that must mean that, "*The double of any multiple of 50 must be a hundreds number.*"

Vocabulary

derive: use known information to find or work out further information.

Look out for!

- Learners who find it hard to move on to multiples of 50. *Use a tens frame to link two fives, then label each square in the tens frame as 10, so that it is now a 100 frame. Show the learners how two fifties (double fifty) is 100. Use several copies of the 100 frame to double multiples of 50.*

10	10	10	10	10
10	10	10	10	10

- Learners whose firm understanding of the number system may extend beyond 1000. *Challenge them to make some thousands place value cards to help them write the larger numbers.*

Tell the learners that you would like them to work in pairs to find out if that is true. Explain that you have a few things that they might find useful, but they do not have to use any of them if they have a better idea. Give each pair of learners a copy of the *1000 square* sheet, a set of ten and hundred Place value *cards* and a calculator. Circulate around the room as the learners work. Support them by asking questions that make them think about what they are doing, for example, *"Is that true? How do you know? How would you convince someone else of that?"* Choose two or three pairs of learners to explain to the rest of the class what they did. Ask the learners, *"Is it true that the double of any multiple of 50 must be a hundreds number?"*

Finish the session by using a *100 square* and then the *1000 square* to show the learners that they already know the five times table and can quickly 'derive' the 50 times table. Read across the 100 square, *"1 × 5 = 5, 2 × 5 = 10, 3 × 5 = 15 and so on to 100."* Then read across the 1000 square, *"1 × 50 = 50, 2 × 50 = 100, 3 × 50 = 150 and so on to 1000."* Explain to the learners that you used the word *derive*. It means using something that you know to find out something else. Go on to explain that in mathematics, you never know just one thing, you can always derive lots more from that one thing.

If there is time, use an example such as double 100 = 200. Ask the learners what else they know from that one fact – half of 200 = 100, double 10 = 20, half of 20 = 10, 2 × 100 = 200 and so on.

Summary

- Learners link doubling with the two times table and extend their understanding of doubling and halving to three-digit numbers.
- They can quickly calculate the double of a multiple of five and 50 and derive the related halves.

Notes on the Learner's Book

Double (and half) trouble (p97): learners ask each other double and half questions, covering the number used on their own page with a counter. Some learners might prefer to work on their own, trying to use all the numbers.

Check up!

- Say a multiple of 50 and ask the learners to tell you its double.
- Then ask for half of the new number and how they are linked.
- Expect learners to use the word **inverse** and be able to explain what it means.

More activities

Place value doubles and halves (pair)

You will need a set of the *Place value cards* photocopy master (CD-ROM) (remove the odd ones cards), per pair.

Learners create a three-digit number using the place value cards: one of the pair halves the hundreds, the other halves the tens and the ones. They add the three halves together to find half of the original number and record it as, for example: **half of 482 is 200 + 40 + 1 = 241** or **half of 368 is 150 + 30 + 4 = 184.** They also find the double of each number, swapping roles, with each other, one finding double the hundreds and the other double the tens and ones. They then add the doubles together to find double the number. So: **double 482 is 800 + 160 + 4 = 964** or **double 368 is 600 + 120 + 16 = 736**. Encourage the learners to use their place value cards to help them add the numbers. Alternatively, some learners could use a calculator. Some learners may need to work with two-digit numbers only.

Quick reference

Core activity 24.1: Complements to 100 (Learner's Book p99)
Learners explore finding complements to 100 and how they can use number pairs for 10 to find out other number pairs.

Core activity 24.2: Assorted addition and subtraction (Learner's Book p102)
Learners explore adding and subtracting one- and two-digit numbers to three-digit numbers.

Core activity 24.3: Sums and differences (Learner's Book p103)
Learners explore sums and differences.

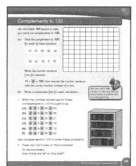
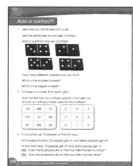

Prior learning	Objectives* – please note that listed objectives might only be partially covered within any given chapter but are covered fully across the book when taken as a whole
• Number pairs for 10. • Multiples of 5 and 10. • Addition and subtraction with single and two-digit numbers.	**3A: Calculation** (*Mental strategies*) 3Nc2 – Know the following addition and subtraction facts: multiples of 100 with a total of 1000; multiples of 5 with a total of 100. **3A: Calculation** (*Addition and subtraction*) 3Nc13 – Find complements to 100, solving number equations such as $78 + \square = 100$. 3Nc14 – Add and subtract pairs of two-digit numbers. 3Nc15 – Add three-digit and two-digit numbers using notes to support. 3Nc17 – Add/subtract single-digit numbers to/from three-digit numbers. 3Nc18 – Find 20, 30, … 90, 100, 200, 300 more/less than three-digit numbers. **3A: Problem solving** (*Using techniques and skills in solving mathematical problems*) 3Pt4 – Check the results of adding two numbers using subtraction, and several numbers by adding in a different order. 3Pt5 – Check subtraction by adding the answer to the smaller number in the original calculation. 3Pt1 – Choose appropriate mental strategies to carry out calculations. 3Pt3 – Make sense of and solve word problems, single (all four operations) and two-step (addition and subtraction), and begin to represent them, e.g. with drawings or on a number line. 3Pt10 – Estimate and approximate when calculating, and check working. 3Pt11 – Make a sensible estimate for the answer to a calculation e.g. using rounding. 3Pt12 – Consider whether an answer is reasonable. **3A: Using understanding and strategies in solving problems** 3Ps2 – Explain a choice of calculation strategy and show how the answer was worked out. 3Ps3 – Explore and solve number problems and puzzles. 3Ps5 – Describe and continue patterns which count on or back in steps of 2, 3, 4, 5, 10 or 100. 3Ps6 – Identify simple relationships between numbers. 3Ps8 – Investigate a simple general statement by finding examples which do or do not satisfy it e.g. when adding 10 to a number, the first digit remains the same. 3Ps9 – Explain methods and reasoning orally, including initial thoughts about possible answers to a problem.

Vocabulary

number pairs • sum • difference

*for NRICH activities mapped to the Cambridge Primary objectives, please visit www.cie.org.uk/cambridgeprimarymaths

---

Resources: You will need the *Blank 100 square* photocopy master (CD-ROM), one per learner. (Optional: paper, pens/pencils.)

Call out or write a two- or three-digit number where everyone can see it. Ask a series of questions such as, "*What is 1, 2, ... 9, 10, 20, 30,...90, 100, 200, 300 more (or less)?*" Remind the learners that they know their number pairs to 10 and use them when they add or subtract. Ask if they can remember their multiples of 10 with a total of 100, then move on to the multiples of 100 with a total of 1000.

$0 + 10 = 10$	$0 + 100 = 100$	$0 + 1000 = 1000$
$1 + 9 = 10$	$10 + 90 = 100$	$100 + 900 = 1000$
$2 + 8 = 10$	$20 + 80 = 100$	$200 + 800 = 1000$
$3 + 7 = 10$	$30 + 70 = 100$	$300 + 700 = 1000$
$4 + 6 = 10$	$40 + 60 = 100$	$400 + 600 = 1000$
$5 + 5 = 10$	$50 + 50 = 100$	$500 + 500 = 1000$

List the multiples and ask the learners to talk with their partner about how they are the same and how they are different. Share the learners' ideas. Make sure that they recognise that the numbers are 10 times bigger in each group.

Begin writing subtraction facts to start three 'subtraction lists':

$10 - 0 = 10$	$100 - 0 = 100$	$1000 - 0 = 1000$
$10 - 1 = 9$	$100 - 10 = 90$	$1000 - 100 = 900$

Ask the learners to copy and complete the three subtraction lists. Remind the learners just how useful it is to know those number bonds to 10 – once they know those they know so much more.

Explain that it is also useful to be able to quickly work out complements to 100. These are all the pairs of numbers which make 100, like 1 and 99, 2 and 98 and so on. Explain that it would be a long list and they would never be able to remember them all, so it is better to know how to find them quickly. To do that they will need a *Blank 100 square*. Ask the learners to check that it is a 100 square. Call out a series of numbers for learners to put a finger in that square. Explain that sometimes the numbers in a 100 square get in the way. Ask the learners to put a finger in 37, then to count on in tens from the bottom, then how many squares to the right of their finger. They should get 63 altogether. Explain that that process is so much easier when the numbers are not there. So they started off with 37 + ☐ = 100 and then found out that ☐ was 63, so 37 + 63 = 100, 37 and 63

Look out for!

- Learners needing help with seeing complements to 100. *They will benefit from cutting blank 100 squares into two pieces, so if they needed to find 37 + ☐ = 100, they could identify 37, cut off that part and count in tens and ones to find out how much more was needed to make 100. So 37 + 63 = 100. Having done this a few times, it is essential that the number pairs to 10 are pointed out, and that one ten, plus the other nine tens makes ten tens, 100.*

- More confident learners. *Encourage them to dispense with the blank 100 square as they can work out the complements mentally, using number pairs to 10 and number pairs of multiples of 10 to 100.*

are complements to 100. Write a series of two-digit numbers where everyone can see them. Ask the learners to work with their partner to find the complement of each number, recording them in a number sentence. So if the number was 59, the complement to 100 is 41 and the number sentence would be 59 + 41 = 100.

After the learners have had sufficient time to find the complements, check their work together. With some of the calculations, ask the learners to check by adding the numbers in a different order.

Tell the learners that they will not always have a blank 100 square to hand, but they can always picture one in their heads if they need to. Explain that they can also think how many are needed to get to the next 10 and then how many more to 100. So if the number they were given was 47, they know that seven and three is ten, so three will get them to 50. They need 50 to get from 50 to 100, so the complement was 53. Explain that what they thought was: 47 → 3→50→53. So 47 + 53 = 100. Ask the learners to draw their thought line for finding the complement of 71. 71 →9→20→29. So 71 + 29 = 100.

Call out a few more numbers for the learners to have a go at finding the complement to 100 without a blank 100 square. Talk through the thought line together.

Summary

Learners can find complements to 100 and use number pairs for 10 to find other number facts.

Notes on the Learner's Book
Complements to 100 (p99): learners explore finding complements to 100 in different ways.

More activities

Number line complements (individual)

You will need paper and pens/pencils.

Give each learner a number (their start number) and ask them to find the complement to 100. The learners draw a number line to 100, mark their start number on it, and use it to explore complements to 100. They draw in a jump to the next multiple of 10 and a jump from there to 100. They add the two jumps together to find the complement to 100 of the start number. They could also draw the matching thought line, to help them see that they are the same.

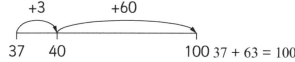

37 + 63 = 100. The matching thought line would be 37 → 3 → 60 → 63.

Some learners may also be able to 'see' the two subtractions, 100 − 37 = 63 and 100 − 63 = 37.

Games Book (ISBN 9781107694019)

Race to 400 (p31) is a game for four to six players. Players compete to add two- and three-digit numbers.

Resources: You will need the *Large Blank 100 square* photocopy master (CD-ROM), one per learner, coloured pencils. The *0 to 9 digit cards* photocopy master (CD-ROM), one per learner. *Number line 0 to 1000 (marked in 10s)* photocopy master (chapter 1, p13), per learner. Place value apparatus. (Optional: two 1–6 dice per group; pens/pencil and paper; double six set of dominoes; counters; pens/pencils; paper.)

Count in multiples of two, three, four, and five to at least 50 with the learners. Use a 100 square for support. End with counting to 100 in multiples of five.

Tell the learners that they just counted in multiples of five to 100. Ask the learners to describe the pattern the multiples make on the 100 square. Give each learner a copy of the *Large Blank 100 square* and ask them to quickly fill in the multiples of five. Once they have done that, ask the learners to ring pairs of multiples of five which make 100. So they should ring 5 and 95, 10 and 90. They might find it helpful to use a different colour for each pair. Ask the learners to make some statements about what they can see. Although they may just suggest that multiples of five have zero or five in the ones place, ask them to look more closely. *"Do there appear to be two sets of pairs? What can we say about each set? If one number in the pair has five ones, does the other number also have five ones? What about zero ones?"* After discussing patterns, tell the learners that you would like them to write one of the subtraction pairs for each of the multiples of five totalling 100. So they might start with $100 - 5 = 95$. Ask them to be systematic so that they know they have written a number sentence for each pair.

Tell the learners that you would like them to practise adding one- and two-digit numbers to a three-digit number, using all the things they know about addition. Give each pair of learners a set of *0 to 9 digit* cards and ask them to remove the zero, then shuffle the cards and put them face down on the table. They then turn over the first three cards, putting them in a row to make a three-digit number. They then turn over the next card and subtract that from the three-digit number. After that, they shuffle all the cards, lay them out in the same way but this time add the single digit number. They then do the same again but after making the three-digit number, they make a two-digit number to subtract. When they have used all the cards, they do the same but add the two-digit number. Provide copies of *Number line 0 to 1000 (marked in 10s)* for support and encourage the learners to make a note of anything they need to remember as they calculate.

Look out for!

- Learners who find adding or subtracting with a three-digit number difficult. *Give them place value apparatus to support their calculations. Make sure they know how to use it. Allow them to choose when to stop using it.*
- More confident learners. *Challenge them to subtract single digit numbers from three-digit numbers such as 304, where all three digits are likely to change.*

As the learners work, circulate around the room asking them how they added (or subtracted) and encouraging them to check using a different method. You should also ask them to estimate the total by rounding the numbers involved.

End the session by working through some of the calculations together, asking learners to estimate before calculating. Focus on just a few calculations, using a range of different methods to find the answer. This could also be the point at which you begin to introduce more formal written methods of calculation using a column layout. This depends upon your school policy. Show learners how to write the same calculation horizontally and vertically.

Summary

Learners can add and subtract a range of numbers using several different methods.

Notes on the Learner's Book
Add or subtract? (p102): learners choose whether to add or subtract a range of numbers. They identify the largest and smallest numbers they can make and answer some addition and subtraction problems.

Check up!
- Say a multiple of five and ask the learners to tell you its pair to make 100.
- Give the learners a three-digit and single-digit addition or subtraction and ask them how they worked out the answer.

More activities

Race to 100 (group)

> You will need two 1–6 dice, pens/pencils and paper.

Players roll the two dice and add the numbers shown. They can do this as many times as they wish during their turn, banking the total when they choose to stop. Once banked, that score is safe and can be added to during their next turn. However, if a double (two identical numbers) is rolled, their score for that round is zero. The target is 100. Which member of the group can get to 100 without going over it first? Can other members of the group get closer to 100, without going over it?

Domino 100 (group, up to nine)

> You will need a double six set of dominoes, counters, pens/pencils and paper.

A set of dominoes is placed face down on a table and mixed up. Each player takes three dominoes and uses them as two-digit numbers. They add the numbers and the closest to 100 earns a counter. The dominoes are returned to the set and mixed up again. The first player to get three counters is the winner.

Core activity 24.3: Sums and differences

> **Resources:** There are no specific resources required for this chapter.

Play a few rounds of *What's in the box?* Draw a box where everyone can see it. Invite learners to give you a number. Write the number in the box if it agrees with your rule (multiples of five, odd numbers, even numbers, numbers where the digits add up to seven and so on) and outside the box if it does not. Once three numbers are in the box, learners can either give you another number or tell you what the rule is. The game is a good opportunity to check learners' understanding of various number properties and pattern spotting.

Ask the learners to give you two two-digit numbers. Write the numbers where everyone can see them. Draw two columns next to the numbers, label them 'sum' and 'difference' and complete them for the numbers given. For example:

	Sum	Difference	Total
23, 45	68	22	90

Ask the learners to explain what sum and difference mean. Once the learners are clear, add the sum and difference together. Tell the learners that you don't think they will be able to find a sum and difference greater than 100 using two different two-digit numbers, so you would just like them to explore the different totals they can make. Circulate around the room as the learners work, encouraging them to check their totals and to try a different method. It should not take long before someone finds a total above 100, so tell the learners that since they have found a total that is more than 100, it must be that they cannot make a total over 200. Ask the learners to keep exploring and find the largest total they can. Remind them that they can only use two two-digit numbers.

After the learners have had plenty of time to explore, find out the highest and lowest totals made. Look at the numbers used with the learners to see if the numbers can be changed to make the total even higher, or lower. The highest total can be made by adding 99 and 10 to get 109, their difference is 89 so the total is 198. They could also make 198 using 99 and 98. The smallest total can be made using 10 and 11. Their total is 22 (sum 21 and a difference of 1). Ask the learners if they have noticed anything about their results. If they haven't, ask

Vocabulary

sum: the answer to an addition calculation. So, for 23 + 19 = 42, 42 is the sum.

difference: how much bigger or smaller one quantity or number is than another.

Look out for!

- Learners who think that the word 'sum' means any calculation. *Correct this misuse of the language so that such misconceptions do not continue. Occasionally ask for the sum of two numbers to check that the learners know what 'sum' means.*
- Learners who are confident about performing additions. *Ask them to make a particular total and once they have done this, ask them to make the same total using different numbers. Go on to challenge them to make the same number in lots of different ways.*

if any of their totals are even, then ask if any of their totals are odd. (None of them are odd). Draw up a chart with the learners to help them understand why this happens.

	Sum	difference	total
Odd, odd	even	even	even
Even, even	even	even	even
Even, odd	odd	odd	even

Summary

Learners can add and subtract pairs of two-digit numbers.

Notes on the Learner's Book

Sums and differences – target 1000 (p103): learners total sums and differences aiming to find a total of 1000. Challenge some learners to change their chosen numbers until they can total exactly 1000.

Check up!
- Ask learners what we mean by sum or difference.
- Give them two numbers and ask them to find the sum or the difference or both.

More activities

Patterns (any number)

Explore sums and differences with different sets of numbers. For example, multiples of 10 or multiples of 100. Ask the learners to look for any patterns in their results.

Games Book (ISBN 9781107694019)

Dice differences (p31) is a game for two players. Players subtract pairs of two-digit numbers.

Blank page

Quick reference

Core activity 25.1: Multiplication with open arrays (Learner's Book p104)
Learners explore using a rectangle to help them multiply teen numbers by 2, 3, 4, 5, 6 and 9.

Core activity 25.2: Division with open arrays (Learner's Book p107)
Learners explore using a rectangle to help them divide two-digit numbers by 2, 3, 4, 5, 6, 9 and 10.

Core activity 25.3: Division stories (Learner's Book p108)
Learners explore the meaning of a remainder to help them interpret a division calculation with a remainder.

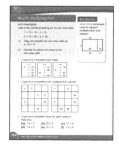
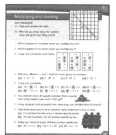

Prior learning	Objectives* – please note that listed objectives might only be partially covered within any given chapter but are covered fully across the book when taken as a whole
• 2, 3, 5, 10 times tables. • Experience of the 4 times table. • Multiplication as an array. • Some understanding of the link between multiplication and division.	**3A: Calculation** (*Mental strategies*) 3Nc3 – Know multiplication/division facts for 2×, 3×, 5×, and 10× tables. 3Nc4 – Begin to know 4× table. **3A: Calculation** (*Multiplication and division*) 3Nc21 – Multiply single-digit numbers and divide two-digit numbers by 2, 3, 4, 5, 6, 9 and 10. 3Nc22 – Multiply teens numbers by 3 and 5. 3Nc23 – Begin to divide two-digit numbers just beyond 10× tables, e.g. 60 ÷ 5, 33 ÷ 3. 3Nc24 – Understand that division can leave a remainder (initially as 'some left over'). 3Nc26 – Understand the relationship between multiplication and division and write connected facts. **3A: Problem solving** (*Using techniques and skills in solving mathematical problems*) 3Pt6 – Check multiplication by reversing the order, e.g. checking that 6 × 4 = 24 by doing 4 × 6. 3Pt7 – Check a division using multiplication, e.g. check 12 ÷ 4 = 3 by doing 4 × 3. 3Pt1 – Choose appropriate mental strategies to carry out calculations. 3Pt3 – Make sense of and solve word problems and begin to represent them. 3Pt10 – Estimate and approximate when calculating, and check working. 3Pt11 – Make a sensible estimate for the answer to a calculation e.g. using rounding. 3Pt12 – Consider whether an answer is reasonable. **3A: Using understanding and strategies in solving problems** 3Ps1 – Make up a number story to go with a calculation. 3Ps2 – Explain a choice of calculation strategy and show how the answer was worked out. 3Ps3 – Explore and solve number problems and puzzles. 3Ps5 – Describe and continue patterns which count on or back in steps of 2, 3, 4, 5, 10 or 100. 3Ps6 – Identify simple relationships between numbers. 3Ps8 – Investigate a simple general statement by finding examples which do or do not satisfy it. 3Ps9 – Explain methods and reasoning orally, including initial thoughts about possible answers to a problem.

Vocabulary

difference • multiplication • multiply • division • divide • array • open array • sum

*for NRICH activities mapped to the Cambridge Primary objectives, please visit www.cie.org.uk/cambridgeprimarymaths

Core activity 25.1: Multiplication with open arrays

Resources: You will need a collection of counters. (Optional: two 1–6 dice (CD-ROM); A4 sheets of paper; pens/pencils; small pieces of paper; a bag or envelope.)

Count on or back with the learners in steps of two, three, four, five, 10 or 100.

Ask the learners to describe the pattern of the numbers they have just said. End the counting by saying the 5 × table and asking the learners some quick times tables questions from the two, three, five and 10 times tables.

Ask the learners to remind you what an **array** is. Check that the learners remember that it is an arrangement of counters (or cubes, crosses or dots) that help you to see multiplication and division facts. Draw a 3 by 4 grid and ask the learners to tell you the related multiplication and division facts. Explain that what they told you is absolutely true, but as you start working with bigger numbers, we might easily run out of counters, cubes or even squared paper. Explain that it is enough to simply label a rectangle. Draw a rectangle and label the longer side four and the shorter side three. Explain that the rectangle can be anything we want it to be. Ask, "*What if we were multiplying five by 12?*" Show the learners how useful it would be to label the rectangle five and 12, then split the 12 into 10 and two. This is helpful because we know that 10 × 5 = 50 and 2 × 5 = 10, so 12 × 5 = 50 + 10 = 60.

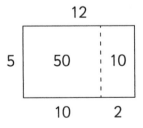

Ask the learners to work with their partner to work out 17 × 5. Talk through what they did, focusing on what they know. They could split the rectangle into 10 × 5 and 7 × 5 or 10 × 5, 5 × 5 and 2 × 5, whatever they find most useful. Explain that this is an **open array**.

Vocabulary

multiply/multiplication: a quicker way of doing repeated addition. For example, 2 + 2 + 2 + 2 + 2 = 10

$$2 \times 5 = 10$$

array: items arranged in rows or columns, as in a grid. For example,

```
                      column
row →   x x x x x  }2 × 5
        x x x x x  }5 × 2
```

open array: rectangle used to support multiplication and division.

$$12 \times 5 = 50 + 10 = 60$$

| | 12 | | $60 \div 5 = 12$ |

```
        12
    +---------+---+
 5  |   50    | 10|
    +---------+---+
       10      2
```

Look out for!

- Learners who find it difficult to liken a rectangle to an array. *Make an array with them and draw around the outside of it. Label the rectangle and remove the counters, then ask the learners to draw one for a similar calculation.*

Write some multiplications using teen numbers multiplied by two, three, four and five (for example: 13 × 3, 16 × 3, 15 × 5, 17 × 2, 14 × 4) and ask the learners to work through them using the rectangle, even if they know the answer. Explain that knowing the answer helps them to get to know the method better, so that they can use it confidently when they don't know the answer. Challenge learners who complete all the calculations you have written to choose one (or more) of their own calculations to solve. Circulate as the learners explore, asking questions such as, "How are you going to split the 17 to help you? Label your rectangle so you don't get in a muddle." Encourage learners to check their calculations by multiplying in a different order. After the learners have had plenty of time to explore, work through one or more of the questions together, checking that everyone understands what they are doing and why they are doing it.

Show the learners that we can use the grid to solve a missing number puzzle too.
Write □ × 15 = 90.
Draw the array then talk through, noticing that 3 × 5 = 15 and 3 × 30 = 90, so I can split the box into three, and each of those three pieces are 30. So, for □ × 5 = 30, I know that □ must be six because 6 × 5 = 30. So if there are six fives in each 30, there must be six fifteens in 90.

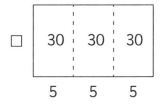

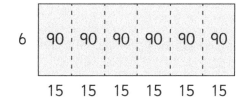

End the session by inviting different learners to tell everyone a story to match one of multiplication calculations.

- Learners who are confident with the correspondence between rectangle and array. *Challenge them to multiply larger two-digit numbers by a single digit number. Some could move on to multiplying two two-digit numbers together or solving missing number problems such as □ × 15 = 90, as demonstrated during the session.*

Summary

Learners can use a rectangle as an open array, to support multiplying teen numbers by two, three, four, five, six and nine.

Notes on the Learner's Book
Much multiplication (p104): learners solve a range of multiplication calculations and problems.

Check up!
- Draw and label a rectangle. Ask the learners what multiplication calculation it could be used for.
- You could give the learners a calculation and ask them to draw the rectangle to help them solve it. It is not always necessary to go on to solve the calculation.

More activities

Multiple bingo (class)

You will need two 1–6 dice (CD-ROM), A4 sheets of paper, pens/pencils.

Complete a 1 to 6 multiplication square with the learners to find out which numbers can be made by multiplying the numbers on the dice together. Then ask learners to fold a piece of A4 paper in half, then half again and a third time. When they open it up, they will have eight spaces. They choose eight numbers from the multiplication square and write one number in each space. Roll the dice and call out the multiplication shown on the dice. Learners work out the total or look it up on the multiplication square. They then cross out the number on their grid if they have it. The winner is the first person to cross out all their numbers.

Tell me a story (group or class)

You will need small pieces of paper, a bag or envelope.

Write a series of multiplication number sentences with or without the answer on small pieces of paper. Put them in a bag or envelope and invite learners to pick out a piece of paper without looking and tell the group (or class) a matching story.

Orchestra (group)

Put the learners into groups and give each group a times table. When you point to a group, they say the multiples in their times table. When they reach the tenth multiple, they start again. Point to different groups. Learners must watch closely so they stop counting when you move your pointer away from them and start counting as soon as you point to them. Alternatively, have the learners seated in groups. Again, give each group a particular times table. Count together from one, with learners standing up for each number that is in their times table. So on four, both the two and four times tables groups should be standing. On 10, the two, five and 10 times table groups should be standing, and so on.

Games Book (ISBN 9781107694019)

Only snakes (p33) is a game for two to four players. Players multiply single-digit and low two-digit numbers by 2, 3, 4, 5, 6, 9 and 10.

Core activity 25.2: Division with open arrays

LB: p107

Resources: You will need counters or cubes. (Optional: one 1–6 dice (CD-ROM) and *1–100 Number cards* photocopy master (CD-ROM); use the teen cards only; A4 sheets of paper and pens/pencils; small pieces of paper and a small bag or envelope; hoops or chalk, mini whiteboards; paper and pens/pencils).

Count on or back with the learners in steps of two, three, four, five, 10 or 100. Ask the learners to describe the pattern of the numbers they have just said. End the counting by saying the three times table and asking the learners some quick times tables questions from the two, three, four, five, six, nine and 10 times tables. It might be helpful to refer back to Core Activity 25.1: Multiplication with open grids.

Tell the learners that they have used an open array for multiplication; now they are going to use the same approach for division. Draw a rectangle and write the calculation 39 ÷ 3. Ask the learners to tell you something they know about 30 and 3. They should be able to tell you that 10 × 3 = 30. Complete the relevant parts of the diagram as below.

39 ÷ 3 =

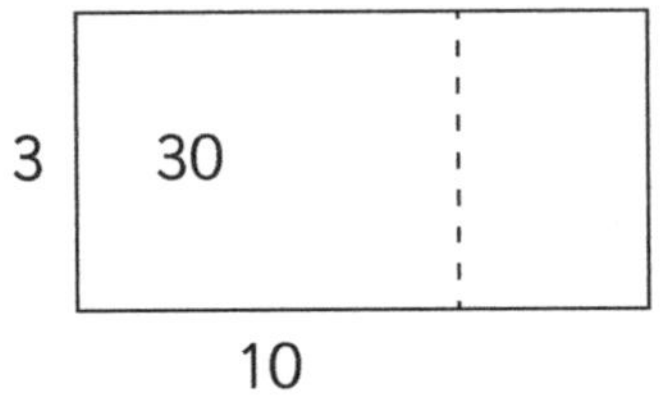

Now ask the learners what 39 – 30 is and mark it on the diagram. Ask the learners, how many threes in nine and mark it on the diagram.

39 ÷ 3 = 13

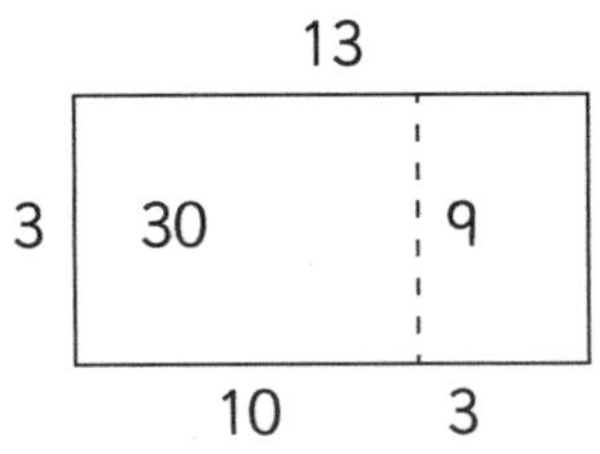

Now the learners should recognise that 10 threes and three threes make 39 so 39 ÷ 3 = 13. If necessary, work through a second example.

Vocabulary

divide/division: grouping or sharing a quantity into smaller, equally sized groups.

Look out for!

- Learners who find it difficult to use an open array as shown here. *Encourage them to draw a large rectangle and use cubes or counters within the rectangle. After a while they may be able to dispense with some or all of the counters or cubes.*
- Learners who find it straightforward to use an open array. *Challenge them to divide random larger numbers so that they have to think about how they will deal with remainders.*

Write a series of two-digit division by two, three, four and five calculations (for example 24 ÷ 2, 72 ÷ 2, 27 ÷ 3, 48 ÷ 3, 68 ÷ 4, 95 ÷ 5) and ask the learners to work through them using the rectangle, even if they know the answer. Remind them that knowing the answer helps them to get to know the method better, so that they can use it confidently when they don't know the answer. Challenge learners who complete all the calculations you have written to choose one (or more) of their own calculations to solve. Circulate, as the learners explore, asking questions such as, *"How are you going to split the 48 to help you? Which multiplication fact do you know that will be useful? Label your rectangle so you don't get in a muddle."* Encourage learners to check their calculations by multiplying.

After the learners have had plenty of time to explore, work through one or more of the questions together, checking that everyone understands what they are doing and why they are doing it.

End the session by inviting different learners to tell everyone a story to match one of multiplication calculations.

Summary

Learners can use a rectangle as an open array, to support dividing by two, three, four, five, six, nine and 10.

Notes on the Learner's Book
Multiplying and dividing (p107): learners solve multiplication and division calculations and division problems.

Check up!
- Draw and label a rectangle. Ask the learners what division calculation it could be used for.
- You could give the learners a calculation and ask them to draw the rectangle to help them solve it. It is not always necessary to go on to solve the calculation.

More activities

Multiple bingo 2 (class)

You will need one 1–6 dice and teen number cards, A4 sheets of paper, pens/pencils.

Extend multiple bingo to include teen numbers. Complete a multiplication square for 11 to 19 × 1 to 6. Learners make a bingo board as before. Use a 1–6 dice and teen number cards to generate the numbers. Learners look up the answer to the multiplication on the multiplication square.

The answer is… (individual)

Give the learners a number between 1 and 50. Tell them that this is the answer and ask them what the question could be. Allow addition and subtraction suggestions from some learners initially, but move on to accept only multiplication and division suggestions. You may need to model this for the learners the first time – $1 \times 50 = 50$, $2 \times 25 = 50$, $5 \times 10 = 50$, $10 \times 5 = 50$, $200 \div 4 = 50$ and so on. 10, 20, 30, 40 and 50 are easier numbers to work with.

Tell me a story (group or class)

> You will need small pieces of paper and a small bag or envelope.

Write a series of division number sentences with or without the answer on small pieces of paper. Put them in a bag or envelope and invite learners to pick out a piece of paper without looking and tell the group (or class) a matching story.

Class division (class)

> You will need hoops or chalk, mini whiteboards.

In a large open space, either place some hoops on the ground or draw them with chalk. The hoops need to be large enough for up to 10 learners to stand inside. Ask the learners to predict if the class can be divided exactly by two, three, four, five, six, nine or 10. Call out two, three, four, five, six, nine or 10. The learners make groups of that number within the hoops or circles. Anyone left over is a remainder. Ask some learners to say the division that has been demonstrated. Alternatively, each hoop could have a mini-whiteboard for learners to record and show the division calculation they are modelling.

What else do you know? (individual)

> You will need paper and pens/pencils.

Give learners a multiplication such as $5 \times 9 = 45$ and ask them to make list of what else they know. This could extend from the fact family to doubling ($10 \times 9 = 90$ or $5 \times 18 = 90$) to multiplying by 10 ($50 \times 9 = 450$ or $5 \times 90 = 450$) to various measures ($5 \times 9 \text{ cm} = 45\text{cm}$).

Resources: You will need the *Large blank 100 square* photocopy master (CD-ROM). (Optional: A4 sheets of paper, pens/pencils; paper and pens/pencils; small pieces of paper, a bag or envelope.)

Count on or back with the learners in steps of two, three, four, five, 10 or 100. Ask the learners to describe the pattern of the numbers they have just said. End the counting by saying the 4 × table, using a large 100 square for support if necessary, and asking the learners some quick times tables questions from the two, three, four, five, six, nine and 10 times tables.

Tell the learners that they have worked really well with the open array earlier in Core Activity 25.1: Multiplication with open arrays, but division doesn't always work out exactly. Sometimes there is some left over. Ask the learners if they can remember what this is called (**the remainder**). Explain that it isn't just a case of finding an answer, you also need to think about what the answer means. Work through 17 ÷ 5 = 3 r2 with the learners. Explain that this calculation could be about learners sitting at tables to eat their lunch. Ask, "*If a table seats five learners, how many tables do you need for 17 learners? You might carry out the calculation and say that the answer is three tables because 17 ÷ 5 = 3 r2. But what about the other two learners? Do they have to sit on the floor? That does not seem fair. So although the answer to the division calculation is 3 r2, we would go on to say four tables were needed.*" Tell the learners another division story, for example, "*48 people need to cross a river. Each boat carries five people. How many boat journeys will be needed to get all the people across the river?*" Ask the learners to carry out the calculation, then consider what the answer actually means.

> Write some division problems that will have remainders where everyone can see them. Make sure some need to be rounded up while others do not. Ask the learners to work through the problems and to check their calculations by multiplying. Circulate as the learners explore asking questions such as, "*What is the calculation you need to do? What does the answer tell you?*"

After the learners have had plenty of time to explore, work through one or more of the questions together, checking that everyone understands why it was sometimes necessary to increase the answer by one. End the session by writing up some calculations with remainders and asking different learners to tell the rest of the class a matching story.

Vocabulary

remainder: what is left over after division.

Look out for!

- Learners who still find it difficult to use an open array to help them. *Encourage them to use cubes or counters and draw around them to produce a rectangle.*
- *Some learners will leave too large a remainder when they divide. For example, 16 ÷ 5 = 2 r6. This is likely to be because they rely heavily on a few facts they know, such as 2 × 5 = 10. Explain that the remainder cannot be bigger than the number they are dividing by. Model the division on a number line with counters and show how another group of five can be made, so 16 ÷ 5 = 3 r1.*
- Learners who find using an open array straightforward. *Challenge them to divide random larger numbers by a single digit number. They may find it helpful to work in chunks as in the open array, but with or without an array.*
  For example
  78 ÷ 4
  10 × 4 = 40
  5 × 4 = 20
  4 × 4 = 16
  So 78 ÷ 4 = 19 r2

Summary

Learners can interpret the answer to a division problem that has a remainder.

Notes on the Learner's Book

What does a remainder mean? (p108): practice questions with remainders and problem solving interpreting the remainder.

Check up!

Tell the learners a division problem with a remainder and ask them to explain what the answer means.

More activities

Division bingo (class or group)

> You will need A4 sheets of paper, pens/pencils.

Complete a 1 to 9 multiplication square with the learners to find out which numbers can be made by multiplying two single-digits together. Then ask learners to fold a piece of A4 paper as before and choose eight numbers 1 to 9, but they can repeat any number two or three times. They write one number in each space. Call out a division calculation that will leave a remainder, for example $26 \div 6$.

Learners use the multiplication square to help them find the remainder. $26 \div 6 = 4\ r2$, so learner can cross out a 2 if they have one. The winner is the first person to cross out all their numbers. Play the game with small groups before playing it with the whole class.

The answer is… (individual)

> You will need paper and pens/pencils.

Give the learners a number between 1 and 20 and a remainder. Tell them that this is the answer and ask them what the question could be. Allow only division answers. So if the number you give is 4 r1, the question could have been $21 \div 5$, $17 \div 4$, $13 \div 3$ and so on.

Tell me a remainder story (group or class)

> You will need small pieces of paper, a bag or envelope.

Write a series of division number sentences with remainders on small pieces of paper. Put them in a bag or envelope and invite learners to pick out a piece of paper without looking and tell the group (or class) a matching story.

Blank page

Quick reference

Core activity 26.1: Finding and drawing right angles (Learner's Book p110)

The core activity 1 revises work already done on angles and introduces learners to the use of a set square to find and draw right angles.

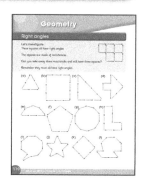

Prior learning	Objectives* – please note that listed objectives might only be partially covered within any given chapter but are covered fully across the book when taken as a whole
• Knowledge of right angles in 2D shape. • Knowledge of right angles in the immediate environment. • Skill of using a ruler.	**3B: Shapes and geometric reasoning** 3Gs8 – Identify right angles in 2D shapes. **3B: Position and movement** 3Gp3 – Use a set square to draw right angles. 3Gp4 – Compare angles with a right angle and recognise that a straight line is equivalent to two right angles. 3Gs1 – Identify, describe and draw regular and irregular 2D shapes including pentagons, hexagons, octagons and semi-circles. 3Gs2 – Classify 2D shapes according to the number of sides, vertices and right angles. 3Gs3 – Identify, describe and make 3D shapes including pyramids and prisms; investigate which nets will make a cube.

*for NRICH activities mapped to the Cambridge Primary objectives, please visit www.cie.org.uk/cambridgeprimarymaths

Vocabulary

make • build • draw • straight line • triangle • square • greater/smaller than a right triangle • right-angled

Core activity 26.1: Finding and drawing right angles

LB: p110

> **Resources:** You will need the *Angle cards* photocopy master (p222), one set in an envelope per group. Set squares (per learner). Paper. Rulers (per learner). *Right angle recording sheet* photocopy master (CD-ROM), per learner, equal strips of cardboard (2 to 3 cm wide) and split pins. (Optional: paper and pens/pencils; two sticks (or similar) and a camera.)

Start the session by revising the properties of 2D and 3D shapes, focusing on right angles. For example, ask, *"Tell me a shape that has four right angles,"* (**square, rectangle**) *"Tell me the name of a shape that has only one right angle,"* (**right-angled triangle**). Demonstrate if necessary.

Then say, *"Look around you. Tell me something that you can see that has right angles."* (**door, cupboard, book**).

Tell the class that today you are going to work on right angles. Give each group an envelope containing the angle cards. Say, *"You have one minute to match the numbers and words up correctly."* Give time for the activity. Then ask, *"What did you find out?"* Discuss the results.

Explain that an **angle** is a measure of turn. Ask the learners to stand behind their chairs and give them instructions. *"Turn one right angle to the right. Turn two right angles to the right. Now turn one more right angle to the right. What do you notice?"*

Now say, *"Turn five right angles to your right."* Watch how the learners respond to this. Did they all turn five right angles or did some realise that they only needed to turn one? Ask, *"How many right angles did you turn? Who turned five? Some of you only turned one. Why was this?"* Establish that to make a complete turn, you turn through four right angles, so to turn five they could have stayed where they were (which would be four) and then turned one more.

Now say, *"I want you to turn nine right angles. Think about what you did when you turned four."*

Show the class a set square, *"A set square is used to find or draw right angles. Which of these corners is a right angle?"*

Look out for!

- Learners who find it difficult to use the set square. *Give them a 'right angle finder' (a circle with a right angle cut out) instead. Alternatively, give each pair two strips of cardboard fixed together at one end using a split pin. Ask the learners to move the strips to make right angles, straight lines, and so on.*
- Learners who are competent with using the set square. *Encourage them to use it to construct more complex shapes that have right angles. Moving on from the straight line they can rotate it and make a square or a rectangle or an irregular pentagon with right angles at the bottom two corners (like a house).*

Ask the learners to draw a large triangle with no sides or angles that are the same. They should then use a ruler to find and mark the mid-point of each side, and join the midpoints to make another triangle. Ask, "*What do you notice about the smaller triangle? Use your set square to see if you have produced a right angle in your smaller triangle.*"

Now ask the learners to use their rulers to draw a line 20 cm long and make a mark at 10 cm. They should then put their set square on that mark and draw a vertical line. Ask, "*What do you see?*" (**two right angles**) Then ask, "*What if you took that vertical line away? What would be left?*" (**a straight line**) "*So, two right angles together make a straight line. If one right angles is 90 degrees, what would two be?*" (**180**) "*So, the angle along a straight line would measure 180 degrees.*"

Ask the learners to draw more right angles using their set squares. Give time for this activity.

Finally, say "*Now you know how to use a set square to make a right angle, use it to find right angles in the classroom. Draw and write what you find.*" Give the learners the *Right angle recording sheet.*

Summary

By the end of this session the learners will have learnt how to use a set square to find and draw right angles.

Notes on the Learner's Book
Right angles (p110): this takes what the learner has learnt about right angles and applies it to puzzles and problems to solve.

Check up!
Ask the learners:
- "*Tell me something that you can see that has a right angle.*"
- "*Tell me something that you can see that does not have a right angle.*"
- "*Tell me something that you can see that has two right angles side by side*" (**straight line**).

More activities

Right angles at home (individual)

You will need paper and pens/pencils.

Ask the learners to look around their houses for different angles and then draw and label them and estimate their measure in degrees (e.g. they could draw the angle of the corner of the kitchen window, label it as a right angle and estimate its measure at 90°).

Right angles outside (individual)

You will need natural materials (e.g. sticks) to make right angles, and a camera.

Take photos to make a 'My book of right angles outside.' This could also be done inside so that comparisons can be made between the two environments.

Angle cards

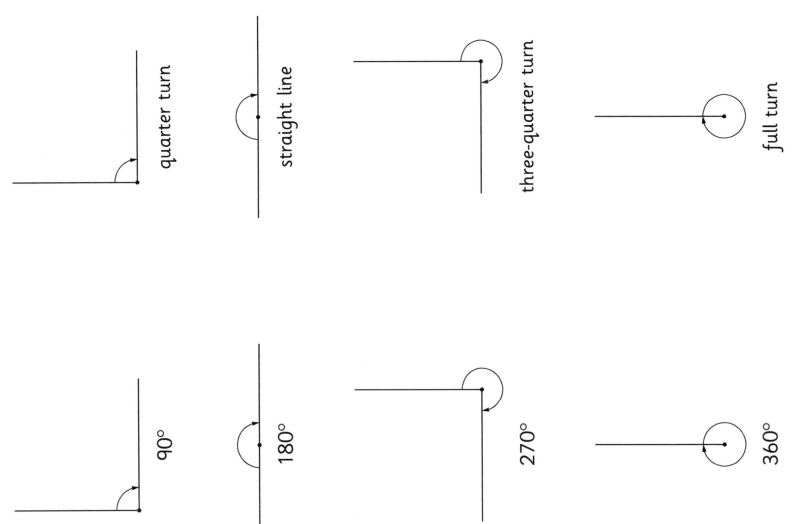

quarter turn — 90°

straight line — 180°

three-quarter turn — 270°

full turn — 360°

Instructions on page 220

Quick reference

Core activity 27.1: Lines of symmetry (Learner's Book p112)

This activity uses paper folding to explore the idea of symmetry. Learners create their own designs and use those to discuss the properties of symmetrical shapes and lines of symmetry.

Core activity 27.2: Identifying symmetrical shapes (Learner's Book p114)

This activity develops symmetry further by using the local environment of the classroom to find and record where symmetry and right-angled triangles feature.

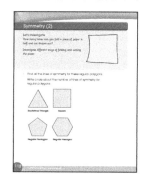

Prior learning	Objectives* – please note that listed objectives might only be partially covered within any given chapter but are covered fully across the book when taken as a whole
Knowledge and understanding of symmetry and associated vocabulary.	**3B: Shapes and geometric reasoning** 3Gs5 – Draw and complete 2D shapes with reflective symmetry and draw reflections of shapes (mirror line along one side). 3Gs7 – Identify 2D and 3D shapes, lines of symmetry and right angles in the environment. **3B: Using understanding and strategies in solving problems** 3Ps7 – Identify simple relationships between shapes, e.g. these shapes all have the same number of lines of symmetry.

*for NRICH activities mapped to the Cambridge Primary objectives, please visit www.cie.org.uk/cambridgeprimarymaths

Vocabulary

symmetrical • line of symmetry • mirror line • reflection

Resources: Paper. Scissors. *Symmetry activity sheet* photocopy master (p228), one copy per learner, Squared paper, (Optional: sheets of paper; scissors; colouring pencils.)

Give each learner a piece of paper and some scissors. Say, *"Fold the paper so that opposite sides are touching. Fold again so the other sides are touching. Open the paper. You have folded it into quarters."* Check that all learners have quarters. Then say, *"Re-fold the paper along the same fold lines. Cut shapes in the paper along the edges that are not folds so that pieces come out. Leave the paper folded and look at the pieces that have come out. What do you notice?"* Establish that there are four identical copies of each shape. Then ask, *"Can you predict what your design will be when you open the paper? Draw what you think it will look like. Use the pieces that you cut out to help you."* Give time for the learners to do this. Open out your folded sheet of paper.

Then ask, *"How close was your drawing? Look at your design. What do you notice about it? Talk to your partner."* Gather feedback and establish that the design has two lines of symmetry.

Then ask, *"How many pieces did you cut out when the paper was folded?"* (Could be one, two, three, four …)? *"How many pieces do you have?"* Write the number of pieces on the board (4, 8, 12, 16 …) Ask, *"What do you notice about these numbers?"* (**multiples of four**) *"Why does that happen?"*

Tell the learners to fold another piece of paper in the same way as before. *"This time, cut shapes from the folded edges. Open out the pieces. What do you notice about these shapes?"* (**They have at least one line of symmetry.**)

Ask, *"What do you think the design on your paper will look like? Will it have lines of symmetry like before? Where will the holes be? Draw it before you open it."* Give time for this to happen.

Then ask, *"What do you notice this time? Is it the same as before or different? Where were the gaps last time when you cut the open edges? Where are they this time when you cut the folded edges? What would you have to do to get some shapes on the edge or some shapes in the middle or some shapes both at the edge and in the middle"?*

Tell the learners they are going to explore cutting paper to make shapes that are symmetrical as well as leaving a pattern that is symmetrical.

Show and explain the *Symmetry activity sheet*.

Vocabulary

reflection: in the context of the line of symmetry, this is the image that is reflected in the mirror line.

Look out for!

- Learners who may have difficulty following folding instructions. *Model them slowly and clearly, next to the learner if necessary. It won't help their learning if it is done for them (unless there are physical difficulties).*
- Learners who find this activity easy and finish it quickly. *Ask them to fold a square of paper diagonally and predict the shapes that will come out and the pattern that is left.*

Opportunities for display!

The completed symmetrical patterns.

At the end of the session, discuss what the learners did and what they found out. Ask, "*Did you find any shapes that, although they looked different, all had the same number of lines of symmetry?*" Tell us about that.

Summary

By the end of this session learners will have drawn and completed 2D shapes with reflective symmetry and drawn reflections of shapes. They will have been able to identify simple relationships between shapes, e.g. these shapes all have the same number of lines of symmetry.

Notes on the Learner's Book

Symmetry 2 (p112): this builds on the activities in the session and allows learners to complete symmetrical patterns for practice and assessment as well as to design some of their own.

Check up!

Ask questions such as:
- "*Can you tell me two shapes that have a line of symmetry? Draw them on the board.*"
- "*Do all shapes have a line of symmetry?*" (**not irregular shapes**)
- "*What types of shapes have a line of symmetry?*" (**regular**)

More activities

Folding (individual)

> You will need sheets of paper and scissors.

Instead of folding the paper as in *Core activity 27.1*, fold it vertically. Make some cuts and predict the shape that will be left. Does it have a line of symmetry? Do the pieces cut out have lines of symmetry?

Real-life patterns (individual)

Explore patterns and designs in real life contexts: wallpaper, fabric, buildings. Where can you see symmetry? Use photographs from magazines or old calendars.

Aliens (individual)

> You will need paper, colouring pencils and scissors.

Make a set of symmetrical aliens for display. Fold a sheet of paper in half and draw the outline of half on alien on one side, then cut it out. Draw and colour symmetrical features (eyes, clothes, buttons) on the alien.

Games Book (ISBN 9781107694019)

Build the pattern (p39) is a game for two players. Players identify simple relationships between shapes and identify lines of symmetry.

Core activity 27.2: Identifying symmetrical shapes

Resources: You will need the *Symmetry recording sheet* photocopy master (CD-ROM), two copies per learner. Mirrors. A selection of symmetrical and non-symmetrical shapes. (Optional: a pack of cards showing both symmetrical and non-symmetrical shapes; paper; paint; paintbrushes; potatoes; knives; fabric.)

Remind the class that in the previous session they made their own symmetrical designs. Tell them that today they are going to look for symmetry around them. "*Look round the classroom. Can you see anything that is symmetrical? Tell your partner what it is.*" Give time for learners to do this activity and then choose some of them to feedback.

Now give each learner a copy of the *Symmetry recording sheet*. "*Each of you will record what you find out about symmetry in the classroom on the sheet, but you are going to work in pairs so that you can share and discuss ideas.*"

Tell the learners to find eight things and draw them. "*They can be 2D or 3D. Count how many lines of symmetry they have and how many right angles. Write that on your sheet. Add the two numbers together to get your score. The score is just for you, this is not a competition. But when we do this activity again, see if you can beat your score of today. Or you could try it at home.*"

As the class is working, walk round to make sure that all learners understand the task. Use it as an opportunity to correct or reinforce language associated with symmetry: symmetrical, mirror line, reflection, line of symmetry.

At the end of the session, ask, "*How many different symmetrical things did you find? Did they all have right angles? Tell me something that was symmetrical with no right angles.*" (e.g. door knob, circle, equilateral triangle)

Then ask, "*I wonder what it would be like to live in a world where everything is symmetrical. Would that be a good idea? Why/why not?*" Encourage discussion.

Finally, ask, "*Why do we need symmetry?*"

Look out for!

- Learners who find it difficult to recognise symmetry. *Give them a mirror to help. Put some shapes on a table for them to explore rather than walking around the room.*
  - *Give learners cut-out pictures or shapes so that they can fold them in half to find if they are symmetrical.*
- Learners who have grasped the concept of symmetry. *Encourage them to work with pictures or shapes that have more than one line of symmetry.*
  - *Use square paper folded into four to give four quadrants.*

Summary

By the end of this session learners will have identified and drawn 2D and 3D shapes with lines of symmetry and right angles from the immediate environment of the classroom.

Notes on the Learner's Book
Symmetry 3 (p114): this asks learners to complete questions on symmetry to give an assessment of knowledge and understanding of what they have learnt in the session.

Check up!

Ask questions such as:
- *"How do you know this shape has a line of symmetry?"*
- *"Find two shapes that have for than one line of symmetry."*
- *"Tell me about a right angle."*

More activities

<u>**Snap**</u> (group or class)

> You will need a pack of cards showing both symmetrical and non-symmetrical shapes (you may need to make your own).

Play snap with the cards. The player at the end of the game with most cards is the winner.

<u>**Paint blobs**</u> (individual)

> You will need paper, paint, paintbrushes.

Fold a piece of paper in half vertically, open it out. Put paint blobs on one half, fold the paper over again and gently press. When the paint is dry, fold the paper in half horizontally and repeat. What can you see when the paper is opened? Describe and discuss.

<u>**Printing**</u> (individual)

> You will need potatoes, knives, paint and paper or fabric.

Cut a potato in half and carve a design. On paper or fabric use the carved potato design dipped in paint to make a symmetrical pattern.

Symmetry activity sheet

These shapes have been made by cutting folded paper.

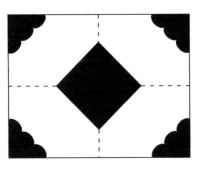

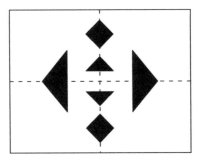

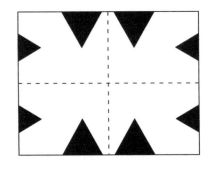

Two shapes cut from open edges.

Three shapes cut from folded edges.

One shape cut from open edge and one shape cut from folded edges

1. Look where the folds are and make cuts to form these patterns.
   Draw your patterns when you have made them.
2. Look at the pieces you cut out to make the patterns.
   Find all the pieces that *do not* have a fold line of symmetry.
   Draw one of each of these pieces on squared paper.
   Draw a line of symmetry and reflect the shape in it.
   For example:

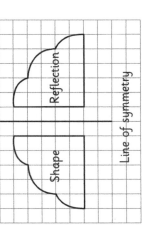

3. Using folded paper, make a design by cutting out just one shape.
   Open out the paper and draw it.
4. Using folded paper, make a design but cutting out two shapes.
   Open and draw it.
5. Look at the lines of symmetry in your shapes.
   Can you find shapes that have the same number of lines of symmetry but don't look the same as each other?
   Draw them on square paper.

Quick reference

Core activity 28.1: Moving and turning (Learner's Book p116)

This activity uses the language and vocabulary of movement starting with a practical activity then moving to group work and problems set by the learners.

Core activity 28.2: Co-ordinates (Learner's Book p118)

This activity examines the use co-ordinates to locate areas in a graph.

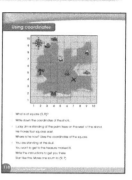

Prior learning	Objectives* – please note that listed objectives might only be partially covered within any given chapter but are covered fully across the book when taken as a whole
Knowledge and understanding of the language and vocabulary associated with movement.	**3B: Position and movement** 3Gp1 – Use the language of position, direction and movement, including clockwise and anti-clockwise. 3Gp2 – Find and describe the position of a square on a grid of squares where the rows and columns are labelled.

*for NRICH activities mapped to the Cambridge Primary objectives, please visit www.cie.org.uk/cambridgeprimarymaths

Vocabulary

co-ordinates • above • below • top • bottom • side • direction • journey • route • map • plan • up • down • grid • row • column • clockwise • anti-clockwise • compass point • north • south • east • west • N, S, E, W • horizontal • vertical • diagonal • whole turn • half turn • quarter turn • angle

Resources: You will need cards reading North, South, East and West. Centimetre squared paper. Pens/pencils. A clip board (per pair). (Optional: *Rescue the robot* photocopy master (CD-ROM), one per learner; pens/pencils; *Where's William?* photocopy master (CD-ROM), one per learner; *This was, that way* photocopy master (CD-ROM), one per learner.)
Before the session, pin up cards reading North, South, East and West in the classroom, one on each wall, using a compass.

Begin the session by saying, *"Look at the compass points. Point to North. Point to East."*

Tell the learners they are going to write instructions to guide someone to a point in the room that is a secret from everybody but them. Give each pair a sheet of centimetre squared paper. Explain that each square on the paper represents one step.

Model the activity using a grid drawn or displayed on the board.
Say, *"If I take three steps I will show it on the grid like this."*

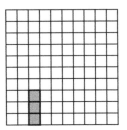

"If I turn a quarter turn clockwise (to the right) and walk three steps I will colour these squares."

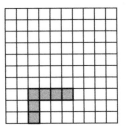

Look out for!

- Learners who find writing or following the instructions difficult. *Prepare a smaller (e.g. 5 × 5) grid with pictorial clues to match the classroom which can be used in the instructions, e.g. "Take two steps forwards, turn to face the door. Take three steps forward, turn to face the window."*
- Learners who find writing and following instructions easy. *Challenge them to plan a more complicated route, e.g. to the next class, the head teacher, the hall, a route outside.*

"If I then make a quarter turn anti-clockwise (to the left) and walk four steps I will colour these squares."

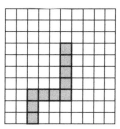

Say, "*You can choose to turn a quarter or a half turn. What would happen if you turned a whole turn?*" (**You'd be facing the way you had come from**)

Give the learners the choice of how to describe their routes. "*Instead of talking about turns you can say, 'Walk north three steps. Walk east three steps.' Plot a route with your partner and write the instructions for another pair to follow. They will only get your instructions not the plan of your route.*" Give time for learners to complete the task (learners might find it useful to clip their instructions to a clip board while they move around).

Now tell the learners to swap their instructions with another pair. Remind them to keep the route plan hidden. "*Each pair must follow the instructions they have been given and complete a route plan for them.*" Give time for learners to complete the task.

At the end of the session, ask pairs to compare their route plans for the same journeys. Ask, "*Do they look the same? Discuss with the others what is the same and what is different. Can you find out where they began to be different?*"
Ask, "*Did you find this activity easy or difficult? What made it difficult?*
Remember, when we write directions we must be very precise about what we mean."

Summary

At the end of this session learners will have used the language of position, direction and movement, including clockwise and anti-clockwise when giving and receiving instructions

Notes on the Learner's Book
Position and movement (p116): this page starts with a puzzle to solve and then uses what has been learnt in the session as reinforcement, practise and assessment.

Check up!
Ask:
- "*Face north. Turn one right angle clockwise. What can you see?*"
- "*Face south, turn two right angles anti-clockwise. What can you see?*"

More activities

Rescue the Robot (individual)

> You will need the *Rescue the robot* photocopy master (CD-ROM), one per learner, pens/pencils.

Learners write directions to get the robot to each picture, starting at the shaded square and then returning there once they have collected all the toys. They use the list of movement words to help them.

Where's William? (individual)

> You will need the *Where's William?* photocopy master (CD-ROM), one per learner, pens/pencils.

Learners work with an activity sheet to reinforce positional vocabulary.

This way, that way (individual)

> You will need the *This was, that way* photocopy master (CD-ROM), one per learner, pens/pencils.

Learners follow instructions for clockwise and anti-clockwise movements.

Begin the session by explaining what co-ordinates are, and how and why we use them. "*The position of any object in the real world can be described using a simple co-ordinate system. For example, you could describe your television as being four metres **across from** the door, two metres **up from** the floor (on a table).*" Model this with a simple graph.

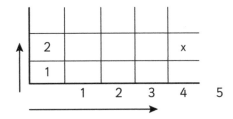

Demonstrate with other objects, such as a book (on a table), a lamp (on a table), a picture (on the wall).

Ask, "*Did anyone notice which way I plotted the first set of numbers? Let's do another one and you look carefully.*"

Reinforce the fact that the horizontal axis is always plotted first ("*You walk along the corridor before you climb the stairs*" often helps learners to remember).

Tell learners they are going to play a game in pairs. Hand out a 6 × 6 grid, 12 counters and a 1–6 dice to each pair. Explain the rules:
Each player places six counters on the grid; each counter goes in a different square of their choosing.

Vocabulary

co-ordinates: a set of values that show an exact position. On maps and graphs it is common to have a pair of numbers to show where a point is: the first number shows the distance along (left or right) and the second number shows the distance north or south.

Look out for!

• Some learners who find it difficult to remember which axis to plot first. *Help them by giving clues: 'You travel along the corridor before you go up the stairs.' A visual image of a street with houses may help.*

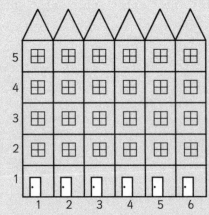

Players take turns to throw the dice twice. The first number thrown tells them how far to move along the horizontal axis, the second number thrown tells them how far to move up the vertical axis. If a player lands on a square with a counter, they take the counter.
Play continues until all of the counters have gone. The player with the most counters is the winner.

Allow learners the play the game at least once, then ask, "*What did you think of the game? Was it a good game or a bad game? Why? What if we change the rules?*"

Make statements such as, "I am house number 2," (move across to the 2nd house in the grid). "I live on the 4th floor." (Move up to the 4th floor level with the number 4.)

- Learners who need more challenge. *Give them a set of co-ordinates which they plot on a graph which will give a picture of a car, bus, house or animal when coloured in. Ask them to design a picture and give the co-ordinates to a friend to plot.*
  - *Using their knowledge of symmetry, ask them to give co-ordinates which will give a picture with one, two, three or four lines of symmetry.*

Summary

By the end of this session learners will have found and described the position of a square on a grid of squares where the rows and columns are labelled.

Notes on the Learner's Book
Using co-ordinates (p118): this page takes the learning from the session and extends knowledge and understanding in order to reinforce the use of co-ordinates.

Check up!
Have a numbered grid on the board. In some of the spaces drawn an animal or shape. Ask:
- "*Give me the co-ordinates for the cat (or square)."*
- "*Give me the co-ordinates for the turtle (or triangle)."*

More activities

<u>Where I live</u> (pair/class)

> You will need a local street map marked as a numbered grid and pens/pencils.

Give the learners a copy of a street map of the area around the school marked as a numbered grid. Help them to orientate themselves with the map by asking them to locate some local features. For example ask them to, "*Mark the school on the map. Mark the local park/sports ground. Mark a local shop (dairy, petrol station, bakery, church etc.)."* Ask them to describe the locations of the school, sports field, shop. Ask them to write the grid references for five locations on the map. Pairs of learners then swap their grid references and see if they can find each other's locations.

Grids again! (teams)

> You will need masking tape.

Mark a large floor grid with co-ordinates. Split the class into two (or four) teams according to numbers.

Choose one learner from each of two teams. Call out a grid reference. The first learner to stand in the square wins one point for their team. Replace those learners with two others and call a different co-ordinate.

Continue until all learners have played the game. The team with most point is the winner.

Gardening (pairs)

> You will need the *10 by 10 grid* photocopy master (CD-ROM), one grid per learner, and colouring pencils.

Learners sit opposite each other so that they can't see the other's grid paper. One learner gives a grid reference to draw a flower. Both plot it on their own paper. The other learner gives a reference for the next flower, which they both plot. They take turns until they have each given five instructions. Compare the gardens to see if they match.

Cross it out (class)

> You will need the *10 by 10 grid* photocopy master (CD-ROM), one per learner, colouring pencils.

Learners choose to colour any 10 squares. The teacher calls out grid references such as (2, 5), and learners cross it out if they have that one coloured. The first learner to cross out five squares is the winner.

Making patterns (pair)

> You will need the *10 by 10 grid* photocopy master (CD-ROM), one per learner, colouring pencils.

Learners each colour a pattern of squares in half of their grid. They give their pattern to their partner who has to write the grid references to make the pattern symmetrical. This can be done horizontally, vertically or diagonally.

Games Book (ISBN 9781107694019)

Find the spider (p42) is a game for two players. Players find and describe the position of a square on a grid of squares where the rows and columns are labelled.

Quick reference

Core activity 29.1: Journey times (Learner's Book p120)

This activity deals with the passage of time and how to measure it. Both digital and analogue times are used.

Core activity 29.2: Time puzzles (Learner's Book p122)

This activity takes the idea of time changing and looks at the impact of that as learners travel through space.

Prior learning	Objectives* – please note that listed objectives might only be partially covered within any given chapter but are covered fully across the book when taken as a whole
• Know how to represent times on digital and analogue clocks. • Understand simple passage of time.	**3C: Measures** 3Mt1 – Suggest and use suitable units to measure time and know the relationships between them. 3Mt2 – Read the time on analogue and digital clocks to the nearest 5 minutes on an analogue clock and to the nearest minute on a digital clock. 3Mt3 – Begin to calculate simple time intervals in hours and minutes. 3Mt4 – Read a calendar and calculate time intervals in weeks or days. **3C: Problem solving** 3Pt2 – Begin to understand everyday systems of measurement in length, weight, capacity, time and use these to make measurements as appropriate. 3Pt10 – Estimate and approximate when calculating and check working 3Ps2 – Explain a choice of calculation strategy and how the answer was worked out. Use ordered lists and tables to help solve problems systematically.

*for NRICH activities mapped to the Cambridge Primary objectives, please visit www.cie.org.uk/cambridgeprimarymaths

Vocabulary

am • pm • time • days of the week: Monday • Tuesday... • months of the year: January • February...
• day • week • fortnight • month • year • century • calendar • date • morning • afternoon • evening
• night • bedtime • dinnertime • playtime • today • yesterday • tomorrow

Resources: You will need the *Aero-chart* photocopy master (p245), one copy per pair, and the *Flight plan* photocopy master (p246), one copy per pair. (Optional: paper and pens/pencils.)
Learner's Book: the *Digital display* photocopy master (CD-ROM) and the *Blank clocks* photocopy master (CD-ROM) one of each per learner.

Introduce the idea of plans to the class. *"It would be very difficult to build a house without a plan. A builder needs a plan to give information about the design and size of a house under construction. Plans can also be used to describe an event such as planning for a celebration."*
Tell the learners that the pilot of an aeroplane depends on a **flight plan** to give information to help get safely to the destination. A flight plan will include the following information (write these on the board as you say them to act as a memory aid later in the session):

- When the flight will leave.
- Where the plane will take off from.
- How the plane will get to where it needs to go.
- Where and when the plane will land.
- How long did the flight take?

Tell the learners that, working in pairs, they are going to design and record a flight plan for their own aircraft. Give each pair a copy of the *Aero-chart*. Explain that they will need to look carefully at the chart as they plan their route. *"You can fly north, south, east or west, but you might need to change direction to avoid the no-fly zone, the mountains or bad weather."*
Ask the learners to choose two airports and work out a flight plan to fly from one to the other. *"Use the compass points when you describe your journey."* Demonstrate how to plot a route.
Then say. *"When you have drawn your route, count the squares to find how long the flight took. Use the key to work out the time for your flight. It takes half an hour to fly over each square on the chart."*
Finally, show the learners the *Flight plan* and explain that once they have worked out their route and how long it takes, they need to plan when to make the flight and fill in all the information on the sheet.
As the class are working, walk round to make sure that they understand the task. Encourage some learners to plan their flight for late at night so that they arrive the following day.

At the end of the session, ask some of the pairs to feedback to the rest of the class information about their flight plans.

Look out for!

- Learners who are having difficulty plotting a flight. *Start them with a simple journey from one airport to another with no deviations.*
- Learners who are finding the task easy. *Challenge them to create their own sheet on which to record their flight plan. Arrange different routes. Which is the shortest/longest if all the airports are visited?*

Opportunities for display!

Large wall display of the map and the learners' flight plans. Ask if learners can predict what future events and designs in aviation might look like, their ideas could form part of a display.

Summary

- By the end of this session learners will have used their knowledge of time (minutes, hours days months) to plan and answer questions about a flight.
- They will have recorded times on both digital and analogue clocks

Notes on the Learner's Book

Passage of time (p120): this page explores the idea of the passage of time by asking learners to calculate time intervals through word problems. Some of them, such as the first question, require learners to use logical strategies. Being systematic is also important, particularly for the second question.

Check up!

Ask
- *"If your plane takes off at 3:15 pm and flies for 12 hours, what time will it arrive?"*
- *"If your plane takes off at 11:45 (digital) what will show on the clock when it lands one hour later?"*

More activities

Flight time line (class)

You will need paper and pens/pencils.

Make a time line showing different flight modes: air balloon, first flight, gliders etc. Learners can decide how each will be displayed: design cards for the time line or build a paper model, or magazine cutouts, pictures, and models made from recycled items found around their home.

Discussion (class)

You will need the flight time line from above.

Learners use research and prepare for a discussion. *"How important was the event you researched to changes in aviation?*
If a particular time line event had never occurred, how do you think this might have changed aviation history?
How did the time line that the class created (above) help you to learn about aviation history?"

What's the time (class)

Ask questions such as, *"Two hours ago, it was as many hours after one o'clock in the afternoon as it was before one o'clock in the morning. What time is it now?"* (**nine o'clock in the evening**)

What's the day (class)

Ask questions such as:

- "*What is the day two days after yesterday?*" (**tomorrow**)
- "*What is the day three days before the day after tomorrow?*" (**yesterday**)
- "*Today is the 24th What is the date three days after four days before yesterday?*" (**22nd**)
- "*Four days after yesterday will be Tuesday. What is today?*" (**Saturday**)

Games Book (ISBN 9781107694019)

Read the clocks (p61) is a game for two to four players. Players read the time on analogue (to the nearest five minutes) and digital (to the nearest minute) clocks.

Resources: *Time travel* photocopy master (p247), per pair. (Optional: paper and pens/pencils.)

Tell learners that NASA (National Aeronautics and Space Administration) has developed a galactic bus to travel into space and visit different planets. Each planet has different times from all of the others.

Write the following information on the board as you say each one so that they can be used as a reference during the activity.
- Planet Zog is six hours in front of us.
- Planet Zig is 10 hours in front of us.
- Planet Porro is eight hours behind us
- Planet Glug has times the same as us.

Now say, "*As a special treat you are allowed to go on the bus.*
You leave home at 9 am on Tuesday 15th May and travel to Zog. It takes three hours. What time do you arrive using Zog time? How can we work that out?"

Give time for discussion and take feedback. Establish that if you leave home at 9 o'clock and travel for three hours, you arrive at 12 o'clock. But then you need to add on six hours – so it is 6 o'clock on Zog. Ask, "*Is it 6 o'clock in the morning or evening? How do you know?*" Write 6 pm on the board.

Now tell the class that they stay for two hours on Zog and then travel from Zog back home. Ask, "*What time will you arrive home using our time?*" Give time for discussion and feedback, writing the suggested answers on the board. If there are different answers ask the learners to explain how they got their answer. Confirm that the correct answer is 5 pm. "*You leave Zog at 8 pm and travel back home for three hours. You arrive home 11 pm Zog time. But there is six hours difference so we need to take six hours off which makes it 5 pm.*"

Give each pair of learners a copy of the *Time travel* sheet and ask them to read the information and find the times when they arrive back home from each of the planets. They should show how they work out their answers. Remind them that some of the times are in front of us and some are behind us.

Vocabulary

am: is the half of the day from midnight to midday. We call it morning. It comes from the Latin ante meridiem, meaning 'before midday'.

pm: is the half of the day from midday to midnight. We call it afternoon and evening. It comes from the Latin post meridiem for 'after midday'.

Look out for!
- Learners who aren't confident counting on and back for time. *Give them a number line or time number line as support. Some learners might also benefit from working in mixed-ability pairs.*
- Learners who are confident with the Learner's Book activity *Time puzzles.* *Ask them to write some problems of their own to do as a class.*

As they are working, walk round the class to make sure that all learners understand the task and are developing strategies to work on the problems. Where learners are not confident show them how to use number or time lines to calculate the time differences asked for.

At the end of the session, ask for some feedback from the work done. Ask, *"Did you all get the same answer? Did anyone have a different answer? Tell us how you worked it out."* Give time for learners to talk and discuss their strategies.

Summary

By the end of this activity learners will have covered the passage of time, and worked on problems involving time, calculating and checking their working.

Notes on the Learner's Book
Time puzzles (p122): this is a page of number puzzles and problems relating to time using information covered so far.

Check up!
Ask questions such as:
- *"What is four hours after 9 am?"*
- *"What is six hours after 2 pm"*

For some learners cross the boundary of midday and midnight.

More activities

Other planets (group of any size)

Explore planets that have five hours in a day, or eight or 10. How does that impact on daily routines? How many days in a week would they have? How many months in a year. Plan a day or a week of activities for the people who live on that planet.

Going on a journey (individual)

> You will need paper and pens/pencils.

Plan a journey (on Earth!) that will take one week from the day you leave to the day you get back home. Make a timetable showing travel times, where you visit, how long you stay. How long in total did you travel? How long was spent on each of the other activities?

School Trip (individual)

> You will need paper and pens/pencils.

Plan a school trip for your class. Decide how you will travel and think about number of driving hours, length of time for stops or rests, length of trip – local trip or a long distance one, what impact might the traffic conditions have, will there be holdups or delays?

The school year (individual)

Explore how many days you spend at school in a year. How many days do you have at home? Do they total 365 (or 366 in a leap year) days? Change the number of days at school to weeks and days. Change the number of days at home to weeks and days.

• Airport

Aero-chart

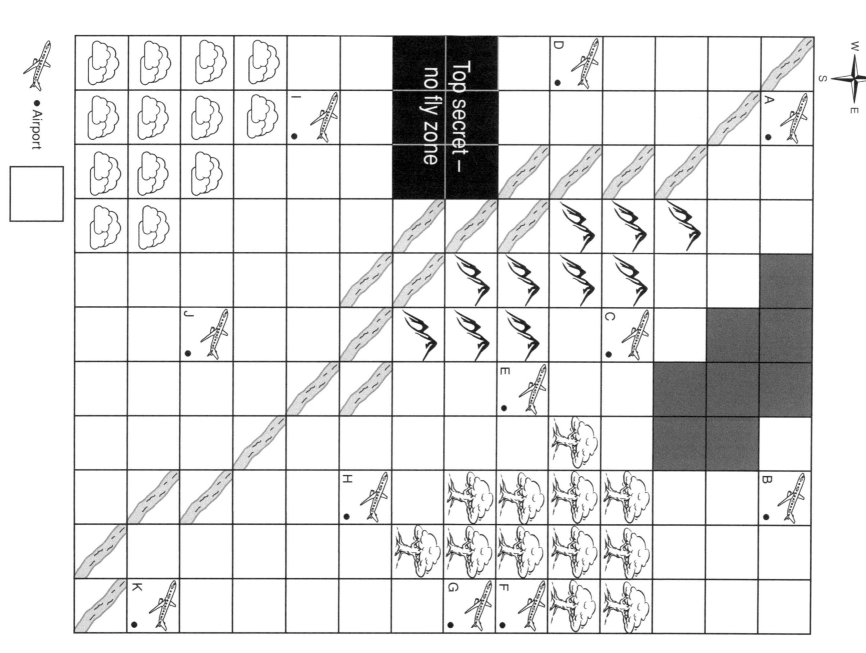

Top secret – no fly zone

Flight plan

Departure airport – which airport will you leave from? _____

Destination of flight – where will you land? _____

Route of flight – which direction will you fly? _____

Estimated flight time – how many hours will it take to get there? _____

Departure time – What time will you leave?	Arrival time – what time will you land?
Show this as analogue and digital time.	Show this as digital and analogue times.

Departure date – What day will you leave? What month?	Arrival date – What day will you leave? What month?
Show the date on a calendar page.	Show the date on a calendar page.

Month: _____

Mon	Tue	Wed	Thu	Fri	Sat	Sun

Month: _____

Mon	Tue	Wed	Thu	Fri	Sat	Sun

Instructions on page 238

Time travel

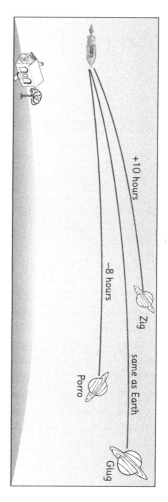

Answer the questions. Use this to help you.

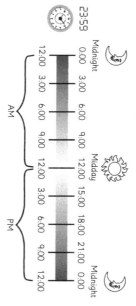

1. You leave home at 6:30 am and travel to Zig. The bus takes one hour to get there.

What time in Zig time do you arrive? _____

You sleep for two hours, then get on the bus to come home.

What time do you leave Zig? _____

What time do you arrive home? _____

2. You leave home at 3:30 pm and travel to Porro. The bus takes four hours to get there.

What time in Porro time do you arrive? _____

You play with your friends for three hours, then get on the bus to come home.

What time do you leave Porro? _____

What time do you arrive home? _____

3. You leave home at 12:20 pm and travel to Glug. The bus takes two hours to get here.

What time in Glug time do you arrive? _____

You go shopping for five hours, then get on the bus to get home.

What time do you leave Glug? _____

What time do you arrive home? _____

Blank page

Quick reference

Core activity 30.1: Adding and subtracting money (Learner's Book p124)

This activity introduces the dollar to the learners and looks at its relationship to cents.

Core activity 30.2: Double your money (Learner's Book p126)

This activity is a number story linked to doubling in the context of a money problem.

Prior learning	Objectives* – please note that listed objectives might only be partially covered within any given chapter but are covered fully across the book when taken as a whole
• Counting to 100 in 5s and 10s. • Familiarity with 100 square.	**3C: Measures** 3Mm1 – Consolidate using money notation. 3Mm2 – Use addition and subtraction facts with a total of 100 to find change. **3C: Problem solving** 3Pt1 – Choose appropriate mental strategies to carry out calculations. 3Ps1 – Make up number story to go with a calculation, including in the context of money. 3Pt11 – Make a sensible estimate of the answer to a calculation. 3Pt12 – Consider whether an answer is reasonable.

*for NRICH activities mapped to the Cambridge Primary objectives, please visit www.cie.org.uk/cambridgeprimarymaths

Vocabulary

money • coin • note • total • amount
value • worth • dollar • cent • least

> **Resources:** *Large Blank 100 square* photocopy master (CD-ROM) and the *100 square* photocopy master (CD-ROM). A selection of coins (1c, 5c, 10c, 4 × 25c, 50c, $1) (or use the *Coins* photocopy master (CD-ROM)). Sticky tack. *Drinks café* photocopy master (p257), one copy per learner. (Optional: the *Money spots* photocopy master (CD-ROM); 1–6 dice (CD-ROM); 1c, 5c, 10c and 25c coins; paper; a 1–3 spinner (or a 1–6 dice (CD-ROM) with labels stuck over 4–6 and renumbered 1–3).)

Start the session by revising the values of the coins from the *Coins* sheet. Show each coin in turn. Ask, "*How much is this worth? And this?*"

Show learners a dollar. "*What do you know about a dollar?*" (**100 cents**) Show just the dollar. "*If I put one cent on each square of this blank grid how many squares would they cover?*"

Take feedback. Some learners may not realise that it is a *Blank 100 square* while others may because it is 10 × 10.

Ask, "*How many squares do you think this grid has? Let's count the squares cross the top: one, two, three,… 10. It has 10 squares across the top. If we know that, we can count in tens to the bottom row. Start counting down: 10, 20, 30 40,… 100. It has 100 squares. Where have you seen a grid with 100 squares before?*" Show the class the *100 square* (numbered 100 grid).

Ask, "*If there are 100 squares on this grid and 100 cents in a dollar, and I put one coin in each space, how may spaces will I cover?*"(**100**)

Show a 25 cent coin. Say, "*This has 25 cents on. Is that more than 100 or less? How many squares do you think this coin would need?*" (**25**) Use the sticky tack to put the 25c coin on the 25 square. Then ask, "*Where would we put the next 25 cents? We need to add on or count on another 25.*" Leave time for learners to work it out. Establish that the second coin goes on 50. Ask, "*How did you work that out? What about the next one and the next?* (**75 and 100**) How many 25 cents make a dollar?*" (**4**)

Now say, "*I have one dollar and I spend 50 cents. How much will I have left?*" (**50 cents**) "*How did you work that out?*" Ask for feedback from several learners.

Vocabulary

value/worth: number given to something to show its size.

Look out for!

- Learners who need a more visual image. *Encourage them to use a 100 square. Some will be able to work with the Blank 100 square while others will need the 100 square (numbered). Suggest that they use them when working on the Burger Bar activities.*
- Learners who are already competent with dollars and cents. *Set them further problems such as:*
  - *There were three sisters and one brother in a family. They shared a certain sum of money equally. If only the sisters shared it, they would have increased the amount they each had by $20. What was the original sum of money?* (**$240**)
  - *Show how you worked it out.*

Give each learner a copy of the *Drinks café* worksheet and ask them to look at the price list at the top. Say, "*I have $4. I want to buy some drinks. What could I buy? How much change will I have? Talk to your partner and find as many different ways for me to spend $4.00.*" Take feedback. Ask several pairs for different ways to spend the money. Record what they say on the board.

For $4.00 dollars I could buy
1.
2.
3.

Ask the learners to work with a partner to answer the questions. As the class is working, walk round to listen and hear what the learners are saying. Use it as an opportunity to correct or reinforce vocabulary.

At the end of the session ask some learners to give their answers. Did everyone get the same answer? For those learners who had different answers ask them how they worked it out. Allow learners to change their minds when they realise that they had made an error.

Finish by asking, "*What would you buy if you went to the Drinks café? Work out how much it would cost.*" Learners feedback by completing the sentence, 'I would buy _____. It would cost _____.'

Summary

By the end of the session the class will have consolidated using money notation and use addition and subtraction facts with a total of 100.

Notes on the Learner's Book
Money 3 (p124): this page gives learners the opportunity to solve problems relating to money as well as closed questions to find out what they know and understand.

Hint
Use 'Tell me' statements:
- "*Tell me different ways of making 5 cents/10 cents.*"
- "*Tell me two different ways to make a dollar.*"

More activities

Money spots (individual or group)

You will need the *Money spots* photocopy master (CD-ROM) and a 1–6 dice.

This is a random choice of activities based on the throw of a dice.

Race to 25 cents (group)

You will need 1c, 5c, 10c and 25c coins, paper, 1–3 spinner (or a 1–6 dice with labels stuck over 4–6 and renumbered 1–3).

This is another version of a previous game where learners are asked to trade coins for larger value ones in order to get to 25 cents. Learners draw four columns and head them 1c, 5c, 10c and 25c. They spin the spinner or throw the 1–6 dice and collect that number of 1c coins, placing them in the 1c column. When they have five 1c coins, they swap them for a 5c coin. When they have two 5c coins, they swap them for a 10c coin. The winner is the first player who can swap two 10c coins and either one 5c coin or five 1c coins for a 25c coin and place it in the 25c column.

Games Book (ISBN 9781107694019)

Clean up the money (p65) is a game for two players. Players use their knowledge of co-ordinates and money notation. They make sensible estimates and use addition facts in the context of money.

Resources: You will need the *Money options* photocopy master (CD-ROM) and calculators. (Optional: the *Blank Venn diagram* photocopy master (CD-ROM), one per learner, or a sheet of paper; pens/pencils; 'bank books'; paper money (real or hand drawn); a collection coins: 1c, 2c and 10c.)

Tell the learners to imagine that, "*You're sitting in a maths session just like this one and a letter arrives to say that the school has been given some money. We can choose how we want the money. We can have 1 cent on the 1st day, 2 cents on the 2nd day and double each day for 30 days.*" Write it on the board to show the patterns of doubling: (day 1, 1 cent; day 2, 2 cents; day 3, 4 cents; day 4, 8 cents; and so on). "*Or we can have exactly $1,000,000*" (one million dollars). "*I would take the million dollars, what would you do?*"

Tell the learners that they are going to work with a partner and test their theory about which the best choice would be, using a table to show their results.
Draw a table on the board and work through week 1 with the class.

Day	Money for that day	Total money (in dollars)
1	.01	.01
2	.02	.03
3	.04	.07
4	.08	.15
5	.16	.31
6	.32	.63
7	.64	1.27

Ask, "*How much would you make in the first week if you chose the 1 cent and doubling option?*" (**$1.27**)
Then ask, "*Based on what you found out about week 1, do you want to change your mind about which option to choose?*" Tell your partner about the option you think is best and why.

Ask the learners to continue the table until they get to day 30. They should then prepare to share their thoughts with the class, explaining about what option they chose to begin with, what they found out, and if (and why) they changed their minds.

Look out for!

- Learners who find spending decisions difficult. *Suggest that they break the problem into smaller parts. Give them the Money options sheet, which has a blank table to fill for each week. Some may like to use a calculator to work on the doubles.*
- Learners who make decisions confidently. *Ask them to design some of their own, "Which would you rather?" questions. Make sure they have worked on the options before they ask so that they know the answer!*

When learners have completed the task, ask, "*Who would choose the million dollars? Why? Who would choose the cent on day 1 option? Why?*" Choose some learners to tell the class what they did, what they found out and if they changed their mind. (The 1 cent and doubling option pays $10,737,418.23 over 30 days.)

Summary

By the end of this session learners will have chosen appropriate mental strategies to carry out calculations within a number story in the context of money.

Notes on the Learner's Book

Money puzzles (p126): this page uses money in real life contexts, as well as in problems to solve using knowledge and understanding of cents and dollars.

Check up!

- Ask other, "*Which would you rather?*" questions such as, "*Would you rather have $5 dollars or 550 cents? Why?*"
- Or ask closed questions such as, "*What is 45 cents more than $1.60?*"

More activities

Venn diagram (individual)

> You will need either the *Blank Venn diagram* photocopy master (CD-ROM), one per learner, or a sheet of paper, and pens/pencils.

Make a statement (e.g. 'All coins are round, all coins have a president on the front') and ask learners to investigate them by comparing and contrasting coins, and sort them using a Venn diagram.

Coin caterpillars (pair)

> You will need a selection of coins. Learners make caterpillars with different coins, and challenge a partner to find the totals.

Using banks (class)

> You will need 'bank books', coins and paper money (real or hand drawn).

Set up a role play bank in the class room. Some learners play customers and others work in the bank. Roles can change. Activities can include paying money in (depositing money) and taking money out (withdrawing money). Each learner needs a bank book where they keep a record of their money transactions. Link with a shop as well so that learners have experience of 'spending' their money. The shop keeper can also pay money in (from the till) or take money out (to buy more goods).

Coin combinations (individual)

> You will need a collection coins: 1c, 2c and 10c, paper and pens/pencils.

Challenge learners to make 20 cents using only 1 cent, 2 cent and/or 10 cents coins, recording the different combinations in a table. This is a complex problem and lends itself well to differentiation. Some learners can be asked to find five ways of making 20 cents, some ten ways, and some all possible ways. Once they see the pattern of numbers it becomes much easier. Some learners can be challenged to make 30 cents, or even 40 cents.

(Answers for 20c: $20 \times 1c$; $4 \times 5c$; $2 \times 10c$; $15 \times 1c + 1 \times 5c$; $10 \times 1c + 2 \times 5c$; $10 \times 1c + 1 \times 1c$; $5 \times 1c + 3 \times 5c$; $5 \times 1c + 1 \times 5c + 1 \times 10c$)

Drinks café

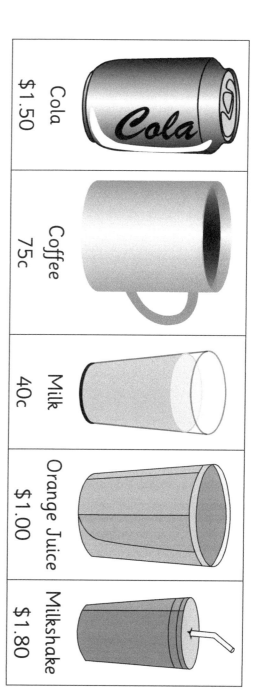				
Cola	Coffee	Milk	Orange Juice	Milkshake
$1.50	75c	40c	$1.00	$1.80

1) How much would it cost Ajit to buy a can of cola and some orange juice? _____

2) Ravinder bought a milkshake and some orange juice.
   How much did it cost? _____

3) Jyoti bought a glass of milk, some coffee and some orange juice.
   How much did it cost? _____

4) Qasim bought a cup of coffee.
   How much change from $1.50 did he get? _____

5) Alma orders a cup of orange juice and a milkshake.
   How much would her order cost? _____
   If Alma pays with $5.00 how much change would she get? _____

6) Safiya had $1 to spend.
   How much more would she need if she wanted to buy a can of cola and a milkshake? _____

If Ajit pays with $4.00 how much change will he have? _____

Blank page

31 Capacity and length

Quick reference

Core activity 31.1: Capacity (Learner's Book p128)

This session involves learners mixing liquids together to create their own 'potion' that totals 125 ml. They then total the different coloured 'ingredients' to make 1 litre.

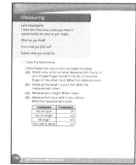

Core activity 31.2: Measuring length (Learner's Book p130)

This activity takes the idea of developing mystery trails that can only be solved by using knowledge and understanding of measurement.

Core activity 31.3: More length measuring (Learner's Book p132)

This activity re-visits the ideas set out in *Core activity 31.1* by asking learners to find their own body measurements and then use them to answer questions.

Prior learning	Objectives* – please note that listed objectives might only be partially covered within any given chapter but are covered fully across the book when taken as a whole
• Skills of using measuring equipment. • Knowing the difference between and relationships of different units of measure. • Knowledge and understand of the language and vocabulary of capacity. • Knowledge of problem solving strategies.	**3C: Measures** 3MI1 – Choose and use appropriate units and equipment to estimate, measure and record measurements. 3MI2 – Know the relationship between kilometres and metres, metres and centimetres, kilograms and grams, litres and millilitres. 3MI3 – Read to the nearest division or half division, use scales that are numbered or partially numbered. 3MI4 – Use a ruler to draw and measure lines to the nearest centimetre. 3MI5 – Solve word problems involving measures.

*for NRICH activities mapped to the Cambridge Primary objectives, please visit www.cie.org.uk/cambridgeprimarymaths

Vocabulary

division • approximately • distance apart/between • distance to... from... • kilometre (*km*) • metre (*m*) • centimetre (*cm*) • kilogram (*kg*) • half-kilogram • gram (*g*) • litre (*l*) • half-litre • millilitre (*ml*) • capacity • full • half full • empty • holds • contains litre (*l*) • half-litre • millilitre (*ml*) • container scale

LB: p128

Resources: Measuring cylinders (in which learners can measure capacities up to 125 ml). Medicine cups (to hold 125 ml). Jugs of water coloured with food colouring (red, blue and green; per group). *Potions recording sheet* photocopy master (pp268–269), per learner. Colouring pencils. 2 litre containers (e.g. water bottle), Pins. Masking tape. Clear containers. Markers. stopwatches. (Optional: the *How Much Water?* photocopy master (CD-ROM); selection of containers of water, labelled alphabetically (capacities to be estimated and measured in millilitres); measuring jugs; the *Estimating millilitres* photocopy master (CD-ROM); water; empty containers; measuring cylinders; the *Capacity colouring* photocopy master (CD-ROM), colouring pencils; the *Capacity word problems* photocopy master (CD-ROM), one per learner; pens/pencils).

Explain to the class that today you are going to look at **capacity**. Remind them of work done previously on capacity. Say, *"Capacity is a measure of how much space something takes up. Measuring spoons, cups or jugs can be used to measure capacity."* Remind them that capacity is measured in millilitres (ml) and litres (l); 1 litre is the same as 1000 ml. Discuss useful strategies for estimating capacity, for example:

- 5 ml is about the capacity of a teaspoon.
- 1l is about the capacity of a large carton of fruit juice.

Ask the learners to look at the measuring cylinders and discuss with a partner what they see. Ask, *"What are the numbers on the measuring cylinder? What do the smaller marks mean? Talk to each other and find out as much as you can."* Give time for pair discussion. Then talk with the class about reading scales, establishing that you first need to work out how much each mark or division on the scale represents. You can then count on from a numbered division to find the value of an unnumbered division. Say, *"Not all jugs will have the same scale. How much will fit in your measuring cylinder?"*

Discuss the fact that millilitres are small parts of a litre. Remind the learners that there are 1000 ml in a litre and ask, *"How many ml in half a litre?"*

Look out for!

- Learners who are having difficulty with the words used. *Make sure they know that only containers have 'capacity'.*
- Learners who have difficulty with the idea of 'conservation of liquid'. *They may believe that the amount of liquid has changed when a set amount has been poured from one container to another of a different size. They may believe that there is more liquid in the one that has the highest level, because it is narrower.*
- Learners who are having difficulty reading the scale. *Make sure that they keep it vertical when they pick the container up.*
- Learners who have problems converting one unit to another. *Lots of practical activities using a mixture of litres and millilitres should be encouraged.*
- Learners who would benefit from making a clock which shows directly how time is passing. *Challenge them to make a water clock (with the support of a classroom assistant or other adult).*
  - *They will need: 2 litre container (e.g. water bottle), pin, masking tape, clear container, marker, stopwatch.*
  - *Make a small hole in the middle of the base of the 2 litre container.*
  - *Put a piece of masking tape down the side of the clear container.*
  - *Fill the 2 litre container with water, putting your finger over the hole.*
  - *Place it over the clear container and take your finger off the hole.*
  - *After 30 seconds mark the level of water on the masking tape.*
  - *Remove the water and measure how much has passed through the hole.*
  - *Make a table to show how much water has emptied in 30 seconds, 60 seconds.*
  - *What happens if you make the hole bigger?*

Explain the task to learners. *"Today you will be working with a partner to make a secret potion. You can mix together as many different colours as you like but the total must be 125 ml."* Demonstrate on the board a 'recipe' for a potion: Blue 10 ml, red, 25 ml, green 90 ml. Ask, *"Is this 125 ml? How do you know?"*
Pour the colours together and show the potion in a plastic cup.
Tell the learners that they need to measure the correct amount of each ingredient (coloured water) and to write the total amount (by adding the amounts together) and the colour of their medicine. Give each learner a copy of the *Potions recording sheet*.
Before learners start on their potions, say, *"You are going to make 1 litre of potion altogether. How many potions will you need to make so that you have 1 litre altogether?"* (8) *"How do you know?"*
As the learners are working, check they understand the task and understand that 1000 ml = 1 litre and that half a litre is 500 ml.

At the end of the session, ask pairs to feedback about what they did and what they learnt. Ask questions such as :
"How did you get your answer?"
"Can you tell us what you did?"
"What did you find out when you were measuring?"

Summary

- This session gave learners opportunities to use appropriate units and equipment to measure and record measurements, using their knowledge of the relationship between litres and millilitres.
- Through the practical activity learners were able to read to the nearest division or half division using numbered scales, solving word problems involving measures.

Notes on the Learner's Book
Capacity (p128): this page has problems to solve as well as closed questions which use what the learners learnt in the session. The answers can be used as the basis of some assessment.

Check up!
Ask questions such as:
- *"Which is more 500 ml or half a litre?"*
- *"Which is less, half a litre or 600 ml?"*
- *"How many ml in a litre?"*
- *"How many ml in 2 litres?"*

More activities

How much water? (pair)

You will need the *How Much Water* photocopy master (CD-ROM), one copy per pair, pens/pencils, a selection of containers of water, labelled alphabetically (capacities to be estimated and measured in millilitres), and some measuring jugs.

A pair of learners decide who is 1 and who is 2. They then pick up one of the containers and write its letter in the table on the recording sheet. They separately estimate its capacity in millilitres and record their estimates. They then choose a measuring jug and together measure the capacity of the container and record it on the sheet. They work out whose estimate was the closer. They then carefully pour the water back into its original container and repeat with the next container.

Estimating millilitres (pair or small group)

You will need the *Estimating millilitres* photocopy master (CD-ROM), water, empty containers, measuring cylinders.

Provide learners with water, empty containers and some measuring cylinders. Working in a pair or small groups, the learners put what they estimate to be 100 ml of water in an empty container (not using a measuring cylinder). They then check their estimate by measuring the water as accurately as they can in a measuring cylinder. They record their results in the table and work out the difference between their estimate and 100 ml. They then put the water back in its container and try again, up to three more times. They then repeat the activity for 500 ml and 750 ml.

Capacity colouring (individual)

You will need the *Capacity colouring* photocopy master (CD-ROM), colouring pencils.

Carrying on from *Core activity 31.1*, learners are asked to colour in different amounts of coloured water. (Teacher CD)

Capacity word problems (individual)

You will need the *Capacity word problems* photocopy master (CD-ROM) one per learner, pens/pencils.

Learners work on word problems before writing some for the rest of the class.

Games Book (ISBN 9781107694019)

Milking the goats (p67) is a game for two to four players. Players compete to add volumes, using the relationship between litres and millilitres.

Resources: You will need a number of flags (one for each group plus one extra) made by fixing a rectangle of paper to a stick or piece of wire, a set of instructions for each flag: similar to the instructions in the box below (label each set of directions with a number). A number of 'mystery objects', one for each group. Selections of measuring equipment (metre sticks, tape measures, trundle wheels). *Metric mystery trail recording sheet* photocopy master (CD-ROM), per group. (Optional: measuring equipment; objects used as markers; a prepared list of instructions; a compass; a mystery object.)

> 1. Start at the door and walk 2 metres forward.
> 2. Turn left and walk 3 metres forward.
> 3. Turn right and walk 1.5 metres forward.
> 4. Turn right and walk 2 metres forward.
> 5. Stop and place the flag.
> Place a mystery object at the destination for each set of instructions; choose objects that would not normally be found in that place e.g. a ball by the sink or a book in the bin.

Tell the class that today they are going to complete a metric mystery trail. Each group will search for a different object, and can do so at the same time or one after another. Give each group one list of directions and say, "You are going to follow the directions to find a mystery object. You will all start in the same place. Use the measuring equipment to accurately measure each of your movements." Explain that the object will be something that is not usually in that place. "When you get to the mystery object, make one guess about what you think it is and why. Talk to all the other members of the group before you make a decision. When you have decided, measure the shortest distance from the start to the mystery object."

Give each group a copy of the *Metric mystery trail* recording sheet and tell them to record their results for each set of directions. Show them that each set of directions is numbered. When they have completed the task, they should remove the flag and take it and the directions back to the start. They can then take another set of directions.

Look out for!

- Learners who are finding this activity difficult. *Put them in mixed ability groups so that they can see and hear higher level work and thinking, especially the correct use of vocabulary and language structures. This will help them when they do a similar activity.*
- Learners who complete the trail quickly. *Ask them to make their own mystery trails. These can be used at a later time by other learners*

At the end of the session, ask groups to share what they did and what they found. Compare results on the information they collected such as the object they chose and the distance from the start. If there are any differences ask the groups to explain why they chose what they did or how they measured the distance.

Summary

- By the end of this session learners will have had opportunities to choose and use appropriate units and equipment to measure and record measurements.
- They will have been asked to read to the nearest division or half division, use scales that are numbered or partially numbered whilst solving word problems involving length.

Notes on the Learner's Book

Length (p130): this page gives learners the opportunity to work on problems and puzzles using what they have learned about linear measurement.

Check up!

Ask questions such as:
- *"A walk to the shop from your house is 300 metres. From the shop to the park is 200 metres. From the park to your house is 500 metres. How far will you have walked?"*
- *"What is another way of saying 1000 metres?"* **(1 kilometre)**
- *"What if you were asked to walk $3\frac{1}{2}$ metre? How many cm would that be?"*
- *"How many metres is the same as 500 cm?"*

More activities

The 50 Metre Race (class)

> You will need measuring equipment, objects used as markers.

Each runner in this race runs (or walks) until he thinks the distance from the starting line is 10/20/30/40/50 metres. When a runner stops, a marker is placed at the stopping point. Runners measure the distance from their markers to the starting line. The runner whose distance is closest to 10/20/30/40/50 metres wins the race.

Mystery object chase (group)

> You will need a prepared list of instructions, a compass, selections of measuring equipment, and a mystery object.

As *Core activity 31.2* but use compass directions and indicate changes in direction by north, south, east, or west, for example, 2 metres East. You could also have the trail outside, using greater distances.

Games Book (ISBN 9781107694019)

Round the track (p70) is a game for two to four players. Players compete to add lengths using the relationship between metres and centimetres.

Resources: Tape measures (per pair). *Certificate of measure* photocopy master (p270), per learner. *My body* photocopy master (p271–272), per learner. String and metre sticks. (Optional: measuring equipment, paper and pens/pencils.)

Tell the class that they are going to find out a much as they can about the measurements of their body. Divide the learners into pairs, and give each pair a tape measure and two copies of the *Certificate of measure. Read out the top part which explains the purpose of the certificate. "Before you begin to measure draw a picture of yourself."*

Now give each learner a copy of the *My body* sheet. Say, *"Estimate some of your measurements and fill in this sheet first. Use a ruler to draw lines to show your estimates. Draw your lines to the nearest centimetre. Then complete the certificate."*

As the class is working, walk round making sure that all learners understand the task.

At the end of the session, ask, *"What did you find out? How close were your estimates to the actual lengths? Were there any surprises?"* Ask the learners to bring their certificates for the official signature.

Look out for!

- Learners who are still having problems reading scales accurately although they have had practical experience of measuring using rulers and tape measures. *Use tape measures with clear colour differences between the divisions.*
- Use string for the initial measurement and then place it against a metre stick. Make sure the end of the string is at 0 on the metre stick
- Learners who are finding the activity easy. *Ask them to draw a scale picture of themselves where 1 cm on their body is shown by 1mm on their drawing.*

Summary

By the end of this session, learners will have used appropriate units and equipment to estimate, measure and record measurements. They will have used their knowledge of metres and centimetres and used that to solve problems. They will also have used a ruler.

Notes on the Learner's Book

Measuring (p132): this page gives learners further experience of measuring themselves and looks at relationships between different measurements.

Check up!

Ask questions such as:
- *"Which is more: the distance round you head or your wrist?"*
- *"Which is more: the distance from your knee to the floor or from your finger tip to finger tip when you stretch out your arms?"*
- *"Which is less: the length of your big toe or the length of your smile?"*
- *"Which is less: the width of your foot or the length of your ear?"*

More activities

Animals (individual)

> You will need measuring equipment, paper and pens/pencils.

Learners find as much information about an animal of their choice as they can. They draw the animal and record its measurements.

Longer than/shorter than (individual)

> You will need a ruler, paper and pens/pencils.

Make a table for length. Find six things longer than 10 cm and six things shorter than 10 cm. Write the actual measurements.

Hands and feet (individual)

> You will need a ruler, paper and pens/pencils.

Investigate if there is a link between the size of people's hands and feet. Measure hand spans and length of foot. Record the results in a table. Then rank the students in order of longest foot to shortest. And then widest hand to narrowest. Do the results show that the learner with the longest foot also has the widest hand span?

Potions recording sheet

Write how much of each colour you used. Show each colour separately in the container.

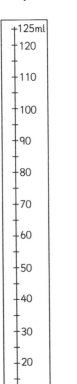
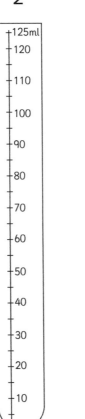
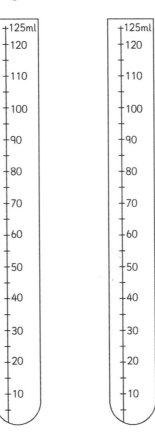

1   **2**   **3**   **4**

Potion 1

We used _____ ml red

We used _____ ml blue

We used _____ ml green

Potion 2

We used _____ ml red

We used _____ ml blue

We used _____ ml green

Potion 3

We used _____ ml red

We used _____ ml blue

We used _____ ml green

Potion 4

We used _____ ml red

We used _____ ml blue

We used _____ ml green

5	6	7	8
+125ml	+125ml	+125ml	+125ml
+120	+120	+120	+120
+110	+110	+110	+110
+100	+100	+100	+100
+90	+90	+90	+90
+80	+80	+80	+80
+70	+70	+70	+70
+60	+60	+60	+60
+50	+50	+50	+50
+40	+40	+40	+40
+30	+30	+30	+30
+20	+20	+20	+20
+10	+10	+10	+10

Potion 5

We used _____ ml red

We used _____ ml blue

We used _____ ml green

Potion 6

We used _____ ml red

We used _____ ml blue

We used _____ ml green

Potion 7

We used _____ ml red

We used _____ ml blue

We used _____ ml green

Potion 8

We used _____ ml red

We used _____ ml blue

We used _____ ml green

We made 1 litre of potion

In total we used

_____ ml red

_____ ml blue

_____ ml green

Certificate of measure

This is to certify than on completion of the information below —— is able to measure objects using metric units of metres and centimetres.

Height —— cm

Height —— m and —— cm

Length of foot —— cm

Extended arms —— cm

Length of big toe —— cm

Width of foot —— cm

One giant step —— cm

Length of thumb —— cm

Length of shoe —— cm

Round my wrist —— cm

Width of hand —— cm

Length of smile —— cm

One walking step —— cm

Length of hand —— cm

Length of ear —— cm

Width of shoe —— cm

Nose to end of finger —— cm

Knee to floor —— cm

Round my head —— cm

This is me

These measurements will change.

Your age ——

Date: ——

Official signature ——

My body

This is me

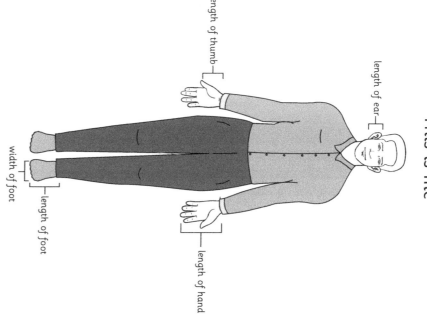

length of thumb

length of ear

width of foot

length of foot

length of hand

I estimate that:

1. The length of my foot is ——— cm

    Draw a line this length here:

2. The length of my hand is ——— cm

    Draw a line this length here:

3. The width of my foot is ——— cm

    Draw a line this length here:

4. The length of my thumb is ——— cm

    Draw a line this length here:

Instructions on page 266

5.   The length of my ear is ———— cm

Draw a line this length here:

Complete the table with your estimate and actual measurements.

Question	My estimate	Actual measurement
1.		
2.		
3.		
4.		
5.		

Quick reference

Core activity 32.1: Units of weight (Learner's Book p134)

This activity focuses on converting from grams to kilograms and back again through practical activities and a worksheet.

Core activity 32.2: Using weight (Learner's Book p136)

This activity takes a real life context and looks at using weight in the work place.

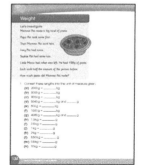 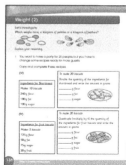

Prior learning	Objectives* – please note that listed objectives might only be partially covered within any given chapter but are covered fully across the book when taken as a whole
• Knows or begins to know the relationship between kilograms and grams. • Knows or begins to know conversion of g to kg and kg to g. • Can discuss and reason with at least one other person.	**3C: Measures** 3MI1 – Choose and use appropriate units and equipment to estimate, measure and record measurements. 3MI2 – Know the relationship between kilometres and metres, metres and centimetres, kilograms and grams, litres and millilitres. 3MI3 – Read to the nearest division or half division, use scales that are numbered or partially numbered. 3MI5 – Solve word problems involving measures.

*for NRICH activities mapped to the Cambridge Primary objectives, please visit www.cie.org.uk/cambridgeprimarymaths

Vocabulary

weigh • weighs • balances • heavy/light • heavier/lighter • heaviest/lightest • kilogram (*kg*) • half-kilogram • gram (*g*) • balance • scales • weight

Resources: *Estimating weight* photocopy master (CD-ROM), one copy per learner. Pairs of objects of comparable weight (as listed on the *Estimating weight* sheet: remove the labels from the cans of beans and soup). Scales (balance and kitchen). 1 litre bottles filled with water, $\frac{1}{2}$ litre bottles filled with water. Paperclips. *Which weight?* photocopy master (p278), one copy per pair, and gram weights (as in the *Which weight?* table). (Optional: bags and scales.)

Tell the class that today's session is about comparing weights, first of all using grams and then kilograms. Say, "*Tell me something about a kilogram. How many grams weigh the same as 1 Kilogram?*" (**1000**) "*Tell me something that weighs about a kilo.*" (**Litre bottle of water weighs about one kilogram.**)

"*When we want to weigh something light we use grams. A paper clip weighs about 1 gram. How many paper clips would we need to weigh a kilogram?*" (**1000**) "*How do you know? How many to weigh half a kilo?* (**500**) *How do you know?*"

Explain that kilograms are good for measuring things that can be lifted by people. "*When you weigh yourself on a scale, you would use kilograms.*"

Give each learner a copy of the *Estimating weight* sheet and explain the task. "*Compare the weights of pairs of objects by holding one in each hand and feeling which is heavier. Record what you think, and then weigh them using either the balance scales or the kitchen scales. Write the actual weight in the last section. You can use the water bottles, paperclips and weights on your tables to help you decide.*"
Allow time for learners to complete the activity, then give out the *Which weight?* sheet. Explain the task. "*Look at the pictures and estimate how much the real ones would weigh. This is an estimate so what you choose will be an approximate answer. Talk with a partner to discuss what you think.*"
Give time for the learners to work on the activity, then ask them to share their estimates with another pair.

At the end of the session, say, "*Tell me of any estimates that were different. Why do you think that was? Give us your reasons for choosing what you chose.*"

As this is a practical task, all learners will be able to estimate, although these estimates may not be very close to the actual.

Look out for!

- Learners who have difficulty reading the divisions on the scales. *If this happens, provide scales with larger dials or tell the learners to work in pairs where one has the responsibility for reading the measurement while the other records it.*
- Learners who need more of a challenge. *Suggest an extension to this activity. Ask them to solve word problems such as:*
  - *Estimate the weight of a wooden brick/block (or a real brick). Weigh it and note the weight. Give facts about a house: Each wall has 400 bricks.*
  - *What will be the weight of the four walls? One wall loses 50 bricks for a window. How much will the bricks weigh on that wall?*

Summary

- By the end of this session learners will have chosen appropriate units and equipment to estimate, measure and record measurements. By doing this they will have reinforced their knowledge and understanding of the relationship between kilograms and grams,
- When testing their own estimates they will have read to the nearest division or half division on the scales
- Further work will have involved solving word problems involving measures.

Notes on the Learner's Book

Weight (p134): this page extends the work done in the session, giving further opportunities to work with units of mass through closed questions as well as problems to solve.

Check up!

Ask questions such as:
- *"How many grams in a litre?"*
- *"How many grams in half a litre?"*
- *"How many litres would weigh the same as 1 kilogram?"*
- *"How many litres would weigh the same as 3 kilograms?"*

More activities

The kilogram race (individual)

> You will need a small bag for each learner and scales.

Each learner fills a bag with items found in the classroom, until the learner thinks the bag weighs one kilogram. Each bag is then weighed and the weight recorded on the bag. The learner whose bag weighs closest to one kilogram is the winner.

The more the better race (individual)

> You will need a small bag for each learner and scales.

This is similar to the kilogram race, except that the winner is the learner whose bag weighs closest to one kilogram *and* contains the greatest number of objects.

The one and only race (individual)

> You will need a small bag for each learner, and scales.

For this race only one item may be placed in the bag. The winner is the learner whose single item weighs closest to one kilogram.

Games Book (ISBN 9781107694019)

Harvest time (p73) is a game for two to four players. Players use the relationship between kilograms and grams.

Resources: *Is your pet overweight?* photocopy master (p279), one copy per pair. *Pet Progress* photocopy master (p280), one copy per pair. *Conversion table* photocopy master (CD-ROM), several copies for the class. (Optional: a collection of recipes; paper; pens/pencils; scales; ingredients for baking.)

Please note: If it is not common place to have animals as pets in your culture, introduce the topic of pets as a cross-curicular activity of learning about the traditions other cultures. You can use examples of normal and overweight pets from the internet.

Introduce the topic of pets by asking, "*Who has a pet at home? Has it ever been ill? Where do you take an animal when it is ill?* (**Vets**) *Did you know that vets use maths every day when they are working with the animals? Tell me something they do that uses maths. Talk to your partner.*" Give time for discussion and feedback. Some of the responses may be amount of food, or number of tablets or amount of medicine.

Explain that, with respect to feeding, the amount of food that an animal has will depend on its size and age. "*If it has too much food, it will become overweight and that may make it ill. If it doesn't have enough it will become underweight and that could make it ill. The vet has to decide how much each animal should have. To do this, animals are weighed and the amount of food they are given is calculated on their weight and age.*"

Give a copy of the *Is your pet overweight?* sheet to each pair (or this can be shown as a slide). Read through the sheet with the class. Then ask learners to look at the facts and talk to a partner: they should find one thing that they can tell the rest of the class. Give time for discussion and then ask for feedback.

Now tell the class that, in pairs, they are going to look at the progress of some of the animals taken to the vet. Give out the *Pet progress* sheet. Explain that it shows the weights of some pets over several months; all of them were very overweight at the beginning. "*With your partner use the information to answer the questions.*"

As the class is working, walk round to listen to the conversations between the pairs. Do you hear correct mathematical vocabulary? Are they able to discuss and reason with each other?

At the end of the session, ask, "*Which pet do you think did the best? Why?*"

Look out for!

- Learners who have difficulty with converting from one unit to another. *Give them a copy of the* Conversion table *to help them.*
- Learners who find this task easy and finish quickly. *Ask them to plot a graph to show the results from the table in the* Pet Progress *sheet. They can then use the graph to decide which pet made the best progress and explain their decision to the rest of the class.*

Summary

- By the end of this session learners will have used the relationship between kg and g to consider the weights of animals.
- They will also have discussed and shared ideas to solve problems involving measures.

Notes on the Learner's Book

Weight 2 (p136): this page explores, to an increasing extent, doubling, quadrupling (× 4 or doubling and doubling again) and conversion of kg and g.

Check up!

Ask questions such as:
- "*Which weighs more a cat at 5000 g or a cat at 12 kg?*"
- "*Which weighs less, a dog at 92 kilos or a dog at 10 000 g?*"
- "*A cat weighs 56 kilos and by the end of a year has doubled in weight. How much does it weigh?*"
- "*A dog weighs 196 kilos and at the end of the year has halved its weight. How much does it weigh?*"

More activities

Cooking (any size)

> You will need a collection of recipes, paper, pens/pencils, scales and ingredients for baking.

Use recipes to discuss the importance of accurate measures including weight. Make the recipes. Make a book of favourite recipes. Organise a bake sale for 'guess the weight of the cake'.

Trail (individual or group)

Learners can look at items as they come to school or around the school and answer questions such as, "*Which is heavier, the car we are in or the truck in front of us?*" They can go on a walk around the school and collect items such as pine cones, sticks, stones, then discuss the relative weights of each and investigate questions such as, "*How many features balance 10 stones? If one feather weighs 1 gram how much will 1000 feathers weigh?*"

Puzzles and problems (groups)

> You will need paper and pens/pencils.

Make a book of puzzles and problems to do with weight, e.g. I need three eggs for this recipe. Each egg weighs 5 grams. The recipe says I need an amount of flour the same weight as 30 eggs. How much flour do I need? Ask learners to make their own puzzles to add to the book. Ask each group to make one puzzles to add to the book.

Which weight?

Choose the best estimate for each animal or object shown.

Work with a partner and talk about what you think.

3 grams 300 grams 3 kilograms	800 kilograms 80,000 kilograms 8000 grams	1 gram 1 kilogram 100 kilograms
18 grams 1000 grams 6 kilograms	30 grams 600 grams 9 kilograms	800 grams 8 kilograms 80 kilograms
590 grams 8 kilograms 28 kilograms	1000 grams 3000 grams 20 kilograms	300 grams 1 kilogram 10 kilograms

Is your pet overweight?

It's easier to tell if pets are overweight by looking at their shape rather than just their weight alone.

Cats should have a smooth tucked in waist.

You should be able to feel their ribs, backbone and hips, but they shouldn't stick out.

This cat is the perfect weight.

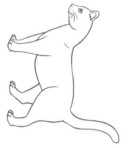

Look at these animals and decide if they are too thin or too fat:

Pet progress

The table below shows the weight of different pets over five months.

| | Medium-sized rabbits | | Large-sized rabbits | | Cat |
	Barney	**Jack**	**Magic**	**Poppy**	**Tilly**
January	19.5 kg	24.5 kg	52.5 kg	51 kg	8 kg
February	18.5 kg	22.5 kg	50.5 kg	50 kg	7.5 kg
March	18 kg	23 kg	48.5 kg	46 kg	7.5 kg
April	17 kg	21.5 kg	46 kg	42 kg	7 kg
May	16 kg	19.5 kg	42.5 kg	36.5 kg	6.5 kg

Look at the table and answer these questions

1. How many rabbits are there? _____

2. (a) (i) What is the combined weight of the medium-sized rabbits in:

    January _____ kg _____ grams

    February _____ kg _____ grams

    March _____ kg _____ grams

    April _____ kg _____ grams

    May _____ kg _____ grams

  (ii) How much weight did they lose together from January
to May? _____

  (b) Make a table to find the same information for the large-sized rabbits.

3. Tilly weighed 8 kg in January.

  (a) How much did she weigh in April? _____

  (b) How much weight had she lost? _____

  (c) By which month had Tilly lost 1500 grams? _____

4. (a) How much weight had each rabbit lost from January
to May? _____

  (b) Which rabbit lost the most weight? Explain how you
know. _____